Open Doors

A Collection of Recipes from
First United Methodist Church
Huntsville, Alabama

Mission Statement

Our mission is to create a source of ongoing funding for Global Missions of United Methodist Women. *Open Doors* is a vision born of our cooking heritage, the generous talents and spirit of our congregants, and the Grace of God.

Additional copies may be obtained at the cost of $27.00 each (including sales tax) plus $5.00 postage and handling for each book.

Cookbook Project
United Methodist Women
First United Methodist Church
120 Greene Street
Huntsville, Alabama 35801
256-539-5738

ISBN: 978-0-9814564-1-6

Bicentennial Edition	3,000 copies	July 2008
Second Printing	3,000 copies	November 2008

WIMMER
COOKBOOKS

A CONSOLIDATED GRAPHICS COMPANY

800.548.2537 wimmerco.com

Share a Meal Together as Friends

Upon first viewing the picture appearing on the front of this cookbook, I was struck by the power of the symbols it displays and how related those symbols are to some words found in the Bible. In Revelation 3:20, we read, *"Look! I stand at the door and knock. If you hear my voice and open the door, I will come in, and we will share a meal together as friends."* (New Living Translation)

In the picture on the front cover of this book, we see the big purple doors standing wide open. Then we see the interior doors of the sanctuary still closed but allowing us a view into our place of communion with God and each other. Through the windows of those doors, we see the lectern and pulpit from which the Word of God is read and proclaimed, preparing our souls to receive the bread and cup from the Lord's Table which is at the front and center.

We can also view the cross which is lifted high and carried down the center of our sanctuary and put in place each Sunday by the young members of our congregation. The story of that cross is enhanced by the fact that Jesus took bread and a cup and said, *"EAT ... DRINK ... ... in remembrance of me."* Then later in Acts 2:46, we discover the disciples *"met in homes for the Lord's Supper, and shared their meals with great joy and generosity."* (New Living Translation)

All these very powerful eating and drinking symbols and images from our worship setting and from scripture certainly give us an important purpose for the contents of this cookbook. My prayer is that through our use of these recipes we can experience the same joy common in the homes of disciples two thousand years ago and in the midst of the fellowship of those who started our own congregation here in Huntsville two hundred years ago. Indeed, in the words of scripture and through our use of this cookbook, *"... we will share a meal together as friends."*

Blessings,
Coy
Rev. Coy J. Hallmark
Executive Pastor, First United Methodist Church

Women at Work

First United Methodist Church
Huntsville, Alabama

The women of First Methodist Church were sending missionary boxes to China even before the twelve-member Woman's Missionary Society was officially organized in April 1889. In May 1890, thirty-two women organized the Ladies' Aid Society, whose stated purpose was to help the pastor with prayers, take charge of the parsonage, minister to the sick, and welcome the stranger.

These two groups merged in 1900, forming the Women's Mission Society. They operated separate treasuries, one for local work and one for conference funds. Conference funds were secured from dues of $3.00 per year plus a voluntary contribution. The women held dinners, bazaars, ice cream suppers, lectures, etc., to provide funding for local work. The Ware brothers, Clarence and Frank, published a cookbook of favorite recipes of church members, designating proceeds to the local treasury. The women proved an invaluable aid to the church. During the next twenty-five years, they provided carpeting for the sanctuary, partial funding for the stained glass windows, and $25,000 of the $42,000 cost to build the 1924 annex.

Fifty-five women organized the Women's Society of Christian Service in 1940, replacing the Woman's Missionary Society. This is the organization that evolved into today's United Methodist Women.

As women at work for over a century, United Methodist Women has become an organization of almost one million members with a $20 million budget worldwide. Projects include providing schools, hospitals, community centers, health clinics, prison ministries, and countless other services to improve the quality of life for children, youth, women, and families. In keeping with this rich tradition, proceeds from *Open Doors* will be used to fund projects supported by United Methodist Women. We strive to know Christ and to make him known throughout the world.

Benefactors

Our heartfelt thanks to our benefactors for their contributions toward publishing costs of *Open Doors*. Your generosity will increase funds for missions supported by the United Methodist Women of FUMC.

Linda and Rob Akenhead
Joyce and Colin Bagwell
Beth and Randy Bailey
Margaret and Walter Batson
Nancy Billings
Marion and Charlie Bishop
Carole and Peter Booher
Glenda Bragg
Robbie and Pat Burlison
Peggy Christian
Virginia Cook
Nancy and Bob Darnall
Faith Sunday School Class
Linda and Woolsey Finnell
Lois and Joe Foster
Mary Evelyn French
Beverly and Larry Fulton
Ann and Miles Greer
Laura Jo and George Hamilton
Anne and Charles Helms
Celeste and Jack Hemby
Liz and Billy Herrin
Virginia Walker Jennings
Kay and Bart Kirchler
Ferne Leonard
Charlene and Jack Lockhart
Pat and Roy Martin
Elizabeth McDonald
Doris R. McHugh
Judy and Fred McLaurine
Helen and Bob Middleton
Jane and Gene Monroe
Linda Montgomery
Syble and Terry Park
Christine Richard
Mary Richardson
Gwen and Don Riley
Paula C. Sanders
Lossie and Ben Small
Jean and Steve Templeton
Nancy W. and Richard Van Valkenburgh
Margaret Anne and Dan Whitsett
Sibyl M. Wilkinson
Lenda Woody

Grace Adkins Franklin

Grace Adkins Franklin was born in Lincoln County, Tennessee, on July 22, 1900. She married L. C. Franklin in 1923. They had one child, a daughter who died at the age of fifteen months.

For many years, the Franklins resided at 1122 Beirne Avenue. Mrs. Franklin was employed as a telephone operator at the Southern Bell Telephone Company. Mr. Franklin sold peanuts to local grocers. Mr. Franklin died in July 1981, and Mrs. Franklin in November 1988.

Grace Franklin loved her church. After remembering specific relatives, a friend, two other churches, and seven charities, Mrs. Franklin bequeathed the remainder of her estate, approximately $392,000, to the First United Methodist Church. Her love and stewardship remains an inspiration and gift to us all.

When the United Methodist Women decided to create a cookbook as a bicentennial treasure, we needed the guarantee of substantial funding to initiate the project. The Church's Administrative Council authorized a loan, if necessary, from the Grace Franklin Permanent Fund. We are grateful to Grace Franklin for helping us carry out Jesus' command to Love One Another. Thank you, Mrs. Franklin.

Cookbook Committee

Pat Martin, *Chair*
Nancy Darnall and Celeste Hemby, *Co-chairs*

Section Chairs
Norma Colbath
Linda Finnell
Barbara Hathcock
Celeste Hemby
Carol Hurst
Judy McLaurine
Denise McLeroy

Recipe Testing Chairs
Pat Cook
Doni Harrison
Natasha McCrary
Camille Vaughan

Photography
Terry T. Lewis

Art Committee Co-chairs
Gail Fay and Helen Middleton

Church History
Nancy Van Valkenburgh

Narrative
Martha Dotzheimer

Finance
Margaret Batson

Tasting Events
Sarah Hereford

Sales and Distribution
Linda Finnell and Sandra Vallely
Glenda Bragg and Lenda Woody

Publicity and Marketing
Nancy Darnall and Judy McLaurine

United Methodist Women President
Pauline Precise

We wish to express our appreciation to the members who so generously shared their favorite recipes. Without you, this book could not have been published. We regret that we were unable to publish all recipes due to similarity or availability of space.

Volunteers

The cookbook committee is grateful to all our volunteers. Whether you typed, proofed, tested recipes, sold cookbooks, served on a committee, or performed any of the many tasks required to make *Open Doors* a reality, we thank you. We have been as diligent as possible in compiling this list, but if your name has been omitted, please know that you are appreciated.

Linda Akenhead
Lucy Armstrong
Marsha Arnold
Joyce Bagwell
Donna Barnes
Gerry Barnes
Cheryl Bence
Nancy Billings
Sarah Blue
Stella Boone
Glenda Bragg
Beth Brandon
Kaylyn Brown
Teri Burgess
Billy Byars
Lea Chaffin
Barbara Chappell
Carole Chase
Richard Chesnut
Peggy Christian
Susan Clanton
Katie Clark
Anne Clough
Norma Colbath
Barbara Cook
Pat Cook
Virginia Cook
Jane Cooper
Renee Cox
Brenda Courtney
Emily Craft
Margaret Anne Crumlish
Karen Cruze
Nancy Darnall
Claudia Davis
Imogene Davis
Lynne Davis
Lonetta Dawson
Sue Day
Linda Dedrick
Shelly DeLay
Melissa Dodgen
Tomalyn Dombrowski
Martha Dotzheimer
Carlene Elrod
Amy Epps
Gail Fay
Linda Finnell
Anna Flesch
Carolyn Fondren
Joe Foster
Lois Foster
Martha Fountain
Mary Evelyn French
Beverly Fulton
Barbie Gardiner
Dee Gibson
Glenda Goldfinger
Clara Goode
Carole Hamm
Doni Harrison
Suzie Harrison
Barbara Hathcock
Rachel Heeschen
Celeste Hemby
Wendy Henshaw
Billy Herrin
Liz Herrin
Nancy Horgen
Carol Hurst
Vicki Irons
Virginia Walker Jennings
Aimee Johnson
Judy Johnson
Mary Susan Johnson

Gina Johnston
Nell Johnston
Betty Lou Jones
Sarah Lauren Kattos
Mona Gay Keith
Jan Kelly
Geneva Kilgore
Shelbie King
Jean Kirby
Jerry Laurine
Virginia Laux
Ferne Leonard
Herb Lewis
Terry T. Lewis
Bettie Lewter
Charlene Lockhart
Julie Malone
Ellen Marks
Greg Martin
Pat Martin
Roy Martin
Natasha McCrary
Shirley McCrary
Elizabeth McDonald
Judy McLaurine
Denise McLeroy
Melanie McRae
Barbara McWilliams

Biddie Merrill
Helen Middleton
Nancy Miles
Mabry Miller
Linda Montgomery
Ellen Moran
Mary Alice Moss
Lakshmi Nallamala
Lola Northington
Alice Ozier
Debbie Packard
Jim Packard
Syble Park
Julia Parker
Gerald Patterson
Lauren Finnell Plott
Linda Finnell Powell
Dale Rhoades
Gwen Riley
Pat Robinett
Rene Robinson
Keith Rogers
Joye Ruffin
Susan Rutenberg
Mary Rutledge
Diane Sammons
Paula Sanders
Shawna Schmitz

Cathy Scholl
Ann Schrimsher
Nancy Seward
Fleming Sharp
Pam Shepard
Erynn Showers
Ben Small
Betty Smith
Lady Smith
Lynda Sobera
Carolyn Spearman
Cindi Stone
Trudy Striplin
Lucy Sutherland
Suzanne Thomason
Anthony Thompson
Brenda Titus
Margaret Tudor
Camille Vaughan
Lady Jane Vowell
Brenda Wagner
Lora Walker
Laura Watson
Cora White
Sibyl Wilkinson
Lil Wood
Emily Wright
John Wright

We extend a special "thank you" to the FUMC staff for all your support and assistance during this project.

A Look Back

Less than 25 years after the organization of Methodism in America, pioneers seeking land began to migrate into the Tennessee Valley. In 1805, an itinerant Methodist preacher, John Ford from South Carolina, led one of the first large groups of settlers.

The Western Conference of the Methodist Episcopal Church met at Liberty Hill, Tennessee, on October 8, 1808, to establish the Flint Circuit and appoint James Gwinn as circuit rider for an area extending approximately from McMinnville, Tennessee, to Chickasaw (Hobbs) Island, Alabama. The society at Hunt's Spring thus was in existence two months before Madison County was created in December.

One of the first acts of the 1819 Alabama legislature in the new state was to empower religious societies to hold real estate. In the following summer, the trustees of the 175 member Methodist Episcopal Church received a grant of land and, by 1821, built a church. By 1822, the new church was overseeing the conference's mission school for Indians.

By 1830, the little frame church in the western part of town seemed inadequate. On March 7, 1832, a new church was built on the present site. This church burned to the ground on January 6, 1864, during the War Between the States, when Federal troops were quartered in the basement and, despite protests by the minister, built fires on the wooden floor to cook their food.

With courage and faith, the Methodists immediately began to rebuild. On August 7, 1867, the cornerstone was laid and the new church was ready for use by the spring. The annex was completed in 1924 and by 1956 the Educational Building was needed. The Wesley Center was dedicated October 27, 1985.

On May 31, 2000, FUMC began a new building program to expand the ministry capabilities of the church. Through this program, the sanctuary and educational buildings were renovated, the church was made more accessible to persons with special needs, a new nursery was built, and a new multi-media worship center was constructed. All of this was dedicated for use in God's service on October 14, 2001, by Bishop Robert Fannin.

Table of Contents

Heritage Recipes, recipes submitted in memory of those saints who have gone before us, are designated by the FUMC steeple.

I WAS GLAD WHEN THEY SAID UNTO ME, "LET US GO INTO THE HOUSE OF THE LORD."

PSALMS 122:1

The cornerstone of the present Sanctuary building was laid on August 7, 1867. The previous circa 1834 church building burned on January 6, 1864. The courage and faith with which these Methodists immediately began to rebuild remained an inspiration to members who have followed. Meeting in a building loaned by the Episcopalians, the members and their friends in the community began many projects to raise money. The main portion of money, however, was raised by the pastor, the Reverend Thomas L. Moody, who made a tour of the surrounding states and came home with $4,500, most of which he raised in Kentucky.

In the 1970's, the Sanctuary's double doors were painted a royal purple matching the colors in the stained glass windows. Purple symbolizes the Kingship of Jesus. The white stucco was added to the church in the 1890's to protect the church's porous 1860's brick. The outstanding contrast between the gleaming white and the royal purple led the church to be known throughout North Alabama and South Tennessee as "the church with the purple doors."

Appetizers & Beverages

Praise ye the Lord. Praise God in his sanctuary....

Psalms 150:1

Until Alabama became a state in December of 1819, there were no churches within the boundaries of Huntsville. One of the first acts of the first legislature was to empower religious societies of every denomination to hold real estate.

On August 29, 1820, the summer following the act of the legislature, the trustees of the Methodist Episcopal Church of Huntsville received a grant of land from John and Johanna Price on Clinton Street. The recorded deed states that the grant was made "For and in consideration of the many benefits received by them through the instrumentality of the Methodist Episcopal Church with the desire that the religion of Jesus Christ may spread and survive everywhere, but more especially in Huntsville and vicinity." Construction began immediately with completion of the church before the next Conference year.

On March 7, 1832, the ground on which the church Sanctuary now stands on the corner of Randolph and Greene Streets was bought from William H. Powers and wife for the sum of $750. Within two years, the church was built. The newspaper reported that the Dr. J. H. Harris came from Nashville for the occasion and he spoke of the church as being "the most commodious and most beautiful church in Huntsville."

In the fall of 1836, the trustees ran into financial difficulties with the Brandon Brothers, the builders of the church. The trustees had depended on subscriptions which were not met, so the Brandons exercised their lien for the amount of $2,221.02 and ½ cent with interest. On the third Monday in October 1836, the property was sold on the public square and was bought by David Moore on behalf of himself and the other trustees for the sum of $2,150.05 which included the auctioneer's fee of $2.00. Thus the church was redeemed and met the first great threat to its existence.

The interior of the Sanctuary is pictured in the year 2008 reflecting renovations made during the year 2000 to expand the ministry capabilities of the church. As churches throughout the nation have been challenged by demographics and have closed or moved, the First United Methodist Church of Huntsville, under the direction of the Holy Spirit, continues to minister "In the Heart of the City in the name of Christ."

Four-Cheese Pâté

- 1 (8 ounce) package cream cheese, softened
- 2 tablespoons milk
- 2 tablespoons sour cream
- ¾ cup chopped pecans, toasted
- 2 (8 ounce) packages cream cheese, softened
- 1 (4½ ounce) package Camembert cheese, softened
- 1 (4 ounce) package crumbled blue cheese, softened
- 1 cup shredded Swiss cheese, softened
- Pecan halves for garnish
- Red and green apple wedges

Line a 9-inch pie plate with plastic wrap and set aside. Combine 1 package of cream cheese, milk, and sour cream in a small mixing bowl. Beat at medium speed of an electric mixer until smooth. Spread into pie plate. Sprinkle with chopped pecans. Combine remaining cream cheese, Camembert cheese (including rind), blue cheese, and Swiss cheese in a small mixing bowl. Beat at medium speed of an electric mixer until smooth. Spoon into pie plate and spread to edge. Cover with plastic wrap and chill up to 1 week. To serve, uncover and invert onto serving plate. Carefully peel away plastic wrap. Garnish with pecans, if desired. Serve with apple wedges or a variety of crackers.

Serves 20 to 25

Barbie Gardiner

Pineapple Cream Cheese Ball

- 1 (8 ounce) can crushed pineapple
- 2 (8 ounce) packages cream cheese, softened
- 2 tablespoons finely chopped onion
- 2 tablespoons finely chopped green pepper
- Garlic salt
- Chopped pecans

Drain pineapple and squeeze out excess juice. Mix pineapple, cream cheese, onion, green pepper, and garlic salt to taste. Form into a ball, wrap in wax paper, and refrigerate until firm. Roll ball in chopped pecans. Serve with assorted crackers.

Serves 30 to 40

Reduced-fat cream cheese may be used.

Pat Martin

Cheese Ring with Jam

16 ounces grated Cheddar cheese
4 green onions, chopped
1 cup mayonnaise
1 cup chopped pecans
½ teaspoon Worcestershire sauce
1 (18 ounce) jar strawberry preserves

Mix cheese, onions, mayonnaise, pecans, and Worcestershire together. Put in a greased 1-quart ring mold and chill. Unmold on a serving plate. Fill center of ring with strawberry preserves. Serve with crackers.

Serves 12 to 14

Jo Nell O'Connor

Healthy Cheese

1 cup sliced pimientos
1 cup crushed pineapple
1 cup raisins
2 pounds Cheddar cheese
1 cup pecan pieces
1½ cups mayonnaise or mayonnaise-type salad dressing

Drain pimientos and set aside. Pour juice from pineapple over raisins and set aside. Cut cheese into wedges that will fit in meat grinder or food processor. Grind together, alternating addition of cheese with pimientos, pineapple, raisins, and pecans. Place in large bowl of mixer. Add mayonnaise and mix thoroughly. With electric mixer, whip the spread until it is creamy. Store cheese spread in serving containers in refrigerator. Serve on crackers, stuff celery, or make a sandwich.

Makes 6 to 8 cups

Variation: If making balls or logs, use 1 cup mayonnaise for stiffer mixture. Shape cheese into balls or logs and coat them with chopped nuts and/or wheat germ. Wheat germ may also be added to the mixture for more nutrition and taste.

Sally Venters

Crab Cream Cheese Spread

- 1 (8 ounce) package cream cheese
- ¼ cup chopped green onion tops
- ¼ teaspoon Worcestershire sauce
- 1 (6 ounce) can lump crabmeat
- 1 cup ketchup
- 3 teaspoons horseradish
- 4 drops hot pepper sauce
- 1 tablespoon lemon juice
- ¼ cup chopped parsley

Cover entire block of cream cheese with chopped green onion tops and sprinkle with Worcestershire sauce. After cleaning crabmeat for boney materials, spread on top of cream cheese. Mix ketchup, horseradish, and hot sauce and spoon over crabmeat. Top with lemon juice and parsley. Chill to let all the flavors merge. Place out ahead of time to soften so it will spread easily on crackers.

Makes 1½ cups

Stella Boone

Shrimp Mold

- 1 (8 ounce) package cream cheese, softened
- 1½ (¼ ounce) envelopes unflavored gelatin
- ½ cup cold water
- ¾ cup chopped celery
- 1 cup mayonnaise
- 2 teaspoons grated onion
- 1½-2 cups fresh cooked shrimp, diced
- Lemon juice
- Salt
- Pepper
- Lettuce

Whip cream cheese in a bowl. Soften gelatin in ½ cup cold water in a small saucepan. Heat water until gelatin is dissolved. Add gelatin to cream cheese and mix until smooth. Add celery, mayonnaise, onion, and shrimp. Add lemon juice, salt, and pepper to taste, and mix well. Pour into a greased gelatin mold and chill until firm. Serve on a bed of lettuce with assorted crackers.

Serves 12

Calvert Sammons

Submitted by Susan Sullins

Salmon Cheese Spread

- **2 (3 ounce) packages cream cheese, softened**
- **3 tablespoons mayonnaise**
- **1 tablespoon lemon juice**
- **½ teaspoon salt**
- **½ teaspoon curry powder**
- **¼ teaspoon dried basil**
- **⅛ teaspoon pepper**
- **1 (7½ ounce) can salmon, drained, bones and skin removed**
- **2 green onions, thinly sliced**

In a mixing bowl, combine cream cheese, mayonnaise, and lemon juice. Add salt, curry powder, basil, and pepper. Mix well. Gently stir in salmon and onions. Cover and refrigerate at least 1 hour. Serve with crackers.

Makes 1½ cups

Paula Sanders

Variation: To make a ball instead of spread, increase cream cheese to 8 ounces and delete mayonnaise. Substitute 1 teaspoon horseradish and ¼ teaspoon liquid smoke for curry powder and basil. Shape into ball and roll in chopped parsley. Wrap in wax paper. Refrigerate.

Barbara Hathcock

Chicken Cheese Ball

- **1 (6¾ ounce) can chunky chicken**
- **1 (12 ounce) carton cream cheese, softened**
- **1 teaspoon grated onion**
- **1 teaspoon finely grated pimiento**
- **6 dashes seasoned salt**
- **4 dashes Worcestershire sauce**
- **1 cup finely chopped pecans, divided**

Blend chicken, cream cheese, onion, pimiento, seasoned salt, Worcestershire, and ¼ cup pecans together. Chill until mixture gets a little firm and can be shaped into a ball or log. Roll in remaining nuts. Serve with small crackers.

Serves 10 to 12

Lynda Sobera

Baked Brie with Tomato Sauce

- **1 frozen pastry shell, thawed**
- **8 ounces Brie, chilled**
- **1 tablespoon olive oil**
- **1 medium onion, chopped**
- **1 clove garlic, crushed (optional)**
- **1 (14½ ounce) can tomatoes, drained and chopped**
- **½ tablespoon chopped fresh basil**
- **1 tablespoon chopped fresh parsley**
- **1 small bay leaf**
- **1 tablespoon raisins**
- **2 tablespoons pine nuts**
- **Salt**
- **Pepper**

With rolling pin, flatten pastry shell and roll out to a size that will completely cover cheese. Wrap cheese in pastry, tucking ends in snugly underneath. Make sure there are no openings in pastry. CHILL WRAPPED CHEESE FOR 1 HOUR. Meanwhile, heat olive oil in a skillet and sauté onion and garlic until tender. Stir in tomatoes, basil, parsley, bay leaf, raisins, pine nuts, and salt and pepper to taste. Allow to simmer 15 minutes. Preheat oven to 350 degrees. Bake chilled cheese on metal pie pan 15 minutes or until browned. Spoon tomato sauce, discarding bay leaf, onto a serving plate and place baked Brie on top in center of plate. Serve with crackers and caraway breadsticks.

Serves 8

Jan Kelly

Tuna Log

- **2 (3 ounce) packages cream cheese, softened**
- **1 ounce blue cheese, crumbled**
- **2 tablespoons finely chopped celery**
- **1 tablespoon finely chopped onion**
- **1 tablespoon mayonnaise**
- **Few drops hot pepper sauce**
- **1 (6 ounce) can tuna, flaked**
- **Chopped pecans or parsley**

In a small mixing bowl, beat together cream cheese and blue cheese. Stir in celery, onion, mayonnaise, hot sauce, and tuna. Shape into logs and chill several hours. Roll logs in chopped pecans or parsley. Serve with crackers. Freezes well.

Serves 8 to 10

Tine Purdy

Nutty Butterscotch Log

- **1 (8 ounce) package cream cheese**
- **1 (12.25 ounce) jar butterscotch sundae sauce**
- **1 cup pecan pieces**

Place cream cheese block in a shallow serving dish. Pour desired amount of sauce over cream cheese. Sprinkle pecan pieces on top of cheese and sauce. Serve with thin wheat crackers.

Serves 8 to 10

Suzanne Thomason

Layered Pesto Torte

- **1 (8 ounce) package cream cheese**
- **2 heaping tablespoons basil pesto**
- **2 heaping tablespoons sun-dried tomato pesto**
- **⅓ cup toasted pine nuts**
- **Fresh basil for garnish**

Let block of cream cheese harden in freezer for a short time so it will slice more easily. Cut cream cheese into half the thickness, making two identical rectangular sections. Make layers by spreading basil pesto on one section and sun-dried pesto on the other. Stack sections so that basil pesto is between the 2 sections of cream cheese with tomato pesto on top. Top with toasted pine nuts. Garnish with fresh basil. Chill overnight in an airtight container. Serve with vegetables, crackers, or bread.

Serves 10

Lakshmi Nallamala

Sherried Pâté

1 (8 ounce) package cream cheese, softened
2 cups grated sharp Cheddar cheese
2 teaspoons curry powder
2 tablespoons sherry
1 (9 ounce) jar chutney
3 green onions, chopped
½ cup chopped peanuts
6 slices bacon, cooked and crumbled
½ cup toasted coconut

Mix cream cheese, grated cheese, curry powder, and sherry until smooth. Pat into a round, flat shape. It should resemble a cake layer. Place between sheets of wax paper and chill. One hour before serving, place cheese mixture on serving plate. On top of cheese, layer in order: chutney, green onion, peanuts, bacon, and coconut. Pat top to press together. Serve with crackers.

Serves 10 to 12

Dale Rhoades

Zesty Pimiento and Cheese

16 ounces Cheddar cheese
1 (10 ounce) can tomatoes with green chiles, drained and chopped
1 (2 ounce) jar pimientos, drained
1 cup mayonnaise
1 teaspoon Worcestershire sauce
Dash of garlic powder

Grate cheese. DO NOT use store-grated cheese. Mix all ingredients and chill before serving. Serve with sturdy chips, assorted crackers, or celery.

Makes 3 cups

Glenda Goldfinger

Marinated Mozzarella

- **1 pound mozzarella cheese, cut in 1-inch cubes**
- **1 (7 ounce) jar roasted red peppers, drained, cut in strips**
- **1 clove garlic, cut in half lengthwise**
- **1¼ cups olive oil**
- **4 teaspoons Italian seasoning**
- **1 teaspoon fresh rosemary leaves, stripped from stem**
- **½ teaspoon crushed red pepper**
- **Rosemary or thyme sprigs (optional)**

In a 1-quart jar, combine cheese, roasted red peppers, and garlic. In a small bowl, combine olive oil, Italian seasoning, rosemary, and crushed red pepper. Pour over cheese mixture. Add a few fresh rosemary or thyme sprigs, if desired. Cover tightly. Turn jar upside down several times to blend ingredients. Refrigerate at least 4 hours. Before serving, let jar stand at room temperature for about 1 hour. Remove cheese and peppers from marinade. Serve with crackers. Any leftovers may be returned to marinade for up to 2 weeks.

Serves 12 to 14

Dottye Montgomery

Hot Cheese Spread

- **1 (8 ounce) package cream cheese, softened**
- **½ cup shredded Swiss cheese**
- **½ cup mayonnaise**
- **3 tablespoons chopped onion**

TOPPING

- **½ (3 ounce) jar bacon bits**
- **½ cup chopped pecans**
- **½ cup crushed round buttery crackers**

Preheat oven to 350 degrees. Mix cream cheese, Swiss cheese, mayonnaise, and onion together and spread in a 9-inch pie plate. Mix bacon bits, pecans, and crushed crackers together. Place on top of cheese mixture. Bake 20 minutes.

Serves 10 to 12

Ann Schrimsher

Cheese Cakes

- **2 cups all-purpose flour**
- **½ teaspoon salt**
- **½ teaspoon red pepper**
- **1 cup margarine, melted**
- **8 ounces grated extra-sharp Cheddar cheese**
- **2 cups crisp rice cereal**

Preheat oven to 300 degrees. Combine flour, salt, and red pepper. Stir in melted margarine. Add grated cheese and mix well. Stir in crisp rice cereal. Shape dough into small balls and place on ungreased cookie sheet. Flatten balls with a fork. Bake 20 minutes. Remove from cookie sheet and cool. Freezes well.

Makes 5 dozen

Barbara S. Chappell

Cheese Wafers

- **2 cups shredded Cheddar cheese**
- **½ cup butter or margarine, softened**
- **1 cup all-purpose flour**
- **½ teaspoon salt**
- **¼ teaspoon ground red pepper**
- **¾ cup finely chopped nuts**

Combine cheese and butter in a mixing bowl and beat well. Add flour, salt, pepper, and nuts. Mix well. Divide dough in half. Shape each half into a 1x 8-inch roll. Wrap in wax paper. Chill at least 2 hours. Preheat oven to 400 degrees. Slice rolls into ¼-inch wafers. Bake 7 to 9 minutes.

Makes 6 dozen

Barbara Hathcock

Green Chile Bites

- **1 (4½ ounce) can chopped green chiles**
- **4 cups grated sharp Cheddar cheese**
- **6 eggs, beaten**

Preheat oven to 350 degrees. Butter a 7x11-inch casserole dish. Layer chiles and cheese in dish. Pour eggs on top. Bake 30 minutes. Cut into small squares.

Makes 25

Lenda Woody

War Eagle Pickled Eggs

(Old Auburn Delicacy)

1¾ cups cider vinegar
¾ cup water
1½ teaspoons salt
Scant teaspoon garlic salt
5 whole peppercorns
⅛ teaspoon dill seeds
⅛ teaspoon coriander seeds
⅛ teaspoon mustard seeds
Sprinkle of red pepper
Sprinkle of celery salt
18 hard-boiled eggs, peeled

Mix vinegar, water, salt, and spices in a pot. Bring to a boil. Let simmer 5 minutes. Cool and pour over eggs in a plastic container with a top. Place in refrigerator. Let marinate at least 7 days. Eat with salt, pepper, and hot pepper sauce.

Makes 18

Billy Bell

Summer Tomato Bruschetta

2 French baguettes
¼ cup extra virgin olive oil
3 large tomatoes or 4 medium tomatoes
2 tablespoons balsamic vinegar
2-3 cloves garlic, peeled and minced
¼ cup thinly sliced fresh basil leaves
1 teaspoon kosher salt
4-5 grinds fresh cracked pepper

Preheat oven to 400 degrees. Slice baguettes diagonally in ⅓-inch slices. Place on cookie sheet and brush generously with olive oil. Toast 5 to 6 minutes or until edges are crisp and brown. Remove from oven and cool. Dice tomatoes, but do not peel them. Squeeze out seeds and extra liquid. Combine tomatoes, balsamic vinegar, garlic, basil, salt, and pepper in a medium-size bowl. Toss gently. Adjust seasonings as needed. Do not refrigerate as cold reduces the flavor of fresh tomatoes. Serve baguette toasts on a platter with bowl of tomato mixture in center. Invite guests to spread tomato topping on toast themselves, so the bread doesn't get soggy.

Serves 6 to 10

A strong, fruity olive oil works best. Use homegrown or farm stand summer tomatoes. Store bought or out-of-season tomatoes simply will not do!

Amanda Vaughan

Zucchini Appetizers

1 cup biscuit baking mix
½ cup finely chopped onion
½ cup grated Parmesan cheese
2 tablespoons chopped parsley
½ teaspoon salt
½ teaspoon ground oregano
⅛ teaspoon pepper
1 clove garlic, minced
¼ cup vegetable oil
4 eggs, beaten
3 cups thinly sliced zucchini

Preheat oven to 350 degrees. Combine all ingredients except zucchini, mixing well. Stir in zucchini. Spread evenly in a lightly greased 9x13-inch baking dish. Bake 30 minutes or until set. Cut into 1½-inch squares. Serve warm.

Makes 48 squares

Imogene Davis

Margherita Tomato Pie

1 pizza crust or 1 pie crust, baked
2 cups grated mozzarella cheese
1 cup grated Parmesan cheese
1 cup chopped fresh basil
3-4 Roma tomatoes, sliced ¼-inch thick
Salt
Pepper

Preheat oven to 350 degrees. Put mozzarella and Parmesan in a bowl with tight-fitting lid and shake until well mixed. Layer on baked crust in order: ½ cheese mixture, ½ chopped basil, sliced tomatoes to cover basil, salt and pepper on tomatoes, remaining basil, and remaining cheese mixture. Bake 30 minutes. Cool 10 minutes before slicing.

Serves 16

Variations: Add 8 slices cooked and crumbled bacon over tomatoes; or sprinkle ½ cup chopped baby spinach over basil, sprinkle ½ cup crumbled feta cheese over tomatoes, and sprinkle ½ cup chopped fresh baby spinach over second layer of basil. Follow other layers as written.

Dale Rhoades

Open-Faced Tomato Sandwiches with Homemade Mayonnaise

1 small loaf French bread, sliced into ½-inch slices
Homemade mayonnaise (recipe follows)
4 fresh tomatoes (small or Roma), thinly sliced
⅓ cup chopped fresh basil
Salt
Coarsely ground pepper
4 slices bacon, cooked and crumbled
Freshly grated Parmesan cheese

Preheat oven to 400 degrees. Spread homemade mayonnaise on bread. Place tomatoes on bread rounds and top with chopped basil. Sprinkle with salt and pepper to taste, crumbled bacon, and Parmesan cheese. Bake 10 minutes. Serve warm.

Makes 12 to 14

Homemade Mayonnaise

1 egg
1 tablespoon Dijon mustard
1 teaspoon salt
1 cup olive oil
Juice of 1 lemon
Red pepper
½ teaspoon garlic powder (optional)

In food processor, combine egg, mustard, and salt. Process until well blended. Slowly add olive oil and lemon juice. Sprinkle with red pepper to taste. Add garlic powder, if desired. Blend.

Makes 1½ cups

Betsy Lowe

Chile Cheddar Pinwheels

- **1 (8 ounce) package cream cheese, softened**
- **1 cup shredded Cheddar cheese**
- **1 (4½ ounce) can chopped green chiles, drained**
- **2 tablespoons picante sauce**
- **½ teaspoon chili powder**
- **¼ teaspoon garlic salt**
- **¼ teaspoon onion powder**
- **2 (8 ounce) cans refrigerated crescent rolls**
- **Additional chili powder (optional)**

In a mixing bowl, beat cream cheese. Add Cheddar cheese, chiles, picante sauce, chili powder, garlic salt, and onion powder. Separate each can of crescent roll dough into 4 rectangles. Press perforations to seal. Spread ¼ cup cheese mixture over each rectangle. Roll up jelly roll style starting with short side. Wrap in plastic wrap and chill for at least 1 hour. Preheat oven to 350 degrees. Unwrap and cut each roll into 8 slices. Place on ungreased baking sheets. Sprinkle with additional chili powder, if desired. Bake 10 to 12 minutes or until golden brown.

Makes 64

Sylvia Bruens

Texas Torte

- **2 eggs**
- **2 tablespoons all-purpose flour**
- **½ teaspoon salt**
- **⅓ cup milk**
- **1 (4½ ounce) can chopped green chiles, or to taste**
- **½ pound sharp Cheddar cheese, grated**
- **½ pound Monterey Jack cheese, grated**

Preheat oven to 350 degrees. Beat eggs. Add flour, salt, and milk. Add green chiles and cheeses. Pour into a greased 9x13-inch dish. Bake 30 to 35 minutes. Cut into squares.

Serves 10 to 12

Lise Wilson

Chinese Meatballs

MEATBALLS

2 pounds ground beef
½ cup all-purpose flour
1 tablespoon salt
1 teaspoon sugar
1 cup finely grated onion
¼ cup sherry
1 teaspoon pepper
2 eggs
1 teaspoon dry parsley
1 teaspoon ginger powder
¼ cup soy sauce

SAUCE

1 cup ketchup
1 teaspoon hot pepper sauce

Combine all ingredients and mix well. Shape into small balls and drop into enough boiling water to cover. When balls rise to the top, they are done. Drain. Combine sauce ingredients and use as a dip with meatballs. Serve hot with picks.

Makes 30 to 40

Lola Northington

Cheese Olivettes

60 green olives
½ cup butter, softened
½ pound sharp Cheddar cheese, finely grated
½ teaspoon hot pepper sauce
1½ cups all-purpose flour

Preheat oven to 375 degrees. Drain olives and spread on a towel to dry slightly. In a large bowl, cream butter and blend in cheese. Add hot sauce and stir to blend. Add flour and stir with a wooden spoon. Use hands to fully blend flour into butter mixture. Roll dough into a log shape and divide into 60 pieces. Wrap each piece of dough around an olive and roll into a ball. Bake on a cookie sheet 15 to 20 minutes.

Makes 60

Olivettes may be frozen before baking in an airtight container for later use. Bake while frozen 30 to 40 minutes.

Ellen Moran

Mushroom Crab Melts

3 bacon strips, diced
1 cup sliced fresh mushrooms
¼ cup chopped onion
1 (6 ounce) can crabmeat, drained, flaked, and cartilage removed
1 cup shredded Swiss cheese
½ cup mayonnaise
⅓ cup Parmesan cheese
2 tablespoons butter or margarine, softened
6 English muffins, split
Dash of cayenne pepper
Dash of paprika

Preheat oven to 400 degrees. In a skillet, cook bacon over medium heat until crisp. Drain on paper towels. Reserve 2 tablespoons drippings. Sauté mushrooms and onion in drippings until tender. In a large bowl, combine mushroom mixture, crab, Swiss cheese, mayonnaise, Parmesan cheese, and bacon. Spread butter over muffin halves. Top with crab mixture. Sprinkle with cayenne and paprika. Place on an ungreased baking sheet. Bake 10 to 15 minutes or until lightly browned.

Makes 12, or cut in quarters 48

One (8 ounce) can refrigerated pasteurized jumbo crabmeat or imitation crabmeat may be substituted.

Sylvia Bruens

Sausage and Bacon Roll-Ups

12 slices bacon, halved crosswise
½ pound pork sausage
1 (8 ounce) package cream cheese, softened
12 slices white bread

Preheat oven to 350 degrees. Fry bacon until transparent. Drain and set aside. Cook sausage until browned, stirring to crumble. Drain. Combine sausage and cream cheese. Stir well and set aside. Trim crust from bread and cut slices in half. Spread cream cheese mixture over bread. Starting with the short end, roll up each slice. Wrap each with 1 piece of bacon and secure with a toothpick. Cook on ungreased cookie sheet 5 to 20 minutes.

Makes 24

If freezing, do not add bacon until cooking time. Do not thaw before cooking.

Jo Nell O'Connor

Sausage Loaf

1 long loaf French bread
2 eggs
½ cup milk
1 pound pork sausage, browned and drained
8 ounces sliced Monterey Jack cheese

Preheat oven to 400 degrees. Split bread loaf lengthwise with an electric knife, so that you have a top and a bottom. Pull bread out of top and bottom (hollow out the loaf). Put bread pieces in a bowl. Set aside. Beat eggs and milk together. Set aside. Brown and drain sausage. Combine egg mixture, sausage, and bread pieces. Spoon mixture evenly into bottom of bread. Bake 15 minutes. Remove from oven and top with cheese. Place top portion of bread over cheese. Bake 5 minutes. Remove from oven and slice.

Makes 15 to 20 slices

Cade Johnston

Lil Reubens

1 (12 ounce) can corned beef
1 (8 ounce) carton sour cream
1 (1 ounce) package dry onion soup mix
Cocktail rye bread
Mustard
1 (16 ounce) jar sliced dill pickles
1 (10 ounce) can sauerkraut

Combine beef, sour cream, and soup mix. Heat in microwave. Spread on cocktail rye bread. Serve with mustard, pickles, and sauerkraut.

Makes 16 to 18

Suzanne Thomason

Ham Roll-Ups

12 ounces cream cheese
½ cup mayonnaise
1 pound (16 slices) packaged ham
16 small scallions

Beat cream cheese with mayonnaise until softened. Spread mixture over ham slices. Place 1 scallion on each cheese-covered ham slice. Roll up and chill until firm. Cut into ½ to ¾-inch sections.

Makes 80

Lenda Woody

Joy's Sausage Stars

- **1 (16 ounce) package won ton shells**
- **1 pound mild breakfast sausage**
- **¾ cup ranch dressing**
- **1 (6 ounce) can black olives**
- **1½ cups shredded Cheddar cheese**
- **1½ cups shredded mozzarella cheese**

Preheat oven to 350 degrees. Spray muffin pans with cooking spray. Press a won ton shell in each muffin cup. Spray shells lightly with cooking spray. Bake 5 minutes or until lightly browned. When done, remove shells from pans. Set aside and cook remaining shells. Some will break or not be stuffable. Fry sausage until browned and drain. Slice olives. Combine sausage, ranch dressing, olives, and cheese. Arrange cooked won ton shells on an ungreased cookie sheet. Stuff each shell about ¾ full with sausage mixture. Bake 5 to 7 minutes or until bubbly.

Makes 25 to 30

Egg roll wrappers cut in fourths may be substituted for won ton shells (available in produce department).

Carlene Elrod

Guacamole Dip

- **4 medium-size ripe avocados**
- **2 tablespoons sour cream**
- **1 tablespoon hot sauce**
- **1½ teaspoons garlic salt**
- **½ teaspoon black pepper**
- **2 tablespoons Italian dressing**
- **1 teaspoon freshly squeezed lemon juice**
- **2 teaspoons Parmesan cheese**
- **1 small sweet onion, finely chopped**
- **1 medium tomato, diced**

Skin and pit avocados. Mash avocados until you reach desired smoothness. Stir in sour cream, hot sauce, garlic salt, black pepper, Italian dressing, lemon juice, and Parmesan cheese. Add chopped sweet onion and diced tomato. Serve with corn chips for dipping or as a topping for your favorite Mexican dinners.

Serves 10

Best served 1 to 2 hours after preparation.

Natasha McCrary

Mayfair Park Cool Breeze Dip

2 (8 ounce) packages cream cheese, softened
1 (9 ounce) jar chutney
12 slices bacon, fried and crumbled
1 bunch green onions, tops and bottoms, chopped

Spread cream cheese about 1/4 to 1/2-inch thick on a large platter. Spread with chutney and sprinkle with bacon and green onions. Serve with corn chips.

Makes 2 cups

Susan Rutenberg

Buffalo Chicken Dip

4 chicken breasts, skinned and boned
2 tablespoons hot pepper sauce
2 (8 ounce) packages cream cheese, softened
1 cup prepared ranch dressing
2 cups grated Cheddar cheese

Cook and cool chicken and cut into chunks. Pour hot sauce over chicken and refrigerate for several hours. Preheat oven to 350 degrees. Mix together cream cheese, ranch dressing, Cheddar cheese, and chicken. Pour into a shallow baking dish and bake 20 to 30 minutes or until hot and bubbly. Mixture may also be cooked in a slow cooker on low about 4 hours. Serve with sturdy chips, such as large corn chips or tortilla chips.

Serves 10

Doni Harrison

Picante Dip

2 (8 ounce) packages cream cheese, softened
1 (16 ounce) jar picante sauce
1/2 cup diced onion
1 tablespoon sugar or sugar substitute

Mix cream cheese, picante sauce, onion, and sugar. Use hand-held mixer to blend. Spoon into serving bowl. Chill. Serve with favorite nacho chips.

Makes 2 to 3 cups

Darla Mason

Curried Vegetable Dip

- 1 clove garlic, mashed
- 2 cups mayonnaise
- 3 tablespoons ketchup
- 1 tablespoon Worcestershire sauce
- 2 tablespoons grated onion
- 3 tablespoons curry powder
- ½ teaspoon hot sauce
- Pinch of salt

Mash garlic and rub inside of bowl to season. Discard garlic. Combine remaining ingredients in bowl and mix well. Chill. Serve with fresh vegetables.

Makes 2¼ cups

Sue Allen

Submitted by Glenda Goldfinger

Corn Dip

- 2 (8 ounce) packages cream cheese, softened
- 1 (1 ounce) package dry ranch dressing mix
- 1 medium red bell pepper, finely chopped
- 2 (11 ounce) cans whole kernel corn, drain one can
- 1 (4½ ounce) can chopped green chiles, drained
- 1 (2¼ ounce) can sliced black olives, drained
- ½ cup mayonnaise

Mix all ingredients together and chill. Best if made the day before serving. Serve with tortilla chips or crackers.

Makes 4 cups

Add a few dashes of hot pepper sauce for a little kick.

Catherine Jones

Black Bean Salsa Dip

1 (15 ounce) can black beans
1 cup prepared salsa
¼ cup chopped green onion
¼ cup chopped red bell pepper
1 tablespoon lime juice
1 tablespoon olive oil
½ teaspoon minced onion
¼ teaspoon ground cumin
2 tablespoons chopped fresh cilantro
1 avocado, chopped

Rinse and drain black beans. Place in a large bowl. Add salsa, green onion, bell pepper, lime juice, olive oil, onion, cumin, and cilantro. Mix well. Cover and chill at least 1 hour. Add avocado just before serving with tortilla chips.

Makes 3 to 4 cups

1 tablespoon dried cilantro may be substituted for fresh cilantro.

Stella Boone

Texas Caviar

2 (15 ounce) cans black-eyed peas
1 (11 ounce) can white shoepeg corn
2 (4½ ounce) cans chopped green chiles
1 (15¼ ounce) can yellow whole kernel corn
1 (15 ounce) can black beans
2 (2¼ ounce) cans chopped black olives
3 tomatoes, chopped small
1 bunch green onions, finely chopped
½ tablespoon minced garlic
1 large bell pepper, chopped
2 fresh jalapeño peppers, seeded and minced
½ cup chopped fresh parsley
1 (16 ounce) bottle Italian dressing

Drain black-eyed peas, shoepeg corn, green chiles, corn, black beans, and olives until as dry as possible. After draining, mix well. Combine tomatoes, green onion, garlic, bell pepper, jalapeño, and parsley. Add to first ingredients and mix. Add dressing. Chill. Serve with tortilla scoops.

Serves 12

Jerry Laurine

Chocolate Chip Dip

1 (8 ounce) package cream cheese, room temperature
1 cup confectioners' sugar
1 teaspoon vanilla extract
1 cup mini chocolate chips

Mix cream cheese, confectioners' sugar, and vanilla until smooth. Fold in chocolate chips. Refrigerate in a plastic container until ready to serve. Serve with chocolate graham cracker sticks for dipping.

Makes 1 cup

This is a great dip for children.

Natasha McCrary

Olive Tapenade

2 cups kalamata olives
2 cloves garlic, finely chopped
1 tablespoon olive oil
1 tablespoon lemon juice
1 teaspoon cracked black pepper

Use small paring knife to pit olives. Place in food processor. Chop 5 seconds. Set aside. Fry garlic in olive oil until golden brown. Mix into chopped olives. Stir in lemon juice and pepper. Refrigerate. Serve on a platter with bagel chips, toast points, slices of party bread, goat cheese, and sliced Roma tomatoes.

Makes 2 cups

Dena Schrimsher

Vidalia Onion Dip

1½ cups chopped Vidalia onions
¾ cup light mayonnaise
1 cup shredded Swiss cheese

Preheat oven to 350 degrees. Mix all ingredients and bake in a lightly greased 1-quart casserole for 30 minutes. Serve with thin wheat crackers.

Serves 8

Mona Gay Keith

Chile con Queso Mexicano

- **6 fresh green chiles, roasted and peeled**
- **1 onion, chopped**
- **2 tablespoons bacon grease**
- **1 clove garlic, minced**
- **2 large fresh tomatoes, peeled and finely chopped**
- **2½ cups grated Monterey Jack or longhorn cheese**
- **Salt**

Cut chiles into lengthwise slices. Sauté chiles and onion in bacon grease. Add garlic and cook until soft. Add tomatoes, cheese, and salt to taste. Heat until cheese melts. Keep warm in chafing dish or on low in slow cooker. Serve with chips or over toast points.

Serves 4 to 6

Canned diced tomatoes may be substituted for fresh tomatoes, and ½ teaspoon canned minced garlic in oil substituted for garlic clove.

Syble Park

Boudreaux's Famous Cheese Dip

- **1 (2 pound) loaf processed cheese**
- **2 (10¾ ounce) cans cream of mushroom soup**
- **2 (10 ounce) cans tomatoes and green chiles**
- **1 pound ground beef**
- **1 pound pork sausage**
- **1 jar jalapeños (optional)**

Cut cheese into cubes and melt in a saucepan or slow cooker. Add soup and tomatoes with chiles. Brown ground beef and sausage. Drain, crumble, and add to cheese. Add jalapeños, if desired. Serve warm with chips.

Makes 5 to 6 cups

Terry T. Lewis

Hot Cheese and Sausage Dip

1 pound hot sausage
1 pound mild sausage
1 pound loaf hot Mexican processed cheese
1 (10¾ ounce) can cream of mushroom soup
1 (10¾ ounce) can nacho cheese soup
1 cup water

Brown sausage in a skillet. Drain well. In a saucepan, combine cheese, mushroom soup, cheese soup, and water. Heat until creamy. Add drained sausage. Serve warm with corn chips.

Serves 30

Daphne Reed

Smoked Oyster Dip

1 (8 ounce) package cream cheese, softened
1 teaspoon fresh lemon juice
½ teaspoon Worcestershire sauce
½ cup sour cream
1 (3.75 ounce) can smoked oysters, undrained

Blend cream cheese, lemon juice, Worcestershire, and sour cream. Combine with undrained oysters. Serve with assorted crackers.

Makes 1½ cups

Lenda Woody

Green Chile Dip

2 (4½ ounce) cans chopped green chiles, well drained
1 cup mayonnaise
1½ cups grated Parmesan cheese
1½ cups grated Monterey Jack cheese
¼ teaspoon ground cumin
⅛ teaspoon chili powder

Preheat oven to 350 degrees. Mix all ingredients well in a casserole dish. Bake 20 minutes. Serve with corn chips.

Makes 4 cups

Sharon Walker

Southwest Dip

- **2 cups sour cream**
- **½ cup mayonnaise**
- **1 (1.4 ounce) package vegetable soup mix**
- **1 cup salsa**
- **1 heaping tablespoon chili powder**
- **½ cup chopped fresh cilantro**

Mix all ingredients and serve with favorite chips.

Makes 2½ cups

Spring vegetable soup mix is not recommended.

Susan Clanton

Easy Hot Cheesy Dip

- **1 (8 ounce) carton cream cheese with pineapple**
- **2-2½ cups grated Swiss or Asiago cheese**
- **½ cup (more if desired) dried fruit of choice**
- **1 tablespoon white cooking wine**

Preheat oven to 350 degrees. Mix all ingredients and put in a 5x8-inch greased casserole. Bake 15 to 20 minutes until bubbly. Spread on favorite crackers.

Makes 1 to 2 cups

I use dried blueberries in summer, dried apples cut up in fall, and dried cranberries at Christmas. Toasted almonds may also be used.

Melissa C. Brinkley

Fruit Dip

- **1 (8 ounce) package cream cheese, softened**
- **¾ cup brown sugar**
- **¼ cup confectioners' sugar**
- **3 tablespoons condensed milk**
- **1 teaspoon vanilla extract**

Mix all ingredients together. Serve with your favorite fruit.

Serves 10 to 12

Sharon Walker

Toasted Microwave Pecans

1 quart pecan halves
¼ cup butter or margarine
1 teaspoon salt

Place butter in microwave-safe dish. Microwave on low to melt butter. Add pecans and salt. Stir to coat pecans with salt and melted butter. Place in microwave and cook 2 minutes on high. Stir pecans. Repeat cooking process 2 more times. Place on wax paper to cool.

Makes 1 quart

Stella Boone

Plantation Tea

2 quarts water
6 peppermint tea bags
½ (12 ounce) can frozen concentrate orange juice (pulp free)
½ (12 ounce) can frozen concentrate lemonade
1 cup sugar

Bring water to a boil. Steep tea bags in water 20 minutes. Add sugar and stir until dissolved. In a gallon jug, mix tea with concentrate orange juice and lemonade. Chill.

Serves 10 to 12

Natasha McCrary

Applewood Julep

4 cups apple juice
1 cup pineapple juice
1 cup orange juice
¼ cup lemon juice

Mix all ingredients and serve over ice.

Serves 6

Virginia Laux

Sparkling Cranberry Punch

8 cups cranberry juice, chilled
½ (12 ounce) can frozen pink lemonade concentrate, thawed
1 (2 liter) bottle lemon-lime carbonated beverage, chilled

Combine cranberry juice and lemonade concentrate. When ready to serve, add lemon-lime carbonated beverage. Serve chilled.

Makes 25 cups

A great punch for a ladies' morning coffee or afternoon tea.

Barbie Gardiner

Tomato Juice Appetizer

1 (46 ounce) can tomato juice
1 cup orange juice
3 tablespoons lemon juice
1 teaspoon salt
1½ teaspoons Worcestershire sauce
1½ teaspoons horseradish
3 teaspoons sugar

Mix all ingredients and chill.

Makes 15 (4-ounce) servings

This is pretty served from a punch bowl with ice ring or over ice cubes.

Hazeline Graves

Submitted by Barbara B. Cook

Hazeline, an extremely gracious hostess, was the wife of the University of Alabama Huntsville's first president. She entertained frequently and was very instrumental in helping the community and university staff get to know each other.

Two-Fruit Frosty

- **1½ cups fresh or frozen blackberries, blueberries, huckleberries, or raspberries**
- **1 cup frozen unsweetened sliced peaches, thawed**
- **1 cup milk**
- **1 cup vanilla yogurt**
- **¼-⅓ cup honey**
- **½ teaspoon ground cinnamon**
- **½ teaspoon ground nutmeg**
- **Cinnamon sticks (optional)**
- **Fresh mint (optional)**

Combine your choice of berry, peaches, and milk in blender. Cover and process on high. Add yogurt, honey, cinnamon and nutmeg. Blend well. Pour into goblets and garnish with a cinnamon stick or mint leaf, if desired. Serve immediately.

Serves 4 to 6

This is a refreshing and colorful drink to serve for brunch. The cinnamon and nutmeg give it just the right amount of zing.

Variation: Add ½ teaspoon coconut extract to above mixture and garnish with a sprinkle of coconut omitting mint leaf.

Syble Park

Hot Cranberry Punch

- **2 cups cranberry juice**
- **2½ cups unsweetened pineapple juice**
- **½ cup water**
- **⅓ cup brown sugar**
- **1½ teaspoons whole cloves**
- **1½ teaspoons whole allspice**
- **3 (2-inch) cinnamon sticks, broken**

Combine juices, water, and brown sugar. Pour into an electric percolator. Put cloves, allspice, and cinnamon sticks in percolator basket. Heat punch until it perks through the cycle.

Makes 5 cups

Camille Vaughan

Russian Tea

- **2 cups sugar**
- **¾ cup lemon juice**
- **1 teaspoon allspice**
- **12 whole cloves**
- **3 large cinnamon sticks**
- **2 cups hot water**
- **8 cups unsweetened tea**
- **4 cups pineapple juice**
- **4 cups orange juice**
- **4 cups hot water**
- **Lemon slices**

In a large pot, heat sugar, lemon juice, allspice, cloves, cinnamon sticks, and 2 cups hot water. Boil for 10 minutes. Add tea, pineapple juice, orange juice, and 4 cups hot water. Bring to boil. Remove from heat. Discard whole cloves and cinnamon sticks. Serve hot with lemon slices.

Makes 2 gallons

Leftover tea may be stored in refrigerator and reheated.

Denise McLeroy

Variation: Omit allspice; add rind of 2 lemons.

Mary Rutledge

Grandaddy's Eggnog

- **3 eggs**
- **6 tablespoons sugar**
- **⅛ teaspoon salt**
- **2 tablespoons vanilla extract**
- **2¼ cups milk**
- **¾ cup water**
- **Fresh ground nutmeg for garnish**

Beat eggs until pale yellow. Gradually beat in sugar, salt, and vanilla. Stir in milk and water. Place in a screw-top jar and allow to ripen in refrigerator for 24 hours. Serve with fresh ground nutmeg on top.

Makes 1 quart

Pasteurized eggs may be used. Substitute evaporated milk for a richer eggnog.

John Harrison

Submitted by Doni Harrison and Susan Lewis

"Silver Spoon" Boiled Custard

- **½ gallon whole milk**
- **5 egg yolks**
- **2 whole eggs**
- **1½ cups plus 2 tablespoons sugar**
- **Dash of salt**
- **2 teaspoons vanilla extract**

Scald milk in a double boiler. (Milk is scalded when a row of tiny bubbles appears around the edge.) In mixer, beat eggs. Add sugar and salt. Beat to combine well. Add small amount of scalded milk to egg mixture to temper mixture before combining ingredients. Pour heated egg mixture into scalded milk. Stir constantly over medium heat 20 to 25 minutes until custard "coats a silver spoon". (A stainless spoon works just as well.) Cool 15 minutes. Add vanilla and stir. When completely cooled, refrigerate. Custard thickens as it gets cold. Serve in bowls or compotes to eat with a spoon or in cups to drink.

Serves 8 to 9

Custard cannot come to a boil or it will curdle. Keeps about a week.

Beverly L. Fulton

Mocktails

- **3 cups pineapple juice**
- **1 (14 ounce) can sweetened condensed milk**
- **½ (12 ounce) can frozen orange juice concentrate, thawed**
- **½ teaspoon coconut extract**
- **1 (32 ounce) bottle ginger ale, chilled**

Combine pineapple juice, condensed milk, orange juice concentrate, and coconut extract in a large pitcher. Stir well. Refrigerate up to one week. To serve, pour ½ cup pineapple juice mixture into individual glasses over crushed ice and top off each glass with ⅓ cup or more ginger ale.

Serves 10

Halea Dardin

Boiled Custard

1 cup sugar
1 tablespoon all-purpose flour
4 eggs
2 teaspoons vanilla extract
1 quart milk

Mix sugar and flour thoroughly and set aside. Use blender to combine eggs and vanilla. In a heavy pan, heat milk to scalding. Reduce heat. Add sugar and flour mixture to milk. Cook 5 minutes but do not allow to boil. Remove from heat. Blend ¼ cup of milk mixture at a time with egg mixture until it measures about 2 cups. Add this to remaining milk mixture in pan. Mix well and return to heat. Stir constantly 5 to 8 minutes or until spoon is coated. Pour into jar(s) and refrigerate.

Makes approximately 1 quart

Mary Etta Vinson

Submitted by Barbara B. Cook

Sarah's Fruit Punch

6 ounces canned unsweetened pineapple juice
12 ounces white grape juice
12 ounces lemon-lime flavored carbonated beverage

Mix all ingredients and chill. Serve over ice.

Makes 3 to 4 cups

May make any amount needed using one part pineapple juice, two parts white grape juice, and two parts lemon-lime beverage.

Henrietta Wooten

AND HE TOOK BREAD,
AND GAVE THANKS, AND BRAKE IT,
AND GAVE UNTO THEM, SAYING,
"THIS IS MY BODY WHICH IS GIVEN FOR YOU:
THIS DO IN REMEMBRANCE OF ME."
LIKEWISE ALSO THE CUP AFTER SUPPER SAYING,
"THIS CUP IS THE NEW TESTAMENT IN
MY BLOOD WHICH IS SHED FOR YOU."

LUKE 22:19-20

The silver chalice engraved "M.E. Church, Huntsville, Ala." is part of the communion service used in the pre-Civil War church building from 1834 to 1864. The communion service, the communion table, and a portion of the communion rail are all that was saved from the 1864 fire.

The church building was occupied by Federal troops during what historians call The War Between the States or the Civil War (1861-1865). The soldiers were quartered in the basement and built fires on the wooden floors to cook their food. Despite the protests of the ministers about the fire hazard to the building, on the night of January 6, 1864, these fires started a blaze that burned the church to the ground.

Soups, Salads, & Sandwiches

AND THE LORD SAID UNTO MOSES, "WRITE THIS FOR A MEMORIAL IN A BOOK...."

EXODUS 17:14

The Ruth Sykes Ford Historical Room is named for our first church historian. Mrs. Ford was responsible for saving much of the history of the church when the church was busy expanding to the needs of a fast growing Huntsville. Few knew what had gone before them. She wrote a church history documenting the first 150 years of the church, even going to Washington, D.C., to research federal documents relating to the church claims for the fire accidentally caused by federal troops during the Civil War.

The photo shows part of the communion rail saved from the 1864 fire, the pulpit Bible used in the Sanctuary prior to renovations made in the 1960's, and the bell wheel used to toll the bell. The bell was installed in the present building when the belfry was complete and rang out over the city for the first time on May 17, 1868.

The bell was removed and donated to the metal drive during World War II. The wheel was removed during the renovation of the bell tower in November, 1965. It was put on the construction scrap heap. Church member G. G. Grimwood, Sr., realized what it was and saved the wheel for the history room.

Quick Shrimp Chowder

2 tablespoons margarine
1 medium onion, chopped
2-3 stalks celery, chopped
½ red bell pepper, chopped
2 (10¾ ounce) cans cream of potato soup
3½ cups milk
¼ teaspoon ground red pepper
1½ pounds medium shrimp, peeled and cut in bite-size pieces
1 cup shredded Monterey Jack cheese
Fresh parsley

Melt margarine in a Dutch oven over medium heat. Add onion, celery, and bell pepper. Sauté until tender, about 8 to 10 minutes. Stir in soup, milk, and ground red pepper. Bring to a boil. Add shrimp, reduce heat, and simmer, stirring often, 5 minutes or until shrimp turn pink. Stir in cheese until melted. Garnish with parsley.

Serves 6

May substitute canned shrimp, crawfish tails, or chicken for fresh shrimp. Substitute half-and-half for a richer soup.

Jean Kirby

Easy Vegetable Beef Soup

1 pound ground beef
1 medium onion, chopped
Salt
Pepper
1 (14½ ounce) can mixed vegetables
1 (10¾ ounce) can tomato soup
1 (14½ ounce) can diced tomatoes
1 (10 ounce) can tomatoes and green chiles
1 (15¼ ounce) can whole kernel corn
1 (15 ounce) can chili with beans
1 (15 ounce) can chili without beans
Grated cheese for garnish

Brown ground beef and onion. Drain. Add salt and pepper to taste. Place all ingredients including liquid from cans in a Dutch oven. Bring to a boil and simmer for about 1 hour, stirring occasionally. Serve with grated cheese on top.

Serves 8 to 10

Suzanne Thomason

Linda Powell's Potato Soup

- **1 (16 ounce) package frozen hash brown potatoes**
- **1 cup chopped onion**
- **1 (14 ounce) can chicken broth**
- **2 cups water**
- **1 (10¾ ounce) can cream of celery soup**
- **1 (10¾ ounce) can cream of chicken soup**
- **2 cups milk**
- **10 ounces grated sharp Cheddar or Colby Jack cheese**
- **Grated cheese**

In a 3-quart pot, combine potatoes, onion, broth, and water. Bring to a boil and simmer 30 minutes covered, stirring occasionally. Add cream of celery soup, cream of chicken soup, milk, and cheese. Cover and continue to simmer about 1 hour. Serve with grated cheese on top.

Serves 8

Linda Finnell

Variation: Increase water to 3 cups, omit cheese, add 1 teaspoon salt, and 1 teaspoon pepper. Heat 10 minutes. Garnish with sour cream and bacon bits, if desired.

Natasha McCrary

Keith's Stuffed Spud Soup

- **½ cup chopped green onion**
- **½ cup butter**
- **1 (10¾ ounce) can cream of chicken soup**
- **1 quart half-and-half or milk**
- **2 pounds frozen hash brown potatoes, thawed**
- **1 cup shredded Cheddar cheese**
- **Salt**
- **Pepper**

Sauté onion in butter. Add soup, half-and-half, and potatoes. Stir in cheese and heat gently on medium low about 45 minutes. Stir frequently to keep from burning. Add salt and pepper to taste.

Serves 4

May be made with low-fat or fat-free ingredients for a lower calorie version.

Suzanne Thomason

Winter Chicken Chili

- 4 cups fat-free chicken broth
- 2 cups cooked and deboned chicken
- 2 (15.8 ounce) cans Northern beans
- 1 (10 ounce) can tomatoes and diced green chiles
- 1 (4 ounce) can chopped green chiles (optional)
- 1 large onion, chopped
- 1 teaspoon lemon pepper
- 1 teaspoon cumin
- 1 teaspoon garlic powder
- 1 teaspoon chili powder
- 1 tablespoon lime juice

Combine all ingredients and simmer 30 minutes or longer.

Serves 6

Even better the second day. A favorite winter meal.

Terry T. Lewis

White Chili

- 1 tablespoon oil
- 1 medium onion, chopped
- 1 clove garlic, chopped
- 2 whole chicken breasts, cooked and chopped
- 1 (15.8 ounce) can white beans
- 1 (16 ounce) can garbanzo beans
- 1 (11 ounce) can whole kernel white corn
- 1 (15½ ounce) can white hominy
- 1 tablespoon chili powder
- 1 teaspoon cumin
- 2 chicken-flavored bouillon cubes
- 2 (4½ ounce) cans chopped green chiles
- 1½ cups water or chicken broth
- Salt

Preheat oven to 350 degrees. On top of stove, cook onion and garlic in oil until tender. Combine onion and garlic with all other ingredients (including liquid from cans) in a covered casserole. Salt to taste and bake 45 minutes or until bubbling. Add more liquid if chili is too thick.

Serves 8

Jean always served this with grated cheese on top. Doubles and freezes well.

Jean Payne

Submitted by Betty Lou Jones

Turnip Green Soup

- ½ pound lean ham steak, diced
- 2 tablespoons hot sauce
- 3 tablespoons olive oil
- 1½ cups chopped onion
- 1 garlic clove, minced (optional)
- 1 (16 ounce) package frozen chopped turnip greens
- 1 small smoked ham hock
- 2 cups diced red potatoes
- 6 cups chicken broth
- 2 (15 ounce) cans crowder peas, rinsed and drained
- 2 (15 ounce) cans field peas, rinsed and drained
- 1 (15 ounce) can black-eyed peas, rinsed and drained
- 2 cups water
- 1 (28 ounce) can diced tomatoes, undrained
- 1 tablespoon vinegar
- Salt
- Pepper
- ½ cup white wine

Combine ham steak, hot sauce, and oil in a large soup kettle. Cook over medium heat until ham is browned. Add onion and sauté until soft. Stir in garlic, turnip greens, ham hock, potatoes, chicken broth, peas, water, tomatoes, and vinegar. Add salt and pepper to taste. Bring to a boil. Reduce heat and simmer 1 hour, stirring often. Add wine and adjust seasonings.

Makes 5 quarts

Freezes well. Any beans or other vegetables may be substituted. For lower sodium, use dried beans and soak overnight. Adjust seasonings to taste.

Liz Herrin

Tomato Basil Soup

- 2 (28 ounce) cans crushed tomatoes
- 2 cups tomato juice
- 2 cups chicken broth
- 12-14 basil leaves, chopped
- 1 tablespoon butter
- ¼ teaspoon salt
- Pepper
- 1 teaspoon lemon juice
- 1 cup whipped cream

Combine tomatoes, juice, and broth in a large saucepan. Simmer 30 minutes. Add basil, butter, salt, pepper to taste, and lemon juice. Heat until hot, but do not boil. Just before serving, stir in whipped cream.

Makes 11 cups

Brenda Titus

Carolyn Vann's Chicken Gumbo

- 1 whole chicken
- 2-3 celery stalks, chopped
- Salt
- Pepper
- 1-2 (10 ounce) cartons frozen whole okra
- 1-2 (14½ ounce) cans tomatoes
- 1 (10 ounce) carton frozen lima beans
- 1 (10 ounce) carton frozen corn
- 1 (10 ounce) carton frozen green beans
- 1 medium onion, chopped
- 2-3 medium potatoes, cubed
- 2-3 bouillon cubes or 2 to 3 (14 ounce) cans chicken broth
- ½ teaspoon basil
- ½ teaspoon marjoram
- Dash of oregano
- Dash of red pepper (optional)
- 1 bay leaf (optional)
- 1 quart water
- ¾ cup uncooked macaroni or spaghetti, broken into small pieces

Place chicken in a large soup pot and cover with water. Add celery and salt and pepper to taste. Cook chicken until tender. Remove chicken, debone, and cut into small pieces. Remove celery, if desired. Return chicken to pot. Thaw okra slightly and chop. Add to pot along with tomatoes, lima beans, corn, green beans, onion, potatoes, bouillon or broth, basil, marjoram, and oregano. Add red pepper and bay leaf, if desired. Add about 1 quart water to cover vegetables and cook 1 to 2 hours. Add macaroni or spaghetti pieces and cook another 30 minutes. Add more seasonings and water if desired.

Serves 8-10

This gumbo is usually served fairly thick. Use fresh vegetables when available.

Carolyn Vann

Submitted by Glenda Bragg and Lenda Woody

On special occasions, Mother would prepare this in a large black iron pot, cooked over a wood fire. She would stir it with a wooden paddle that a man on the farm made for her. She loved to cook this for church picnics that were held at our father's farm. Mother would never debone the chicken. She served it bones and all!

Chicken Soup

- **Baked hen**
- **1 large onion, chopped**
- **1 large bay leaf**
- **3 stalks celery, chopped**
- **3-4 tablespoons uncooked oatmeal**
- **Leftover broth or gravy**
- **¼ cup uncooked rice**
- **1 (10¾ ounce) can tomato soup**
- **3-4 tablespoons uncooked oatmeal**
- **2 cups milk**
- **Salt**
- **Pepper**
- **Cayenne pepper**
- **Paprika**

When most of the meat of a baked hen has been used, cover the remainder with water in a large pot. Add onion, bay leaf, celery, and 3 to 4 tablespoons oatmeal. Cook at low heat until meat comes off the bones. Add any leftover broth or gravy. Cool, remove bones, and cut up the pieces of chicken. Chill mixture in refrigerator. Skim off fat. Return mixture to heat, and when it begins to simmer, add rice. Stir occasionally to prevent sticking. Add tomato soup and remaining oatmeal. When the tomato soup and oatmeal are absorbed, stir in milk. Season to taste with salt, pepper, and cayenne pepper. Simmer on low heat before serving with a dash of paprika.

Serves 6 to 8

Oatmeal serves as a thickening agent in this recipe.

Barbara Hathcock

Santa Fe Slow Cooker Soup

2 pounds ground beef
1 (15 ounce) can pinto beans, undrained
1 (16 ounce) can kidney beans, undrained
1 (11 ounce) can black beans, undrained
2 (15¼ ounce) cans whole kernel corn, drained
1 (1¼ ounce) package taco seasoning mix
1 (1 ounce) package dry ranch salad dressing mix
2 cups cold water
Tortilla chips
Sour cream
Grated sharp Cheddar cheese

Brown ground beef in a frying pan. Drain well and place in a 4 or 5-quart slow cooker. Add beans, corn, taco seasoning mix, salad dressing mix, and water. Mix well. Cook 2 hours or until hot on high setting. Serve in large soup bowls. Garnish each serving as desired with crumbled chips, a dollop of sour cream, and a sprinkle of cheese.

Makes almost 3 quarts

Helen C. Bishop

Variation: Brown 1 medium onion, chopped, with ground beef; substitute 1 (11 ounce) can of shoepeg corn for 2 (15¼ ounce) cans corn; add 1 (10 ounce) can tomatoes and green chiles, and 1 (14½ ounce) can diced tomatoes; salt and pepper to taste. Simmer in a Dutch oven on stove top for 2 hours.

Bebe Fleming

Summer Shrimp Gumbo

- **4 quarts water**
- **2-3 pounds large fresh shrimp**
- **3 ounces shrimp crab boil**
- **3 tablespoons bacon fat**
- **3 tablespoons butter**
- **1 cup diced celery**
- **1 cup diced onion**
- **1 cup diced green bell pepper**
- **3 (14½ ounce) cans peeled whole tomatoes**
- **1 large garlic clove, minced**
- **2 teaspoons Worcestershire sauce**
- **1 teaspoon salt**
- **½ teaspoon pepper**
- **1½ teaspoons thyme**
- **1 large bay leaf, crushed**
- **8 ounces frozen cut okra**
- **½ cup uncooked rice**
- **3 teaspoons gumbo filé powder**

In a large pot, bring water to a boil. Add shrimp and crab boil. Return to a boil, reduce heat, and simmer 10 minutes. Turn heat off. Let stand 10 minutes. Drain shrimp, reserving 5 cups of stock. Peel and devein shrimp. Cover and refrigerate. Put butter and bacon fat in a Dutch oven or large pot. Add celery, onion, and pepper. Cook slowly until tender (not brown). Add 4 cups of stock, reserving 1 cup for reheating. Add tomatoes, garlic, Worcestershire, salt, pepper, thyme, and bay leaf. Simmer 45 minutes. Add okra, rice, and shrimp. Simmer an additional 30 minutes or until rice is tender. Add gumbo filé powder just before serving. Stir well.

Serves 6 to 7

Do not use crushed tomatoes. Use whole tomatoes and crush yourself. Keeps well and may be made ahead. Heat slowly when reheating. Add the last cup of stock, if needed.

Barbie Gardiner

Cream Cheese Chicken Soup

- 1 small onion, chopped
- 1 tablespoon butter
- 3 cups chicken broth
- 3 medium carrots, cut into ¼ inch slices (or 2 cups frozen)
- 3 medium potatoes, peeled and cubed
- 2 cups cubed cooked or canned chicken
- 2 tablespoons minced fresh parsley
- ½ teaspoon garlic powder
- Dash of chili powder
- Salt
- Pepper
- ¼ cup all-purpose flour
- 1 cup milk
- 1 (8 ounce) package cream cheese, cubed

In a large saucepan, sauté onion in butter. When clear, add broth, carrots, and potatoes. Bring to a boil. Reduce heat to medium low. Cover and simmer 15 to 20 minutes or until veggies are tender. Add chicken, parsley, garlic powder, chili powder, and salt and pepper to taste. Combine flour and milk until smooth. Add to soup mixture. Bring to a boil. Cook and stir 2 minutes or until thickened. Reduce heat. Add cream cheese and stir until cheese is melted.

Serves 8

Syble Park

Chicken Noodle Soup

- 4 cups water
- 1 (2.1 ounce) envelope chicken noodle soup mix
- 1 (10¾ ounce) can cream of chicken soup
- 1 (10 ounce) can boneless chicken, undrained
- ½ (16 ounce) bag medium egg noodles

In a large saucepan, bring water to boil. Add soup mix to boiling water. Stir in soup and chicken. Return to boil. Add egg noodles. Turn heat down and simmer slowly until noodles are soft, about 10 minutes.

Serves 6

Serve with our family favorite, peanut butter and honey sandwiches!

Angela Stahl

Sunday Night Chili

4 pounds ground round
3 cups chopped onion
½ teaspoon garlic powder
8 tablespoons chili powder
4 teaspoons all-purpose flour
4 teaspoons cocoa
3-4 teaspoons salt
2 tablespoons ground cumin
2 tablespoons sugar
4 cups water
2 (15 ounce) cans tomato sauce
1 (14½ ounce) can diced tomatoes
2 (16 ounce) cans kidney beans

Cook meat with onion. Drain if needed. Mix garlic powder, chili powder, flour, cocoa, salt, cumin, and sugar together in small bowl. Add seasoning mixture to cooked meat, stirring with a fork to infuse seasonings into meat. This is the key to this chili. Add water, tomato sauce, and tomatoes. Simmer 45 minutes. Add beans and cook an additional 20 minutes.

Serves 12 to 15

Trudy Striplin

Vegetable Chili

1 large onion, chopped
1 tablespoon olive oil
1 (28 ounce) can diced tomatoes
⅔ cup picante sauce, mild or medium
1½ teaspoons ground cumin
1 teaspoon salt
½ teaspoon dried basil or 2 teaspoons chopped fresh basil
1 (15 ounce) can black beans
1 large red or yellow bell pepper, chopped
1 large zucchini or yellow squash, sliced
Cilantro
Shredded Cheddar cheese
Sour cream

Sauté onion in oil in a large pot until tender. Add tomatoes, picante sauce, cumin, salt, and basil. Simmer over medium heat 5 minutes. Add black beans, bell pepper, and squash. Cover and simmer 15 minutes. Top with cilantro, cheese, or sour cream.

Serves 6

Camille Vaughan

Chili

1 pound hamburger
½ cup chopped onion
1 (16 ounce) can light red kidney beans, undrained
2 (8 ounce) cans tomato sauce
1 teaspoon salt
1-2 teaspoons chili powder

Brown meat and chopped onion in a large saucepan. Drain excess grease. Stir in beans, tomato sauce, salt, and chili powder. Bring to a boil, cover, reduce heat to low, and simmer 45 minutes. Stir occasionally.

Serves 4

Linda Dedrick

Spanish Bean Soup

3 tablespoons olive oil
1 green bell pepper, chopped
1 onion, chopped
1 clove garlic, minced
1 (16 ounce) can garbanzo beans, undrained
1 (1/28 ounce) packet Spanish flavoring and coloring mix
1 chorizo sausage, thinly sliced
2 potatoes, peeled and sliced
3 cups water
Salt
Pepper

In a 4-quart kettle, heat olive oil. Add green pepper, onion, and garlic and sauté until soft. Add beans, flavoring and coloring mix, sausage, potatoes, and water. Bring to a boil, stirring well. Add salt and pepper to taste. Reduce heat and simmer until thickened, 45 minutes to 1 hour.

Serves 3 to 4

This soup is easy to make and freezes well. May also be made ahead or doubled. If chorizo sausage is not available, substitute kielbasa.

Barbara Cook

Camille Vaughan's Chicken Pasta Salad

DAY 1

- **2 chicken breasts, or 4 halves, cooked and chopped**
- **4 tablespoons balsamic vinegar**
- **1½ teaspoons salt**

Sprinkle chicken with vinegar and salt. Refrigerate.

DAY 2

- **8 ounces linguine**
- **1 tablespoon olive oil**
- **1 cup mayonnaise**
- **½ teaspoon dill weed**
- **⅛ teaspoon black pepper**
- **1 cup finely chopped celery**
- **½ cup red or yellow bell pepper, chopped**
- **½ teaspoon celery seed**
- **½ cup chopped fresh parsley**
- **¼ teaspoon Creole seasoning**
- **2 teaspoons lemon juice**

Cook linguine and toss with olive oil. Set aside. Mix mayonnaise, dill weed, black pepper, celery, bell pepper, celery seed, fresh parsley, Creole seasoning, and lemon juice together. Toss well with chicken and pasta. Keep refrigerated.

Serves 8 to 10

Pasta of your choice may be substituted for linguine.

Julia Parker

Chicken Salad

- **3 cups mayonnaise**
- **1 tablespoon curry powder**
- **2 tablespoons soy sauce**
- **2 tablespoons lemon juice**
- **8 cups diced, cooked chicken**
- **1 (8 ounce) can sliced water chestnuts, drained**
- **2 pounds seedless grapes**
- **2 cups chopped celery**
- **2 cups slivered almonds, toasted**

In a very large bowl, mix mayonnaise, curry, soy sauce, and lemon juice. Add chicken, water chestnuts, grapes, celery, and almonds and mix well.

Serves 12 to 14

Jean Hinson

Nancy's Chicken and Pasta Salad

DAY 1

- **1 (16 ounce) package angel hair pasta**
- **2 cups zesty Italian dressing**
- **2 tablespoons lemon pepper**
- **Salt**
- **2 (6 ounce) jars marinated artichokes, chopped**
- **4 tablespoons finely chopped flat leaf parsley**
- **2 teaspoons basil**
- **2 teaspoons oregano**
- **2 bunches spring onions, finely chopped**
- **2 cups mayonnaise**
- **6 cups cooked, chopped (in large pieces) chicken breasts**

Cook pasta according to package directions. Drain well. Combine dressing, lemon pepper, and salt to taste. Add dressing to pasta. Mix well, cover, and refrigerate overnight. In another bowl, combine artichokes, parsley, basil, oregano, onion, and mayonnaise. Mix well. Add to chicken and stir well. Cover and refrigerate overnight.

DAY 2

- **1 red bell pepper, chopped**
- **1 green bell pepper, chopped**
- **1 yellow bell pepper, chopped**
- **1 (4 ounce) jar chopped black olives**
- **1½ cups small cherry tomatoes, halved**
- **2 cups grated Parmesan cheese**

Using a large mixing bowl to ensure a good mix, combine pasta and chicken mixtures. Add peppers, black olives, and tomatoes. Mix well. Just before serving, add Parmesan cheese and mix again.

Serves 20

Gladys Sullins

Mandarin Pasta Salad

DRESSING

- **1 teaspoon peeled finely chopped gingerroot**
- **1 clove garlic, pressed**
- **⅓ cup rice vinegar or white wine vinegar**
- **¼ cup orange juice**
- **¼ cup vegetable oil**
- **1 teaspoon sesame oil**
- **1 (1 ounce) envelope onion soup mix**
- **2 teaspoons sugar**

SALAD

- **8 ounces uncooked bow tie pasta**
- **½ cucumber, scored, seeded, and sliced**
- **½ cup diced red bell pepper**
- **½ cup coarsely chopped red onion**
- **1 (6 ounce) package fresh baby spinach**
- **1 (11 ounce) can Mandarin oranges, drained**
- **2 cups diced, cooked chicken**
- **½ cup sliced almonds, toasted**

Whisk together gingerroot, garlic, vinegar, orange juice, vegetable oil, sesame oil, soup mix, and sugar. Refrigerate until ready to use. For salad, cook pasta according to package directions. Drain and rinse under cold water. Cut cucumber slices in half. Combine cucumber, bell pepper, onion, spinach, oranges, chicken, and almonds. Add to pasta. Pour dressing over salad and toss. Serve immediately.

Serves 12

Linda Finnell

Crab Louis

DRESSING

1 cup mayonnaise
2 tablespoons lemon juice
1 tablespoon finely chopped chives
1 tablespoon finely chopped green onion
1 tablespoon minced green bell pepper
½ cup chili sauce
¼ teaspoon hot pepper sauce
1 teaspoon Worcestershire sauce
⅛ teaspoon cayenne pepper
Salt

SALAD

4 (6 ounce) cans lump crabmeat, or 1 (16 ounce) can, drained
Lettuce
6 tomatoes, cut into wedges
6 hard-boiled eggs, cut into wedges

To make dressing, combine mayonnaise, lemon juice, chives, onion, green pepper, chili sauce, hot sauce, Worcestershire, and pepper. Mix well. Add salt to taste and chill. Pick through crabmeat, removing any bits of shell. For each serving, arrange a bed of lettuce on a plate and place a generous serving of crabmeat in center. Surround with tomato wedges and egg wedges. Drizzle generously with chilled dressing.

Serves 6

Make salad dressing ahead of time and chill to allow seasonings to meld properly. Dressing keeps well in refrigerator.

Carol Hurst

Mexican Cornbread Salad

1 (8½ ounce) box cornbread mix
1 (4½ ounce) can chopped green chiles, drained
½ cup light mayonnaise
½ cup chopped fresh cilantro
¼ cup lime juice
1 teaspoon ground cumin
½ teaspoon salt
½ head iceberg lettuce, chopped
1 head romaine lettuce, chopped
1 (15 ounce) can black beans, rinsed and drained
1 (11 ounce) can shoepeg corn, drained
8 ounces shredded sharp Cheddar cheese
1 large red bell pepper, chopped
1 small sweet onion, chopped
2 tomatoes, chopped or grape tomatoes
2-3 grilled chicken breasts, chopped (optional)

Prepare cornbread mix according to package directions, adding chiles. Cool and crumble. Process mayonnaise, cilantro, lime juice, cumin, and salt in food processor until smooth. Refrigerate. At least 2 hours before serving, combine cornbread, mayonnaise mixture, lettuce, beans, corn, cheese, pepper, onion, and tomatoes. Cover and refrigerate. If using chicken, marinate with 2 to 3 tablespoons olive oil, 2 to 3 tablespoons lemon juice, and 1 to 2 teaspoons lemon pepper seasoning. Grill until done. Add to salad.

Serves 8

Judy McLaurine

English Cucumber Potato Salad

SALAD

4-5 medium red potatoes, boiled, peeled, and thinly sliced
2 medium English cucumbers, unpeeled and thinly sliced
1 medium sweet onion, thinly sliced

DRESSING

½-1 cup light mayonnaise
1 cup sour cream or plain yogurt
1 tablespoon dried dill weed
2 teaspoons salt
3-4 tablespoons white wine vinegar
Dash Worcestershire sauce

Drain potatoes on a paper towel for at least 1 hour. In a large bowl, combine potatoes, cucumbers, and onion. In a separate bowl, mix all the dressing ingredients. Pour over salad, mix, and chill.

Serves 4

Beverly McCulloch

Party Chicken Salad

4 boneless, skinless chicken breasts
½ cup chopped pecans, toasted
½ cup finely chopped celery
½ Red Delicious apple, finely chopped
¾ cup mayonnaise
Lettuce leaves
Tomato wedges
Grapes

Preheat oven to 350 degrees. Place chicken breasts in a large pan and cover with water. Boil approximately 20 minutes after water comes to a boil. Remove chicken from water and set aside to cool. While chicken cools, place chopped pecans in oven for about 5 minutes to toast. Cut chicken into ½-inch cubes. In a large bowl, combine chicken, pecans, celery, and apple. Stir in mayonnaise. If mixture is too dry, stir in additional mayonnaise. Cover and place in refrigerator to allow flavors to mix. Serve on a bed of lettuce leaves and garnish with a wedge of tomato on top and grapes on the side.

Serves 6 to 8

Goes well with small sandwiches made from date-nut bread with cream cheese filling.

Lossie Small

Potato Salad

5 large potatoes
5 boiled eggs, grated
1 medium green bell pepper, chopped
1 medium onion, chopped
2 whole dill pickles, chopped
5 tablespoons sweet pickle relish
1 (2 ounce) jar chopped pimiento
1 tablespoon yellow mustard
1½-2 cups mayonnaise
1½ teaspoons salt
½ teaspoon pepper

Preheat oven to 400 degrees. Bake potatoes for 1 hour or until done. Cool until they can be comfortably handled. Peel and cut into 1½-inch cubes. Add eggs, bell pepper, onion, pickle, relish, pimiento, mustard, mayonnaise, salt, and pepper. Mix until potatoes are completely coated. Refrigerate. If potato salad seems too dry when ready to serve, add more mayonnaise and mix well.

Serves 12

Best made a couple of days ahead.

Love Burroughs

Submitted by Linda Finnell

My sister always had a big 4th of July party for our family and we all looked forward to her potato salad.

Cold Peanut Rice Salad

1½ cups water
1½ cups instant rice
1 teaspoon salt
1 cup frozen green peas
½ cup chopped celery
1 tablespoon chopped onion
1 tablespoon dried parsley
¼ cup chopped dill pickle
¼ cup chopped green bell pepper
¼ cup grated carrot
1 cup mayonnaise
2 teaspoons Dijon mustard
1 cup salted peanuts

Cook rice according to directions on box. Add salt, peas, celery, onion, parsley, pickle, green pepper, carrot, mayonnaise, and mustard. Mix gently and refrigerate. Just before serving, add peanuts.

Serves 6

Sue Day

Shrimp Pasta

4½ cups salted water
1½ pounds unpeeled medium shrimp
2 cups cooked elbow macaroni
1 cup frozen English peas, thawed
2 hard-boiled eggs, chopped
1 small green bell pepper, chopped
¼ cup chopped pimiento stuffed olives
2 tablespoons chopped pimiento
1 tablespoon chopped green onion
1 cup mayonnaise
Salt
Pepper
Lettuce leaves
Tomato wedges
Canned asparagus spears, chilled

Bring water to a boil. Add shrimp and cook for 3 to 5 minutes. Drain. Peel and devein. Chill. Combine shrimp, macaroni, peas, eggs, bell pepper, olives, pimiento, and green onion. Mix well. Stir in mayonnaise and salt and pepper to taste. Toss gently. Chill. Serve on lettuce with a garnish of tomato and asparagus.

Serves 4

One pound cooked and peeled shrimp may be used instead of raw shrimp.

Glenda Bragg

Shrimp and Mango Salad

DRESSING

¼ cup mayonnaise
2 tablespoons prepared horseradish
1 tablespoon white vinegar
⅛ teaspoon black pepper

SALAD

¾ pound large shrimp, cooked, peeled, and deveined
1 cup peeled and cubed mango
¾ cup cooked white rice
¼ cup chopped red bell pepper
¼ cup chopped green bell pepper

In a small mixing bowl, whisk together mayonnaise, horseradish, vinegar, and black pepper. Set aside. In a large bowl, toss together shrimp, mango, rice, and bell pepper. Pour dressing over shrimp mixture. Toss gently. Thoroughly chill before serving.

Serves 2

Judith Austin

Curried Chicken Salad

1 cup mango chutney
1½ cups mayonnaise
1 tablespoon sandwich and salad sauce
2 teaspoons curry powder
Pinch of cayenne pepper
2 teaspoons salt
6-8 large chicken breasts, cooked and cut into bite-size chunks
3-4 green onions, chopped
1½ cups diced celery
1 cup raisins
1½ cups roasted, salted cashews

In the bowl of a food processor, combine chutney, mayonnaise, salad sauce, curry powder, pepper, and salt. Pulse until well combined. Set aside. Combine chicken, green onions, celery, raisins, and ¾ of the curry sauce. Refrigerate salad and remaining ¼ of the curry sauce. When ready to serve, add cashews and remaining sauce if needed.

Serves 8 to 10

Katie Clark

Chicken and Wild Rice Salad

1 cup wild rice
4 cups chopped cooked chicken
1-1½ cups sour cream
1-1½ cups mayonnaise
1 teaspoon curry powder
1 cup chopped celery
1 cup sliced water chestnuts
1 cup sliced almonds
Salt
2 (11 ounce) cans Mandarin oranges, drained
2 (8 ounce) cans pineapple chunks in its own juice, drained

Wash wild rice, cook according to directions, and chill. Combine rice, chicken, sour cream, mayonnaise, curry powder, celery, water chestnuts, and almonds. Add salt to taste and chill. Just before serving, add Mandarin oranges and pineapple.

Serves 8 to 10

May prepare ahead except for oranges and pineapple. Pretty served in trifle or crystal bowl placed in center of lettuce covered tray surrounded by sliced or balled cantaloupe, honeydew, white grapes, raisins, bananas, etc.

Joy Smith

Fiesta Romaine Salad

SALAD

10-12 cups bite-size romaine lettuce
2 pears, unpeeled and thinly sliced
2 apples, unpeeled and thinly sliced
1 (6 ounce) bag dried sweetened cranberries
1 (6 ounce) can cashews, chopped
1 cup shredded Swiss cheese

DRESSING

⅔ cup canola oil
⅓ cup lemon juice
½ cup sugar
1 teaspoon Dijon mustard
1 tablespoon poppy seed

In a large bowl, combine salad ingredients. In a small bowl, whisk dressing ingredients together. Pour over salad and mix well.

Serves 12

Doris Hagefstration

Speedy Spinach, Cranberry and Cashew Salad

1 (6 ounce) bag fresh baby spinach, washed
1 (6 ounce) package dried cranberries
1 (6 or 9 ounce) container roasted cashews
1 (6 ounce) package shredded Swiss cheese
1 bottle raspberry vinaigrette salad dressing

Place spinach in a large salad bowl. Add as many cranberries, cashews, and cheese as desired. Add enough salad dressing to lightly coat.

Serves 4 to 6

Mary Evelyn French

Gourmet Salad and Dressing

DRESSING

1 cup vegetable oil
½ cup vinegar
⅔ cup sugar
½ teaspoon dry mustard
½ teaspoon garlic salt
2 green onions, thinly sliced

SALAD

2 bags romaine lettuce
½ cup sliced almonds, toasted
1 (3 ounce) jar real bacon bits
8-10 sliced strawberries or 2 (8.25 ounce) cans Mandarin oranges, drained
4 ounces shredded Parmesan cheese

Mix all ingredients for salad dressing and chill overnight. Assemble salad just before serving. Serve dressing on the side or toss salad with dressing as needed to coat all the lettuce.

Serves 8

Dressing makes enough to cover 3 bags of lettuce.

Carol Hurst

Spinach Salad "My Way"

SALAD

1 (10 ounce) package baby spinach
½-1 cup julienned sun-dried tomatoes packed in oil, drained
⅓ cup golden raisins
½ cup toasted pecans
½ cup crumbled blue cheese

DRESSING

5 tablespoons olive oil
3 tablespoons jalapeño pepper jelly or bell pepper jelly
2 tablespoons balsamic vinegar

Toss together spinach, tomatoes, raisins, pecans, and blue cheese. Mix oil, jelly, and vinegar well, making sure jelly has dissolved. When ready to serve, add dressing to spinach mixture and toss well.

Serves 4 to 6

Trudy Striplin

Mother's Frozen Fruit Salad

1 (14 ounce) can sweetened condensed milk
¼ cup lemon juice
1 (20 ounce) can crushed pineapple and juice
1 (16 ounce) can cherry pie filling
2 bananas, chopped
½ cup chopped pecans
½ cup chopped canned pears
½ cup chopped canned peaches
1 (8 ounce) carton frozen nondairy whipped topping, thawed

Beat milk and lemon juice until thick. Fold in remaining ingredients and spoon into a 9x13-inch casserole dish or 3-quart mold. Freeze.

Serves 12 to 16

Betty Peeler

Variation: For a smaller salad, omit lemon juice, bananas, pecans, pears, and peaches. Drain pineapple well. Pour into an 8-inch dish or paper-lined muffin tins and freeze. Remove from freezer 10 minutes before serving.

Pat Smith

Frozen Fruit Salad

2 (8 ounce) cartons sour cream
¾ cup sugar
Dash of salt
2 tablespoons fresh lemon juice
4 slices canned pineapple rings
6 maraschino cherries, chopped
⅓ cup chopped pecans
1 banana, cut into small pieces
Lettuce leaves

Combine sour cream, sugar, and salt. Add lemon juice. Cut pineapple slices into bite-size pieces. Add to sour cream mixture along with cherries, pecans, and banana. Pour into muffin tins lined with paper baking cups, filling each cup ¾ full. Freeze. Unmold and serve on lettuce.

Serves 12 to15

Doris Anne Little

Submitted by Margaret Anne Whitsett

Pink Arctic Salad

1 (8 ounce) package cream cheese, softened
2 tablespoons mayonnaise
2 tablespoons sugar
1 (8 ounce) can whole berry cranberry sauce
1 cup crushed pineapple, drained
½ cup English walnuts or pecans, chopped
1 cup whipped topping

Blend cream cheese with mayonnaise, sugar, cranberry sauce, pineapple, and nuts. Fold in whipped topping. Place foil liners in muffin tins and fill with salad mixture. Freeze. When frozen, remove from muffin tins, place in a freezer bag, and store in freezer. Remove from freezer 10 minutes before serving.

Serves 8 to 10

Barbara Hathcock

Variation 1: Reduce cream cheese to 6 ounces. Use one (16 ounce) can whole berry cranberry sauce, and one (8 ounce) cartoh whipping cream, whipped.

Jean Hinson

Variation 2: Increase sugar to ¼ cup; use one (20 ounce) can crushed pineapple, drained; increase pecans to ¾ cup and whipped topping to 12 ounces.

Bessie Monroe

Submitted by Jane Monroe

Nutty Cabbage Slaw

½ cup mayonnaise
2 tablespoons sugar
2 tablespoons vinegar
4 cups coarsely chopped cabbage
1 cup salted Spanish peanuts, chopped
Cabbage leaves (optional)

Combine mayonnaise, sugar, and vinegar. Mix well. Chill 2 hours. Combine cabbage and peanuts. Add dressing and toss gently. Serve on cabbage leaves if desired.

Serves 6

Great with barbecue.

Barbie Gardiner

1000 Island Dressing

1 cup mayonnaise
¼ cup ketchup
1 thin slice of onion
1 teaspoon dried parsley flakes
1-2 stalks celery, chopped
2 sweet pickles, chopped

Place all ingredients in a blender or food processor. Blend until almost puréed.

Makes about 1½ cups

May substitute 2 teaspoons sweet pickle relish for chopped sweet pickles. Great over sliced tomato topped with boiled shrimp or fresh crab.

Camille Vaughan

Roquefort Salad Dressing

1 quart mayonnaise (regular or low fat, but NOT non-fat)
6 ounces Roquefort or blue cheese
1 teaspoon Worcestershire sauce
3 teaspoons lemon juice
2 cloves garlic, minced fine
2-4 shakes of hot pepper sauce

Combine half of mayonnaise with other ingredients in a blender or food processor. Blend well. Combine with the remaining half of mayonnaise in a large bowl. Cover and refrigerate 12 to 24 hours before serving.

Makes 1 quart

Doni Harrison

Caesar Salad Dressing

1 quart mayonnaise
6 eggs
1 (1 ounce) envelope dry onion soup mix
2 heaping teaspoons anchovy paste
½ teaspoon curry powder
1½ cups grated Parmesan cheese

Combine all ingredients in bowl of mixer. Blend at medium speed 3 to 5 minutes. Refrigerate.

Makes 1 quart

Excellent served over a mixture of romaine and iceberg lettuce. Add croutons if desired.

Kay Brotherton

Poppy Seed Dressing

1½ cups sugar
2 teaspoons dry mustard
⅔ cup vinegar
2 teaspoons salt
3 tablespoons onion juice
2 cups vegetable oil
3 tablespoons poppy seed

Mix sugar, mustard, vinegar, and salt in food processor. Add onion juice and mix thoroughly. Add oil slowly with processor running until thick. Add poppy seed and process a few times. Serve over fruit. Store in refrigerator. Do not freeze.

Makes 3½ cups

Lady Jane Vowell

Variation: Substitute 3 tablespoons chopped onion for onion juice.

Martha Dotzheimer

Carolina Coleslaw

1 teaspoon salt
¼ teaspoon pepper
½ teaspoon dry mustard
½ teaspoon celery seed
2 tablespoons sugar
3 tablespoons canola oil
⅓ cup white vinegar
4 cups finely shredded cabbage (½ head)

Place all ingredients in a large bowl in the order listed. Mix well as you add each ingredient. Cover and refrigerate at least 3 hours. Before serving, mix again and drain excess liquid.

Serves 6 to 8

May be made the day before. Keeps quite well for several days in the refrigerator. Wonderful served with barbecue.

Ferne Leonard

Coleslaw with Cranberries

SLAW

5 cups shredded cabbage
1½ cups dried cranberries
½ cup diced celery
½ cup chopped green onions, white and green parts
½ cup chopped green bell pepper
½ cup almonds, toasted

DRESSING

½ cup mayonnaise
1 tablespoon sweet pickle relish
1 tablespoon honey mustard
1 tablespoon honey
Salt
Pepper

Combine cabbage, cranberries, celery, green onion, and green pepper in a large plastic bowl with a cover. For dressing, combine mayonnaise, relish, mustard, honey, and salt and pepper to taste. Refrigerate until ready to serve. Add almonds and dressing just before serving. Stir well.

Serves 10 to 12

You may buy cabbage already shredded in the produce department. Angel hair shredded cabbage is not recommended. It becomes too limp when dressing is added.

Gina Martin Johnston

Shoepeg Corn Salad

1 green bell pepper, diced
2 tomatoes, diced
2 (11 ounce) cans shoepeg corn, drained
¼ purple onion, diced (do not substitute)
½ cup sour cream
4 tablespoons mayonnaise
2 tablespoons white vinegar
1 teaspoon dry mustard
¼ teaspoon pepper
1 teaspoon salt, or to taste

Combine all ingredients. Chill overnight or several hours before serving.

Serves 6 to 8

Jerry Laurine

Variation: Mayonnaise and salt and pepper, to taste, may be substituted for dressing ingredients.

Gwen Riley

Betty Lee's Kraut Salad

1 cup sugar
½ cup vinegar
10 ounces canned shredded kraut, drained
½ cup sliced green olives
1 cup grated carrots
½ cup chopped green bell pepper
½ cup chopped celery
¼ cup chopped onion
¼ teaspoon celery seed
⅛ teaspoon pepper

Combine sugar and vinegar in a small saucepan. Cook about 5 minutes until syrupy. Set aside to cool some. Combine drained kraut, olives, carrots, green pepper, celery, onion, celery seed, and pepper. Pour sugar mixture over kraut mixture and refrigerate for several hours.

Serves 6 to 8

Traci Conner

Marinated Vegetable Salad

1 head cauliflower
1 bunch broccoli
1 bunch green onions, sliced
½ cup mayonnaise
½ cup sour cream
Garlic powder
1 (10 ounce) package frozen peas, thawed

Cut cauliflower and broccoli florets into bite size pieces. Add onion, mayonnaise, sour cream, and a dash of garlic powder. Add thawed peas. Stir well. Refrigerate overnight.

Serves 6 to 8

Marguerite Simpson

Apple Walnut Coleslaw

- **1 cup mayonnaise**
- **½ cup sugar**
- **¼ cup vinegar**
- **1 teaspoon salt**
- **2 Red Delicious apples**
- **1 bag coleslaw mix**
- **1 cup chopped walnuts or pecans**

In a bowl, combine mayonnaise, sugar, vinegar, and salt. Chop apples into bite-size pieces and add to dressing mixture. Add slaw mix and walnuts. Toss and serve.

Serves 8

Karen Stahl

Rainbow Shrimp Salad

- **1 pound raw shrimp**
- **3 cups cooked rice**
- **½ cup mayonnaise, or as desired**
- **¼ cup chopped green olives**
- **¼ cup chopped pimiento**
- **¼ cup chopped celery**
- **¼ cup chopped green bell pepper**
- **¼ cup chopped onion**
- **Salt**
- **Pepper**
- **Lettuce**
- **Sour cream**
- **1 lemon, cut in wedges**

Bring 2 to 3 quarts of water to a boil in a large pot. Add shrimp, cook 3 to 5 minutes or just until pink. Drain and rinse with cold water. Peel shrimp and chop coarsely. Combine shrimp, rice, mayonnaise, olives, pimiento, celery, green pepper, and onion in a large bowl. Add salt and pepper to taste. Stir gently until well mixed. Serve on lettuce with a dollop of sour cream and a lemon wedge.

Serves 6 to 8

Lenda Woody

Broccoli Salad

SALAD

- **1 large bunch broccoli florets**
- **¾ cup white raisins or dried cranberries**
- **½ cup sunflower seeds**
- **4 tablespoons chopped red onion**
- **½ pound bacon, cooked and crumbled**

DRESSING

- **1 cup mayonnaise**
- **2 tablespoons apple cider vinegar**
- **2 tablespoons sugar**
- **4 tablespoons milk**

Combine broccoli, raisins or cranberries, sunflower seeds, and onion. Mix dressing ingredients and pour over salad. Chill for 4 hours. Add bacon just before serving.

Serves 4 to 6

Henrietta Wooten

Colorful Vegetable Salad

- **¼ cup sugar**
- **½ cup cider vinegar**
- **½ cup vegetable oil**
- **1 teaspoon salt**
- **1 teaspoon paprika**
- **2 (14½ ounce) cans French style green beans, drained**
- **2 (15½ ounce) cans black-eyed peas, drained**
- **2 (15 ounce) cans small green peas, drained**
- **2 (4 ounce) jars diced pimientos, drained**
- **1 cup sliced green onion**
- **1 (16 ounce) package frozen shoepeg corn, thawed**
- **1 green bell pepper, diced**
- **1 cup diced celery**

Bring sugar, vinegar, oil, salt, and paprika to a boil over medium heat, stirring until sugar dissolves, about 5 minutes. Remove from heat and cool 30 minutes. In a large bowl, stir together beans, peas, pimiento, onion, corn, green pepper, and celery. Gently stir in cooled dressing. Cover and refrigerate at least 8 hours. Serve with a slotted spoon.

Serves 8 to 10

Helen Lewis

Sweet and Sour Cucumber Salad

- **2 medium cucumbers, unpeeled**
- **1 medium sweet onion**
- **1 medium green bell pepper, chopped**
- **¼ cup sugar**
- **½ cup cider vinegar**
- **½ teaspoon salt**
- **¼ teaspoon coarsely ground black pepper**

Slice cucumbers and onion as thin as possible in large salad bowl. Add green pepper. Whisk sugar, vinegar, salt, and pepper together and pour over cucumber mixture. Marinate several hours before serving.

Serves 4 to 6

Even better the next day.

Judy McLaurine

West Indies Salad - Almost

- **1 pound freshly caught bream**
- **1 (3 ounce) package crab boil seasoning**
- **1 medium onion, finely chopped**
- **Salt**
- **Pepper**
- **4 ounces vegetable oil**
- **3 ounces cider vinegar**
- **3 ounces ice water**
- **1 bunch mixed salad greens**

Poach bream in water with crab boil. Remove bones. Spread half of chopped onion in bottom of bowl. Add bream and spread with remaining onion. Salt and pepper to taste. Add oil, vinegar, and then water. Cover and place in refrigerator to marinate for 2 to 12 hours. When ready to serve, toss lightly but do not stir. Place over mixed greens and serve as a luncheon salad.

Serves 6 to 8

May also be served as an appetizer with crackers.

Elgin Geron

Submitted by Paula Sanders

Variation: For a true West Indies Salad, substitute 1 pound select lump crabmeat, washed and cleaned, for the bream; increase ice water to 4 ounces. Marinate for 2 days.

Monica Bell

Tomato Aspic

- **1 green bell pepper, finely chopped**
- **3 stalks celery with some leaves, finely chopped**
- **1 green onion, thinly sliced**
- **1 cup sliced olives**
- **3 (¼ ounce) envelopes plain gelatin**
- **1 (46 ounce) bottle tomato-vegetable juice**
- **2-3 drops hot pepper sauce (optional)**
- **Mayonnaise and parsley for garnish**

Coat a 9x13-inch glass baking dish with cooking spray. Mix pepper, celery, onion, and olives in dish and set aside. In a small pan, soften gelatin in 1 cup of the juice and heat until gelatin dissolves. Add gelatin mixture and remaining juice to the dish. Add hot pepper sauce and stir well. Refrigerate until congealed. Put a dollop of mayonnaise and a sprig of parsley on each serving.

Serves 10 to 12

Dale Rhoades

Molded Chicken Salad

- **1 (¼ ounce) envelope unflavored gelatin**
- **¼ cup cold water**
- **1 chicken bouillon cube**
- **1 cup boiling water**
- **1 cup mayonnaise**
- **1 teaspoon salt**
- **Pepper**
- **4 cups chopped cooked chicken**
- **4 medium stalks celery, finely chopped**
- **½ pound seedless white grapes, cut in half**

Soak gelatin in cold water for 5 minutes. Dissolve bouillon cube in boiling water, add gelatin mixture, and cool. Stir slowly into mayonnaise until smooth. Add salt, pepper to taste, chicken, celery, and grapes. Turn into a greased 8x8x2-inch square container. Chill until set. Cut into squares and serve on lettuce. Serve with stuffed eggs, carrot curls, and ripe olives. Or, turn into a mold with a large open center. Pile carrot curls and ripe olives in the center.

Serves 8

Recipe may be doubled for a large luncheon or buffet supper, or placed in individual molds.

Virginia Cook

Pretzel Strawberry Salad

- **2 cups crushed pretzels**
- **1 tablespoon sugar**
- **¾ cup melted butter**
- **1 cup sugar**
- **2 (8 ounce) packages cream cheese, softened**
- **1 (8 ounce) carton frozen whipped topping, thawed**
- **1 (6 ounce) box strawberry flavored gelatin**
- **2 cups boiling water**
- **2 (10 ounce) packages frozen strawberries**

Preheat oven to 350 degrees. Coat a 9x13-inch glass dish with vegetable spray. Combine pretzels, 1 tablespoon sugar, and melted butter. Mix well and press into dish. Bake 8 minutes. Cool. Cream remaining sugar, cream cheese, and whipped topping. Pour over cooled crust. Dissolve gelatin in water. Add frozen strawberries and mix well. Chill until thickened. Pour over cream cheese mixture. Chill.

Serves 12 to 16

Paula Sanders

Spiced Peach Congealed Salad

- **1 (1 pound 9 ounce) jar pickled peaches, diced**
- **1 (6 ounce) box lemon flavored gelatin**
- **1½ cups orange juice**
- **1 cup chopped pecans**
- **Mayonnaise**

Drain peaches, adding enough water to syrup to make 2 cups. Heat syrup and water mixture. Add gelatin and stir until dissolved. Add orange juice. Cool until mixture begins to thicken. Add peaches and pecans. Pour into greased individual molds and refrigerate until congealed. When ready to serve, unmold and top each serving with a teaspoon of mayonnaise.

Serves 10-12

Doni Harrison

Sugar-Free Strawberry Surprise Salad

3 (3 ounce) packages sugar-free strawberry gelatin
3 cups boiling water
1 (10 ounce) package unsweetened frozen sliced strawberries, partially thawed
1 (15¼ ounce) can crushed pineapple in natural juice, drained
3 bananas, mashed
½ cup chopped pecans
1 (8 ounce) carton sour cream
1 (8 ounce) carton sugar-free frozen nondairy whipped topping
Fresh strawberries

Dissolve gelatin in boiling water. Stir in fruit and pecans. Pour half of gelatin mixture into a lightly greased 9x13-inch dish. Chill until firm. Store remaining gelatin mixture at room temperature. Remove gelatin from refrigerator and spread sour cream over gelatin. Spoon remaining gelatin mixture over sour cream. Cover and refrigerate until firm. Slice into squares and serve with a dollop of whipped topping and a fresh strawberry on top.

Serves 12 to 15

Sugar-free ingredients do not have to be used.

Lois Bruce

King Salad

1 (3 ounce) package lime gelatin
1 (3 ounce) package lemon gelatin
1 cup boiling water
1 (20 ounce) can crushed pineapple, undrained
1 tablespoon vinegar
1 (10 ounce) carton cottage cheese (small curd)
1 (14 ounce) can sweetened condensed milk
¾ cup mayonnaise

Dissolve gelatin in boiling water. Add pineapple, vinegar, cottage cheese, milk, and mayonnaise. Mix and pour into a 9x13-inch pan. Refrigerate.

Serves 12

Patricia Brandon

Black Cherry Congealed Salad

- **1 (16½ ounce) can pitted dark sweet Bing cherries in heavy syrup**
- **1 (20 ounce) can crushed pineapple**
- **1 (3 ounce) package black cherry flavored gelatin**
- **1 (3 ounce) package orange flavored gelatin**
- **2 (8 ounce) packages cream cheese, softened**
- **13 ounces cola-flavored carbonated beverage**
- **1 cup chopped pecans**

Drain juice from cherries and pineapple into saucepan. Heat to boiling point and mix with gelatin. Stir until dissolved. Set aside to cool. Cut up cherries and mix with crushed pineapple. Mix fruit with cream cheese. Combine with cooled gelatin mixture and add carbonated beverage and pecans. Pour into a 9x13-inch glass baking dish and refrigerate until set.

Serves 12

This makes a big salad. Size may be reduced by using only 8 ounces of cream cheese.

Joyce Plaster

Submitted by Virginia Walker Jennings

Light and Lively Salad

- **1 (14 ounce) can sweetened condensed milk**
- **1 (8 ounce) carton frozen nondairy whipped topping, thawed**
- **1 (21 ounce) can cherry pie filling**
- **1 cup flaked coconut**
- **1 (8 ounce) can pineapple tidbits, drained**
- **1 cup miniature marshmallows**
- **½ cup chopped pecans**
- **½ cup maraschino cherries, halved**
- **½ cup pecan halves**

Gently combine condensed milk, whipped topping, pie filling, coconut, pineapple, marshmallow, and chopped pecans. Pour into a 9x13-inch casserole or pretty serving bowl. Decorate the top with cherries and pecans. Chill at least 2 hours.

Serves 12 to 16

To use as a dessert, divide between 2 graham cracker pie crusts. Chill as above.

Peggy Christian

Marcy's Fruit Salad

- **2 (20 ounce) cans pineapple chunks, drained**
- **2 (11 ounce) cans Mandarin oranges, drained**
- **4 bananas, sliced**
- **1 (10 ounce) package frozen strawberries, thawed**
- **1 (21 ounce) can peach pie filling**

In large bowl, mix pineapple, oranges, bananas, and strawberries. Pour pie filling over fruit. Stir until mixed. Chill before serving.

Serves 8 to 10

For variety, try cherry pie filling.

Virginia Laux

Variation: Garnish with 2 kiwi, peeled and sliced. May add cubed apple and/or sliced grapes.

Karen Cruze

Orange Fruit Cup

- **¾ cup water**
- **¼ cup sugar**
- **1 cinnamon stick**
- **1 (4-inch) lemon rind strip**
- **1 (4-inch) orange rind strip**
- **4 oranges, peeled and sliced**
- **1 apple, unpeeled and cut into thin wedges**
- **1 pear, unpeeled and cubed**
- **1 tablespoon lemon juice**
- **2 bananas, peeled and sliced**

Combine water, sugar, cinnamon stick, lemon rind, and orange rind in a small saucepan. Bring to a boil, cover, and reduce heat. Simmer 8 minutes. Cool. Remove and discard cinnamon stick and citrus rinds. Combine sugar mixture, orange slices, apple wedges, pear cubes, and lemon juice in a shallow dish. Cover and chill at least 3 hours. Add banana slices and serve immediately.

Serves 6 to 8

Julia Talbot

Submitted by Jerry Laurine

Fresh Apple Salad

3 medium Golden Delicious apples, diced
1 cup diced celery
1 cup seedless grapes, halved
½ cup chopped pecans or walnuts
1 (8 ounce) carton lemon flavored yogurt

Combine apples, celery, grapes, and nuts. Stir in yogurt. Mix well and chill.

Serves 4 to 6

Apples of your choice may be used. Lime flavored yogurt in place of lemon is a nice variation.

Betty Lou Jones

Shelbyville Fruit Salad

1 (20 ounce) can pineapple chunks, drained (reserve juice)
1 (16 ounce) can maraschino cherries, drained (reserve juice)
1 (15 ounce) can peach chunks, drained
2 (11 ounce) cans Mandarin oranges, drained
1 (3 ounce) package vanilla pudding mix
1 banana (optional)

Combine the reserved pineapple and cherry juice to make 1½ cups. Add juice mixture to pudding mix in saucepan and cook over low heat until thickened. Let cool completely. Mix pineapple, cherries, peaches, and oranges with the cooled pudding and refrigerate overnight. Slice banana into pudding before serving if desired.

Serves 8

Fruit proportions may be adjusted to personal taste. Salad may also be served as a dessert.

Carol Cooper

Best Grilled Cheese Ever

- **½ cup softened butter**
- **½ cup freshly grated Parmesan cheese**
- **16 slices Italian bread**
- **16 slices Provolone cheese**
- **Marinara sauce for dipping**

Preheat griddle to 375 degrees. Mix together butter and Parmesan cheese. Spread mixture onto 1 side of each slice of bread. Place 8 slices of bread, buttered side down, on griddle, and top each with 2 slices of Provolone cheese. Place remaining 8 slices of bread buttered side up, on top of Provolone. Cook until bottom is lightly browned. Turn over, and cook the other side until lightly browned. Cut each sandwich in half. Pass the marinara!

Makes 8 sandwiches

Pre-packaged pesto may be used instead of the butter-cheese mixture.

Brianna Darnall

Pimiento Cheese, "The Pâté of the South"

- **1½ pounds New York extra sharp Cheddar cheese, grated**
- **6 ounces cream cheese, room temperature**
- **¾ cup mayonnaise**
- **1 tablespoon grated onion**
- **½ teaspoon cayenne pepper**
- **6 ounces diced pimiento**

Place Cheddar cheese, cream cheese, mayonnaise, onion, and cayenne pepper in bowl of electric mixer. Beat 1 to 2 minutes on medium speed, only until mixed. Add pimiento, and continue mixing until mixture is somewhat smooth. Be careful not to over mix. Place in an airtight container and refrigerate. Remove from refrigerator at least 30 minutes before serving.

Makes approximately 2 pounds

Katie Clark

Bacon Tomato Sandwich Spread

1 (8 ounce) package cream cheese, softened
½ cup mayonnaise
½ cup diced tomatoes
½ cup sliced spring onions
6 slices bacon, crisp and crumbled

Mix all ingredients together. Chill and serve.

Makes 4 to 6 sandwiches

Also delicious served on crackers.

Kay Brotherton

Open-Faced Cowboy Sandwiches

16 slices lean bacon
8 slices wheat bread
1 (15 ounce) can pork and beans
8 ounces shredded sharp Cheddar cheese

Partially cook bacon, and cut each slice in half for 32 pieces. Toast bread. Cover each bread slice with ⅛ of the beans. Top beans with ⅛ of the cheese. Place 4 pieces of bacon on cheese. Place sandwiches on a cookie sheet and broil until the bacon is crisp.

Makes 8 sandwiches

Ronald Barnes

French Dip

1 (2½-3 pound) eye-of-round roast
3 (10½ ounce) cans beef broth
2 tablespoons Worcestershire Sauce
Salt
Pepper
Hoagie rolls

Preheat oven to 350 degrees. Place roast in Dutch oven. Pour soup and Worcestershire over roast. Bake 2½ to 3 hours, turning roast over once during baking time. Wrap roast in foil for 5 to 10 minutes before slicing. Add salt and pepper to taste. Serve au jus for dipping.

Serves 4 to 6

Julia Parker

Mrs. C's Pimiento Cheese

1 (12 ounce) block sharp Cheddar cheese, grated
1 (4 ounce) jar chopped pimientos, drained
1 teaspoon mustard
3 tablespoons mayonnaise-type salad dressing
Dash of hot sauce
Pinch of sugar

Combine all ingredients. Mix well with electric mixer. Refrigerate.

Makes about 1½ cups

Al Cruze

Greek Tomato and Chick-Pea Salad Sandwiches

2 large fresh, fully ripe tomatoes
1 (16 ounce) can chick-peas, drained and rinsed
1 cup chopped green bell pepper
¼ cup diced red onion
2 tablespoons olive oil
2 tablespoons lemon juice
½ teaspoon crushed oregano leaves
½ teaspoon minced garlic
⅛ teaspoon ground black pepper
3 ounces feta cheese, crumbled or cut in cubes
6 pita loaves, cut in half

Core tomatoes. Cut in pieces and drain. Set aside. In a large bowl, combine chick-peas, bell pepper, and onion. In a small bowl, combine oil, juice, oregano, garlic, and black pepper. Whisk to combine well. Add to chick-pea mixture and stir until coated. Stir in feta cheese and tomatoes. Spoon salad into warm pita bread halves.

Serves 6

Also great as a salad.

Carol Hurst

I can do all things through Christ which strengtheneth me.

Philippians 4:13

The stained glass window in the Clinton Street foyer to the Sanctuary building depicts the story of the Church. Starting with the founder of Methodism, John Wesley, it follows the progression of this congregation from 1808 when Bishop Asbury and the Liberty Hill Conference appointed circuit riding Missionary James Gwinn to minister to the Methodist Society at Hunt's Spring.

The path continues past the first church located on the present-day site from 1834 until the fire that destroyed it in 1864. With courage and faith, the Methodists immediately began to rebuild, which is depicted in the white church where we worship today.

The last building is the first Wesley Center which was dedicated October 27, 1985, and sits on the east side of Greene Street. The path ultimately leads to the Kingdom of Heaven through the resurrection of Christ as illustrated by the radiant light at the top of the window. The Cross and Flame is the emblem of the United Methodist Church.

Breakfast, Brunch & Breads

...Jesus...said unto them,
"Suffer the little children
to come unto me,
and forbid them not:
for of such is the kingdom of God."

Mark 10:14

Ethel DeArmond was honored with a reception held May 15, 1977, when the nursery in the original Sanctuary building was named "The Ethel DeArmond Nursery," recognizing her work in many areas of the church, but more particularly her devotion to the care and nurture of the children in the church and in the community.

The stained glass window picturing Jesus and the children was donated by Mrs. DeArmond when the first Wesley Center was constructed in 1985. The facility accommodated the church's top priorities: new nursery, children's Sunday School classes, and space for pre-school and Mother's Morning Out programs.

In 2000, the Wesley Center building was renovated and expanded. The long-awaited Day Care program, the Susannah Wesley Early Education Ministry (SWEEM) opened for the 2001-2002 year. Still working with children and calling each child by name was Ethel DeArmond. Until her passing, she was the embodiment of the pledge of "surrounding each child with steadfast love" that church members pledge at the baptism of every child in the church.

Quick Three-Vegetable Frittata

- 1 large red bell pepper, chopped
- 1½ cups sliced white mushrooms
- 1 bunch thin asparagus, cut into 1-inch pieces
- ½ cup mayonnaise
- ¾ teaspoon salt
- ½ teaspoon pepper
- 3 tablespoons chopped fresh basil
- 7 large eggs, beaten
- ¼ cup grated Parmesan cheese
- ¾ cup grated sharp Cheddar cheese
- ½ cup grated colby/Monterey Jack cheese

Preheat oven to 375 degrees. Place chopped bell pepper in sieve to drain excess liquid. Coat a glass or ceramic deep dish pie pan with cooking spray. Layer bell pepper, mushrooms, and asparagus on bottom of dish. In a medium-size bowl, combine mayonnaise, salt, pepper, basil, and beaten eggs. Whisk until smooth. Add Parmesan cheese to the egg mixture. Pour mixture over vegetables. Sprinkle Cheddar and colby/Jack cheeses on top. Bake 40 minutes until eggs are set and the cheese begins to brown on top. Cool 10 minutes before serving.

Serves 8

Amanda Vaughan

Eggs in Skillet

- 6 bacon slices
- ¼ cup finely chopped green pepper
- ¼ cup finely chopped onion
- 3 cups frozen hash-brown potatoes
- 6 eggs
- ½ cup grated Cheddar cheese

Fry bacon in a large skillet. Remove bacon from skillet and set aside. Sauté pepper and onion. Remove from skillet and set aside. Add potatoes to skillet, adding oil if needed. Fry potatoes on 1 side until brown. Turn and add onions and pepper. After potatoes begin to brown on the bottom, break open eggs, one at a time, and place on top of potatoes. Cover. Cook until eggs are done to your liking. Crumble bacon. Sprinkle bacon and cheese over top just before serving. Cheese will melt.

Serves 6

Kay Brotherton

Sausage-Filled Crêpes

CRÊPES

- 1 cup whole milk
- 1 cup water
- 4 large eggs
- ¼-½ teaspoon salt
- 4 tablespoons butter, melted
- 2 cups sifted all-purpose flour

FILLING

- 1 pound pork sausage
- 1 small onion, diced
- 1 cup shredded Cheddar cheese
- 1 (3 ounce) package cream cheese
- ½ teaspoon dried marjoram or oregano

TOPPING

- ½ cup sour cream
- ¼ cup butter, softened
- ¼ cup chopped fresh parsley
- 1 cup shredded Cheddar cheese
- Parsley

The day before serving, put all crêpe ingredients in a food processor. Mix for 10 seconds. Scrape down sides of the container and mix again for another 40 seconds. Refrigerate batter for 24 hours. To cook crêpes, brush crêpe pan or small non-stick skillet with oil. Heat pan over medium heat. Pour a small amount of batter into pan. Tilt pan to spread batter over bottom of pan. Crêpe should be thin. Cook until lightly browned on one side. Flip over and cook other side. Place crêpes on a towel to cool. Preheat oven to 350 degrees. Prepare filling. Cook sausage and onion; drain. Add 1 cup Cheddar cheese, cream cheese, and marjoram or oregano. Stir until cheese melts. Spoon 3 tablespoons of this mixture down the center of cooked crêpes. Roll up and place seam side down in a lightly greased 9x13-inch pan. Bake for 15 minutes. Mix sour cream, butter, and parsley for topping. Spoon over crêpes. Bake another 5 minutes. Sprinkle with remaining 1 cup of cheese and parsley.

Makes 10 to 12 (8-inch) filled crêpes, 16 to 20 unfilled

Any leftover unfilled crêpes can be frozen for later use.

Dottye Montgomery

Grits and Cheese Casserole

- 3 cups cooked grits
- 1 pound processed cheese loaf, cut in slices or chunks
- ½ cup butter
- Dash of red pepper
- 6 eggs
- ½ cup milk
- 2 teaspoons baking powder

Preheat oven to 350 degrees. Cook grits according to package directions. Cut cheese and butter into hot grits. Add red pepper. Beat eggs in separate bowl and add milk and baking powder. Stir into cheese mixture and pour into buttered 8x11-inch baking dish. Bake 45 to 60 minutes.

Serves 8

Ruth Sykes Ford

Submitted by Martha Dotzheimer

Potato Omelet Casserole

- 1 (20 ounce) package frozen pepper and onion hash browns, thawed
- 1 (16 ounce) package hot pork sausage, cooked, crumbled, and drained
- 10 slices bacon, cooked and crumbled
- 4 ounces shredded mozzarella cheese
- 4 ounces shredded Cheddar cheese
- 10 large eggs
- 2 cups half-and-half
- 1 teaspoon dried basil
- 1 teaspoon dried oregano

Preheat oven to 350 degrees. Lightly grease a 9x13-inch baking dish. Gently press hash browns in prepared dish. Layer sausage, bacon, and cheese on top. In a separate bowl, whisk together eggs, half-and-half, basil, and oregano. Pour evenly over casserole. Bake for 35 to 45 minutes or until lightly browned and set. Serve immediately.

Serves 12

Mild sausage may be substituted for hot sausage. May be prepared the night before and refrigerated. The next morning, remove from refrigerator 15 minutes before baking.

Pat Martin

Sausage Cheese Grits Casserole

1 pound sausage
1 clove garlic, minced
4 drops hot pepper sauce
½ teaspoon salt
⅛ teaspoon pepper
1 cup quick-cooking grits
4 cups boiling water
1 cup grated extra-sharp Cheddar cheese
2 large eggs, well beaten

Preheat oven to 350 degrees. Brown sausage and drain. Add garlic, pepper sauce, salt, and pepper. Set aside. Cook grits in boiling water. Add grits, cheese, and eggs to sausage mixture. Mix well. Pour into a buttered 9x9-inch dish. Bake uncovered for 1 hour.

Serves 6 to 8

Lise Wilson

Zipper Bag Omelet

2 large or extra large eggs
Grated cheese
Diced ham
Chopped onion
Diced green bell pepper
Chopped tomato
Salsa

Crack eggs into a quart-size zipper bag. Zip bag and shake to mix eggs. Add choice of ingredients. Squeeze out excess air and zip bag. Place bag in rolling boiling water for 13 minutes. Open bag and omelet will roll out.

Makes 1 omelet

You can usually cook 6 to 8 omelets in a large pot. It's fun to have guests prepare their own omelet and write their name on the bag with a permanent marker. Can be prepared the night before, refrigerated, and cooked the next morning.

Mary Richardson

Scrambled Egg Casserole

½ pound bacon

SAUCE

¼ cup butter
½ pound fresh mushrooms, sliced
Salt
Pepper
½ cup all-purpose flour
4 cups whole milk
1½-2 cups grated Cheddar cheese
3 cups chopped ham

SCRAMBLED EGGS

18 eggs
1 cup evaporated milk
½ teaspoon salt
½ cup melted butter

Preheat oven to 275 degrees. Cut bacon into pieces, sauté in a large skillet, and set aside to drain. Add butter and mushrooms to bacon grease in skillet and sauté. Sprinkle in flour and salt and pepper to taste. Stir in whole milk and cook until thickened. Stir in cheese until it melts. Add ham and set aside. Combine eggs, evaporated milk, and salt. Beat with mixer. Melt butter in a separate skillet and scramble eggs. In a 9x13-inch casserole, alternate eggs and sauce making 2 layers of each. Garnish with bacon. Bake 1 hour.

Serves 12 to 16

May be prepared the day before and baked the next morning.

Joan Rice

English Muffin and Ham Strata

- 6 cups diced English muffins
- 2 cups diced ham
- 2 cups shredded taco cheese blend
- 1½ cups skim milk
- 1½ cups egg substitute
- ¼ cup Dijon mustard
- ½ teaspoon black pepper
- ¼ teaspoon salt

Coat a 9x13-inch baking dish with nonstick cooking spray. In bottom of dish, place half of muffin pieces. Top with half of ham. Sprinkle half of cheese over top. Repeat layers of muffin pieces, ham, and cheese using all the ham and cheese. In a large bowl, whisk milk, egg substitute, mustard, pepper, and salt. Pour over top of strata. With a large spatula, gently press down on top so all ingredients are moistened. Cover and refrigerate overnight. When ready to bake, preheat oven to 350 degrees. Bake uncovered 45 to 60 minutes until cheese is melted and golden and strata registers 160 degrees on an instant-read thermometer. Allow to stand 10 minutes before serving warm or at room temperature.

Serves 8

Serve with sliced fresh fruit. May be wrapped tightly and frozen for up to 2 months. To cook, thaw in refrigerator overnight.

Carole Chase

Breakfast Casserole

- 1 (8 ounce) can crescent rolls
- 1 pound sausage, browned and drained
- 4-6 eggs, beaten
- Salt
- Pepper
- 1 (8 ounce) box processed cheese loaf
- 1 (8 ounce) can crescent rolls

Preheat oven to 350 degrees. Unroll and flatten 1 can of crescent rolls on bottom of a 9x13-inch baking dish that has been coated with nonstick cooking spray. Put browned sausage on top of roll layer. Combine eggs with salt and pepper to taste, and pour over sausage layer. Slice cheese and place in a single layer on top of eggs. Cover with remaining can of unrolled and flattened crescent rolls. Bake 30 minutes.

Serves 8

May be made the night before. Remove from refrigerator 30 minutes before cooking. Reheats well. Light or Mexican flavored processed cheese may be substituted.

Suzanne Thomason

Meg's Sausage Breakfast Casserole

6 slices thin bread
Butter
1 pound pork sausage
6 ounces longhorn cheese, grated
6 eggs, beaten
2 cups half-and-half
1 teaspoon salt

Remove bread crusts and spread slices with butter. Put in bottom of a 9x13-inch baking dish. Cook sausage, stirring to crumble. Drain sausage and crumble over bread. Sprinkle cheese on top. Combine eggs, half-and-half, and salt. Pour over cheese. Cover and refrigerate overnight. Remove 15 minutes before baking. Bake uncovered at 350 degrees 45 minutes or until set.

Serves 12 to 14

Betty Peeler

My Special Breakfast

8 ounces sharp Cheddar cheese, shredded
1 (2 ounce) jar diced pimiento
3 tablespoons mayonnaise
1 slice whole wheat bread
1 egg
Dash of salt and pepper

Preheat toaster oven (or oven) to 350 degrees. Combine cheese, pimiento, and mayonnaise. Mix well. Spread a thin layer of cheese spread on bread. Place in toaster oven until cheese bubbles and melts. While bread and cheese spread are cooking, scramble egg with salt and pepper. Place cheese toast on plate and top with scrambled egg.

Serves 1

Variation: May substitute different breads or waffles. Crumble crisp bacon over top.

Leftover cheese spread keeps a couple of weeks in refrigerator and can be used for sandwiches and baked potatoes. Purchased pimiento cheese can be used.

Rosa Belle Van Valkenburgh

French Toast Casserole

CASSEROLE

1 large loaf French bread
8 eggs
2 cups half-and-half
1 cup milk
2 tablespoons sugar
1 teaspoon vanilla extract
¼ teaspoon cinnamon
¼ teaspoon nutmeg

TOPPING

1 cup butter, softened
1 cup chopped pecans
½ teaspoon cinnamon
1 cup light brown sugar
2 tablespoons corn syrup
2 teaspoons nutmeg
Maple syrup

Slice bread into 1-inch slices. Arrange in single layer in generously buttered baking dishes (one 9x13-inch dish and one smaller dish). Combine eggs, half-and-half, milk, sugar, vanilla, cinnamon, and nutmeg. Pour over bread. Cover and refrigerate overnight. Preheat oven to 350 degrees. Combine all topping ingredients and top casserole evenly with dollops of mixture. Bake 40 minutes. Serve with maple syrup, if desired.

Serves 12 to 16

Lady Vowell Smith

Crème Brûlée French Toast

½ cup unsalted butter
1 cup packed brown sugar
2 tablespoons light corn syrup
1 loaf French bread
5 eggs
1½ cups half-and-half
1 teaspoon vanilla extract
1 teaspoon orange-flavored liqueur
¼ teaspoon salt

Melt butter in a saucepan. Add sugar and syrup. Stir until smooth. Pour into a lightly greased 9x13-inch glass dish. Slice bread into 1-inch pieces. Place snugly over sugar mixture. Mix eggs, half-and-half, vanilla, liqueur, and salt. Pour over bread. Refrigerate at least 8 hours. Remove from refrigerator and allow to reach room temperature before cooking. Preheat oven to 350 degrees. Bake 35 to 40 minutes.

Serves 4 to 6

Sarah Lauren V. Kattos

Variation: Sprinkle sugar syrup mixture with ½ cup chopped pecans; substitute Texas toast for French bread; use 1¾ cups milk instead of half-and-half; eliminate orange-flavored liqueur.

Pauline Precise

Apricot Casserole

3 (15 ounce) cans apricots, drained
1 (16-ounce) box light brown sugar
2 stacks round buttery crackers
Butter

Preheat oven to 325 degrees. Grease a 2-quart casserole dish. Layer half of apricots, half of sugar, and half of crackers. Dot with a lot of butter. Repeat layers, ending with crackers. Dot with more butter. Bake 1 hour.

Serves 8 to 10

Paula Sanders

Ham and Asparagus Quiche

1 pound fresh asparagus, tough ends removed
1 pound sliced deli ham
2 cups shredded Swiss cheese
½ cup chopped green onion
6 eggs, beaten
2 cups milk
1½ cups biscuit baking mix
¼ teaspoon black pepper
2 tablespoons fresh parsley

Preheat oven to 375 degrees. Cook asparagus in boiling water 3 minutes. Drain and cool. Spray a 9x13-inch baking dish with cooking spray. Cut asparagus and ham into bite-size pieces. Layer ham, asparagus, cheese, and onion. In a separate bowl, beat eggs and milk. Add biscuit mix, pepper, and parsley. Pour over layered ingredients. Bake 30 to 40 minutes or until brown on top.

Makes 10 to 12 squares

Frances Reynolds

Mushroom and Bacon Quiche

8 slices bacon
½ pound fresh mushrooms
2 tablespoons green onion
3 tablespoons butter, melted
1 teaspoon lemon juice
1 teaspoon salt
½ teaspoon pepper
1½ cups half-and-half
3 eggs, slightly beaten
¼-½ cup grated Swiss cheese
1 (9-inch) unbaked pie crust

Preheat oven to 375 degrees. Cook bacon until crisp. Drain well and crumble. Wipe mushrooms with a paper towel and slice thin. Sauté mushrooms and green onion in a skillet with butter. Sprinkle with lemon juice, salt, and pepper. Add half-and-half to eggs. Add bacon, mushrooms, and onion to cream mixture. Sprinkle with grated cheese. Pour into pie crust. Bake 25 to 30 minutes. Cool 5 minutes before slicing.

Serves 6 to 8

Refrigerated pastry dough works just fine. For the last 5 minutes of baking, you may need to put on lower rack to ensure that bottom crust is done.

Camille Vaughan

Easy Quiche

2 deep-dish pie shells, baked and cooled
10 eggs, beaten
2½ cups milk
1 pound hot sausage, cooked, crumbled, and drained
2 cups grated sharp Cheddar cheese, divided
Salt
Pepper

Preheat oven to 350 degrees. Combine eggs, milk, sausage, 1½ cups cheese, and salt and pepper to taste. Pour into pie shells. Sprinkle with ½ cup cheese and bake 30 to 40 minutes. Cover with foil if crust becomes too brown during cooking.

Serves 12 to 16

Bell pepper, mushrooms, and onion may be added if desired. Ham may be substituted for sausage. Share one quiche with a friend or slice into individual servings and freeze.

Lenda Woody

Chicken Quiche

1 (9-inch) deep-dish pie shell
Shredded Swiss cheese
2 cups cubed cooked chicken
¼ bell pepper, minced
4 large eggs
2 cups milk
½ (1 ounce) package onion soup mix (stir well before dividing)
½ teaspoon salt, or to taste
¼ teaspoon pepper, or to taste

Preheat oven to 425 degrees. Cover bottom of pie shell with Swiss cheese. Add chicken and sprinkle bell pepper over chicken. Mix eggs, milk, soup mix, salt, and pepper in blender and pour over chicken. Bake 15 minutes. Reduce heat to 350 degrees and cook 30 to 35 minutes longer or until quiche is set.

Serves 6

Julia Sutton

Hot Browns

- ½ cup butter
- ½ cup all-purpose flour
- 3 cups milk
- 1 teaspoon salt
- 2 egg yolks, beaten
- 3 English muffins, split and toasted (6 halves)
- ¾ pound sliced turkey breast (more or less to your taste)
- ½ cup grated Cheddar cheese
- 6 slices tomato
- 6 tablespoons butter
- 2 tablespoons brown sugar
- 1 cup sliced mushrooms
- 1 tablespoon butter
- 1 tablespoon fresh lemon juice
- 6 slices bacon, fried

Melt ½ cup butter in saucepan and stir in flour. Cook 2 minutes over medium heat. Gradually add milk, stirring until mixture begins to thicken. Stir in salt. Add a spoonful or 2 of sauce to egg yolks, stirring thoroughly to temper. Return mixture to the remaining sauce in saucepan. Heat thoroughly and keep warm on low heat. Arrange turkey breast on top of each English muffin half. Add a layer of sauce, cheese, tomato, and 1 tablespoon butter. Sprinkle with brown sugar. Sauté mushrooms in 1 tablespoon butter and lemon juice and set aside. Broil English muffins 3 to 5 minutes, or until lightly browned. Remove from oven and garnish with mushrooms and bacon.

Makes 6

This dish can be prepared the night before up to the point of broiling. Cover tightly and refrigerate. The next morning, broil and garnish with mushrooms and bacon.

Doni Harrison

Don's Never Fail Cornbread

- 2 tablespoons corn oil
- 1 egg
- 1 teaspoon sugar
- 1 cup self-rising buttermilk cornmeal mix
- 1 cup buttermilk

Preheat oven to 450 degrees. Put oil in an 8-inch iron skillet. A hot, hot skillet and oil are most essential. In a small bowl, combine egg, sugar, cornmeal, and buttermilk. Stir just until mixed. Pour into hot skillet. Bake 20 minutes. If cornbread looks done but not brown on top, flip over for about 5 minutes to brown.

Serves 6

Donald Lewter

Mexican Cornbread

- 2 eggs
- ⅓ cup vegetable oil
- 1 cup self-rising cornmeal
- ¼ teaspoon salt
- 1 (8 ounce) carton sour cream
- 1 (8¼ ounce) can cream style corn
- 1 (4½ ounce) can chopped green chiles, drained
- 2 cups grated sharp Cheddar cheese

Preheat oven to 425 degrees. Heat an oiled iron skillet in the oven for 10 minutes while mixing ingredients. Beat eggs in vegetable oil. Mix with cornmeal and salt. Add sour cream, corn, and green chiles. When skillet is hot, pour half of batter into skillet, sprinkle with cheese, and pour remaining half of batter over cheese. Bake 25 to 30 minutes.

Serves 8

Good served with homemade vegetable soup. Also very good served with salsa on top. Hot peppers may be added for extra zing!

Frances Ann Foster

Submitted by Linda Finnell

Broccoli-Cheese Cornbread

- 4 eggs
- 1 (8.5 ounce) box cornmeal mix
- ½ cup milk
- ½ cup butter, melted
- 2 cups shredded Cheddar cheese
- 1 (10 ounce) package frozen broccoli, thawed and patted dry
- 1 onion, chopped

Preheat oven to 350 degrees. Whip eggs well and stir in cornmeal mix, milk, butter, cheese, broccoli, and onion. Pour into a 9x13-inch glass dish. Bake 35 minutes or until light brown, and inserted toothpick comes out clean. Cut into 2-inch squares.

Serves 12 to 14

Linda Steed

Variation: Omit milk; substitute ¾ cup creamy lite cottage cheese for shredded Cheddar cheese. Bake 40 to 45 minutes at 400 degrees.

Norma Colbath

Rudd's Mother's Rolls

1 (¼ ounce) package active dry yeast
1 tablespoon sugar
¼ cup buttermilk, warmed to 105-110 degrees
2½ cups all-purpose flour
2 tablespoons sugar
½ teaspoon salt
½ teaspoon baking soda
½ teaspoon baking powder
⅓ cup shortening
¾ cup buttermilk, room temperature
½ cup all-purpose flour

Mix yeast, sugar, and ¼ cup buttermilk in a cup and set aside. In a large bowl, mix 2½ cups flour, sugar, salt, soda, and baking powder. Cut in shortening. Stir in ¾ cup buttermilk. Stir in yeast mixture. Place in a greased bowl and cover. Leave overnight in refrigerator. Preheat oven to 375 degrees. Using ½ cup flour, sprinkle on dough board and knead dough about 5 times. Allow dough to rest about 5 to 10 minutes. Roll out dough and cut into desired shapes. Place on a very lightly greased pan, and let rise until double in size. Bake 10 minutes, or until lightly browned.

Makes 20 to 24

Libby Loder

Mini Cinnamon Rolls

ROLLS

1 (8 ounce) can crescent rolls
¼ cup margarine or butter, softened
2 tablespoons ground cinnamon
4 tablespoons sugar
Raisins or chopped pecans (optional)

ICING

1 cup confectioners' sugar
2 tablespoons milk

Preheat oven to 375 degrees. Roll crescent rolls into a large rectangle. Spread with butter or margarine. Mix cinnamon and sugar and sprinkle over butter. Sprinkle on either raisins or chopped pecans (or both). Roll up dough rectangle long ways and slice. Bake in an 8x8-inch greased pan 20 minutes. Mix icing ingredients and spread over cooked rolls while still warm.

Makes 20

Daphne Reed

Mahan's Rolls

2 rounded tablespoons sugar
2 rounded tablespoons shortening
1 teaspoon salt
1 cup boiling water
1 egg
1 (¼ ounce) package active dry yeast
¼ cup warm water
2½ cups all-purpose flour
Flour
½ cup margarine, melted

Combine sugar, shortening, and salt in a large bowl. Pour in boiling water and stir until dissolved. Allow mixture to cool. Beat in egg. Add yeast, which has been dissolved in ¼ cup warm water. Add 2½ cups flour and mix well. Dough will be sticky. Cover and refrigerate several hours or overnight. When ready to make rolls, put a scoop of flour into a small bowl and melted margarine in another. Pinch off walnut-sized portions of dough and dip in flour. Flatten into circle, dip in melted margarine, and place in greased pan. As each roll is placed into pan, fold in half to form a half circle. Cover rolls with a tea towel and let rise 30 to 45 minutes. Preheat oven to 425 degrees. Bake 10 to 15 minutes or until golden brown.

Makes 2 dozen

These rolls may be made up and placed back in refrigerator for up to 2 days prior to baking. After removing from refrigerator, cover with a tea towel, let rolls come to room temperature, and rise for 2 to 3 hours before baking as directed.

Mahan Rutland Harrison

Submitted by Doni Harrison and Susan Lewis

Cheddar Garlic Biscuits

2 cups biscuit baking mix
⅔ cup milk
½ cup shredded sharp Cheddar cheese
2 tablespoons melted butter
⅛ teaspoon garlic powder

Preheat oven to 450 degrees. Mix baking mix, milk, and cheese to form soft dough. Drop 9 spoonfuls of dough onto ungreased cookie sheet. Bake 8 to 10 minutes or until lightly browned. Mix butter and garlic powder. Brush over warm biscuits.

Makes 9

Peggy Christian

Parsley Crescent Ring

½ cup butter
3 (8 ounce) cans crescent rolls
¼-½ cup snipped parsley

Preheat oven to 375 degrees. Put butter in a Bundt pan and place in oven until the butter melts. Unroll the 3 cans of crescent rolls. Sprinkle parsley over dough and re-roll. Place rolls in Bundt pan, end to end. Bake about 25 minutes. Remove from oven. Cool 5 minutes and invert the bread ring onto a platter.

Serves 12

Anne Clough

Sally Lunn

1 (¼ ounce) package active dry yeast
¼ cup lukewarm water
¾ cup milk
½ cup butter or margarine
⅓ cup sugar
3 eggs, beaten
1 teaspoon salt
4 cups all-purpose flour, sifted

Dissolve yeast in water. Heat milk until lukewarm and mix with yeast and water. Cream butter and sugar in a separate bowl. Add beaten eggs and mix. Combine salt and flour. Add to egg mixture alternately with milk mixture. Beat well with wooden spoon and turn into a buttered bowl. Let rise 1 to 1½ hours or until doubled in bulk. Beat again with spoon and pour into a heavily buttered 10-inch tube pan or two 5x9-inch loaf pans. Let rise another 40 minutes, or until again doubled in size. While bread is rising, preheat oven to 350 degrees. Bake 45 minutes. Remove from pan and serve warm.

Makes 12 to 16 slices

Marjorie Peeler

Submitted by Betty Peeler

Sour Dough Bread

STARTER

6 tablespoons instant potatoes
2 cups boiling water
1 teaspoon salt
1 (1/4 ounce) package active dry yeast
1/2 cup water

Combine instant potatoes, boiling water, salt, yeast, and water and mix well. Put in refrigerator 3 to 5 days. Remove 1 cup of starter 12 hours or overnight before making bread. The 1 cup of starter remaining should be refrigerated in a plastic container with several holes in the lid. It must be fed every 3 to 5 days with 3/4 cup sugar, 3 tablespoons instant potatoes, and 1 cup of very warm water, mixing well with a non-metallic spoon. As starter grows, share with a friend or neighbor.

BREAD

1/4 cup sugar
1/2 cup vegetable oil (safflower, corn, etc.)
1 1/2 teaspoons salt
1 cup starter
1 1/2 cups warm water
6 cups bread flour
Vegetable oil

Day 1: Prepare bread dough by placing sugar, oil, salt, starter, warm water, and bread flour in a mixer bowl. Thoroughly mix and knead several minutes. Dough will be relatively stiff. It is almost impossible to over mix. Place dough in a very large non-metallic bowl. Coat dough well with oil and turn over, making sure all sides are oiled. Cover with plastic wrap and let sit at room temperature overnight. Day 2: Punch down dough and knead a few times. Divide dough into 3 equal parts. Knead each part on a floured board about 10 times. Mould the dough by flattening and rolling each part into a loaf that fits the pan. Turn into 3 greased 9x5-inch loaf pans. Coat tops of loaves with oil. Cover with plastic wrap. Let rise in a warm place for 5 hours or more (all day is good). The dough rises slowly. The warmer the room, the shorter the rise time will be. Preheat oven to 325 degrees and bake 30 to 45 minutes. Remove from pan and brush tops with butter. After cooling thoroughly on racks, place in plastic bags with ties.

Makes 3 loaves

Mixing with a large stand-type mixer with a dough hook makes the kneading job much easier than kneading by hand.

Ben Small

Carolina Coffee Cake

CAKE

1/3 cup shortening
3/4 cup sugar
2 eggs
3/4 cup milk
1 3/4 cups sifted self-rising flour
1/3 cup chopped pecans

TOPPING

1/2 cup firmly packed brown sugar
2 tablespoons self-rising flour
1 teaspoon cinnamon
2 tablespoons butter or margarine, softened

ICING

1 1/2 cups sifted confectioners' sugar
2 tablespoons hot milk
1/2 teaspoon vanilla extract

Preheat oven to 375 degrees. Cream shortening and sugar together until light and fluffy. Add eggs one at a time, beating well after each addition. Blend in milk. Stir in flour and pecans, blending well. Grease a 10-inch iron skillet or 9-inch baking pan. Pour batter into prepared pan. Prepare crumb topping by combining ingredients in a bowl using fork or pastry blender. Sprinkle topping evenly over batter. Bake 30 to 35 minutes or until cake begins to pull away from sides of pan. Cool in pan 15 minutes. Prepare icing by combining all ingredients in a bowl, stirring until smooth. Drizzle cake with icing.

Serves 12 to 15

Norma Colbath

Breakfast Cheesecake

2 (8 ounce) cans crescent rolls
2 (8 ounce) packages cream cheese softened
1 egg, separated
¾ cup sugar
1 teaspoon vanilla extract
2 tablespoons sugar

Preheat oven to 350 degrees. Place one can of crescent rolls flat in the bottom of a 9x13-inch pan. Mix cream cheese, egg yolk, ¾ cup sugar, and vanilla. Spread over first layer of rolls in pan. Place second can of crescent rolls over cream cheese mixture. Whip egg white and spread over rolls. Sprinkle with 2 tablespoons sugar. Bake 30 to 35 minutes. May be topped with preserves or cherry pie filling.

Serves 12 to 15

Celeste Hemby

Apricot-Almond Coffee Cake

CAKE

4 ounces cream cheese, softened
½ cup apricot preserves
1 (16 ounce) package pound cake mix
1 (8 ounce) container sour cream
½ cup milk
2 large eggs
½ teaspoon almond extract
½ cup sliced almonds

GLAZE

1 cup confectioners' sugar
½ teaspoon vanilla extract
2 tablespoons milk

Preheat oven to 350 degrees. Mix cream cheese, preserves, and 1 tablespoon cake mix. Set aside. Mix sour cream, milk, eggs, almond extract, and remaining cake mix with mixer on medium speed. Pour into a greased 9x13-inch or two 8x8-inch pans. Drop cream cheese mixture by tablespoon evenly over batter. Swirl batter gently up and down and side to side with a knife. Sprinkle almonds on top. Bake 25 to 28 minutes. Prepare glaze by stirring all ingredients together, adding more milk if needed. Drizzle glaze over warm cake. Cool before cutting.

Serves 12 to 16

Great for breakfast or to take to neighbors.

Chris Bragg

Sour Cream Coffee Cake

CAKE

- **1 cup margarine**
- **2 cups sugar**
- **2 eggs**
- **1 cup sour cream**
- **½ teaspoon vanilla extract**
- **2 cups all-purpose flour**
- **1 teaspoon baking powder**
- **¼ teaspoon salt**

TOPPING

- **½ cup chopped nuts**
- **½ teaspoon cinnamon**
- **2 teaspoons sugar**

Preheat oven to 325 degrees. Cream together margarine, sugar, and eggs. Carefully fold in sour cream and vanilla. Sift flour, baking powder, and salt. Add to egg mixture. Spoon half the batter into a greased tube pan. Prepare topping. Combine nuts, cinnamon, and sugar. Cover batter with ½ of topping. Repeat layers. Bake 50 to 60 minutes. Cool almost completely before removing from pan. Freezes well.

Serves 14 to 16

Tine Purdy

Lynn Smith's Oatmeal Coffee Cake

- **1¼ cups hot water**
- **1 cup uncooked oatmeal**
- **1 cup sugar**
- **1 cup brown sugar**
- **½ cup butter, softened**
- **1½ cups all-purpose flour**
- **1 teaspoon baking soda**
- **2 tablespoons ground cinnamon**
- **½ teaspoon salt**
- **2 eggs**

Preheat oven to 350 degrees. Pour hot water over oatmeal and set aside. Cream together sugar, brown sugar, butter, flour, soda, cinnamon, and salt. Beat in eggs. Blend in oatmeal mixture and pour into a greased Bundt pan. Bake about 35 minutes.

Serves 12 to 14

Carolyn Blue

Jelly Roll

- **3 eggs**
- **1 cup sugar**
- **3 tablespoons cold water**
- **1 cup all-purpose flour**
- **⅓ teaspoon salt**
- **1 teaspoon baking powder**
- **½-1 cup confectioners' sugar**
- **½-¾ cup grape jelly**

Preheat oven to 350 degrees. Beat eggs and sugar until thick and lemon color. Add water. Sift together flour, salt, and baking powder. Combine with egg mixture. Pour batter into a 15x10x1-inch jelly roll pan lined with wax paper. Bake 12 minutes. Loosen edges of cake and turn onto a damp cloth. Remove wax paper. Roll cake and towel together. Cool cake on rack, seam side down, for 10 minutes. Unroll and sprinkle with confectioners' sugar. Stir jelly well and spread on cake. Re-roll cake and sprinkle outside with confectioners' sugar.

Serves 8 to 10

Best served second day. Jelly of your choice may be substituted for grape jelly.

Cooked cake may also be turned out onto a dry towel that has been dusted with confectioners' sugar to prevent cake from sticking while being rolled.

Evelyn Dickson

Cinnamon Roll-Ups

- **2 cups sugar**
- **1 tablespoon cinnamon**
- **1 cup butter, softened**
- **2 (8 ounce) packages cream cheese, softened**
- **2 egg yolks**
- **½ cup sugar**
- **48 slices fresh white bread**
- **½ cup butter**

Mix 2 cups sugar and cinnamon. Set aside. Cream together 1 cup butter, cream cheese, egg yolks, and ½ cup sugar. Trim crusts from bread. Melt ½ cup butter. Spread cream cheese mixture on slices of bread and roll up. Brush each roll with melted butter and roll in cinnamon/sugar mixture. Freeze the roll-ups. This step is essential. When ready to serve, preheat oven to 400 degrees. DO NOT thaw before baking. Bake 15 minutes. Serve warm.

Makes 48

Lucy Gross

Homemade Granola

- **3 cups old-fashioned oats (not instant)**
- **1 cup chopped almonds, slivered almonds, or chopped pecans**
- **¾ cup shredded sweetened coconut**
- **⅓ cup sesame seeds**
- **⅓ cup sunflower seeds**
- **6 tablespoons maple syrup**
- **6 tablespoons packed dark brown sugar**
- **¼ cup vegetable oil**
- **2 tablespoons warm water**
- **¼ teaspoon salt**
- **½ teaspoon cinnamon or ½ teaspoon vanilla extract (optional)**
- **1 cup golden raisins or dried cranberries**

Preheat oven to 250 degrees. Spray a rimmed baking sheet with nonstick spray. Stir oats, nuts, coconut, sesame seeds, and sunflower seeds in a large mixing bowl. Whisk syrup, brown sugar, oil, water, salt, and cinnamon or vanilla in a small bowl. Pour over oats mixture and stir. Spread out in an even layer on baking sheet. Bake until brown, about 1 hour, stirring occasionally. Cool. Transfer mixture to large bowl and toss with raisins. Keep in an airtight container.

Makes 20 servings

May serve as cereal with milk or eat with yogurt. We eat it by itself as a snack.

Diana Finley

Banana Bread

- ½ cup shortening, vegetable oil sticks, or margarine
- 1 cup sugar
- 2 eggs, unbeaten
- 1½ cups all-purpose flour, sifted
- 1 teaspoon baking soda
- ¼ teaspoon salt
- 3 bananas, mashed
- ¼-½ cup chopped pecans or walnuts

Preheat oven to 375 degrees. Cream shortening and sugar. Add eggs and beat well. Sift flour, soda, and salt together and stir into creamed mixture. Add bananas and nuts. Bake in a lightly greased 8x4-inch loaf pan 45 minutes or until done.

Makes 1 loaf

For muffins, bake about 30 minutes. For miniature muffins, bake about 20 minutes. This is moist and tastes more like cake than bread. I have used this recipe for 60 years.

Virginia Walker Jennings

Strawberry Bread

- 3 cups all-purpose flour
- 1 teaspoon baking soda
- 1 teaspoon salt
- 1 tablespoon cinnamon
- 2 cups sugar
- 4 eggs, lightly beaten
- 2 (10 ounce) packages frozen strawberries, thawed and diced
- 1½ cups vegetable oil
- 1 cup chopped pecans

Preheat oven to 350 degrees. Stir together flour, soda, salt, cinnamon, and sugar. Combine eggs, strawberries, and oil, and add to dry ingredients. Mix well. Gently fold in pecans. Pour into 2 greased 9x5-inch loaf pans. Bake 1 hour and 15 minutes or bake in mini loaf pans for 30 minutes.

Makes 2 loaves

Two cups of sliced fresh strawberries may be substituted for frozen strawberries.

Debbie Packard

Easy Banana Nut Bread

5-6 ripe bananas, mashed
4 eggs
½ cup margarine, softened
½ cup milk
4 cups biscuit baking mix
2 cups uncooked quick-cooking oats
1½ cups sugar
1 teaspoon vanilla extract
½ cup chopped black walnuts

Preheat oven to 350 degrees. In a large mixing bowl combine bananas, eggs, margarine, and milk. Use mixer to mix thoroughly. Add baking mix, oats, and sugar. Mix well. Add vanilla and walnuts to batter and mix. Pour into three 4x8-inch or two 5x9-inch greased loaf pans. Bake 50 to 60 minutes or until toothpick comes out clean. Cool before removing from pans. Freezes well.

Makes 2 or 3 loaves

Denise McLeroy

Zucchini Bread

1 (18.25 ounce) box spice cake mix
2 cups shredded zucchini
½ cup chopped pecans or walnuts

Preheat oven to 250 degrees. Toast nuts and set aside. Increase oven temperature to 350 degrees. Mix cake according to package directions. Squeeze excess liquid from zucchini. Stir zucchini and nuts into cake batter. Pour batter into 2 greased 9x5-inch loaf pans. Bake 50 to 60 minutes. Cool 10 minutes in pans. Remove bread from pans. Place on wire racks to finish cooling.

Makes 2 loaves

Wrap in plastic wrap and then in foil to freeze. May freeze up to 3 months.

Lois Bruce

Apple Nut Bread

- **1½ cups vegetable oil**
- **2 cups sugar**
- **4 eggs**
- **3 cups all-purpose flour**
- **1 teaspoon baking soda**
- **1 teaspoon cinnamon**
- **¼ teaspoon salt**
- **1 teaspoon vanilla extract**
- **3 cups peeled and chopped Red Delicious apples**
- **1 cup whole nut meats**

Preheat oven to 325 degrees. Cream oil, sugar, and eggs. Sift flour, soda, cinnamon, and salt together. Add to creamed mixture. Beat until thoroughly mixed. Add vanilla. Stir in apples and nut meats. Bake in 2 greased and floured 8x4-inch loaf pans 1 hour and 20 minutes. Cool and turn out of pans.

Makes 2 8x4-inch loaves

Wanda Groome

Banana Walnut Bread

- **1½ cups all-purpose flour**
- **½ cup sugar**
- **1 teaspoon baking soda**
- **1¼ cups mashed bananas**
- **1 teaspoon vegetable oil**
- **⅓ cup buttermilk**
- **2 teaspoons vanilla extract**
- **¼ cup chopped walnuts**
- **Pinch of salt**

Preheat oven to 350 degrees. Coat a 9x5-inch loaf pan with nonstick cooking spray. Blend flour, sugar, soda, and salt. Mix bananas, oil, buttermilk, vanilla, and walnuts. Combine with flour mixture and pour into loaf pan. Bake 45 to 50 minutes. Turn out and let cool.

Serves 12

Pauline Precise

Squash Bread

- **3 cups all-purpose flour**
- **1 teaspoon baking soda**
- **1 teaspoon salt**
- **½ teaspoon baking powder**
- **1 teaspoon cinnamon**
- **½ teaspoon nutmeg**
- **3 eggs**
- **2 cups sugar**
- **1 cup vegetable oil**
- **2 teaspoons vanilla extract**
- **2 cups squash (zucchini, acorn, or butternut), grated, mashed in blender or cooked**

Preheat oven to 350 degrees. Sift together flour, soda, salt, baking powder, cinnamon and nutmeg. Add to eggs, sugar, oil, and vanilla. Mix well. Stir in squash. Pour into 2 greased 9x5-inch loaf pans. Bake 1 hour.

Makes 2 loaves

Lois Foster

Pumpkin Bread

- **3 cups sugar**
- **4 eggs, beaten**
- **1 (16 ounce) can pumpkin**
- **1 cup vegetable oil**
- **3½ cups all-purpose flour**
- **2 teaspoons baking soda**
- **2 teaspoons salt**
- **½ teaspoon cloves**
- **1 teaspoon baking powder**
- **1 teaspoon nutmeg**
- **1 teaspoon cinnamon**
- **1 teaspoon allspice**
- **⅔ cup water**

Preheat oven to 350 degrees. In a large bowl, combine sugar, eggs, pumpkin, and oil. Mix well. In a separate bowl, combine flour, soda, salt, cloves, baking powder, nutmeg, cinnamon, and allspice. Add to pumpkin mixture alternately with water. Pour into two 9x5-inch greased loaf pans or three smaller ones. Bake large loaves 60 minutes and small loaves 40 minutes. Turn out of pan and cool. Refrigerate. Freezes well.

Makes 2 or 3 loaves

Melanie Kettle

Lemon Bread

- 1 cup sugar
- ½ cup vegetable shortening
- 2 eggs, beaten
- 1 teaspoon baking powder
- ½ cup milk
- 2 tablespoons lemon extract
- 1⅔ cups all-purpose flour
- ½ cup chopped nuts
- Pinch of salt

TOPPING

- 2 tablespoons reconstituted lemon juice
- ¼ cup sugar

Preheat oven to 350 degrees. Cream sugar and shortening. Add eggs, baking powder, milk, lemon extract, flour, nuts, and salt. Pour into a greased 9x5-inch loaf pan. Bake 1 hour. Combine topping ingredients and pour over bread while still warm.

Makes 1 loaf

May bake in smaller loaf pans (two 6x4½ or three 5x3½-inch) for 45 minutes.

Lois Foster

Pumpkin Date Nut Bread

- 2 cups canned pumpkin
- 4 eggs
- ⅓ cup water
- 3 cups sugar
- 1 cup vegetable oil
- 3½ cups all-purpose flour
- 2 teaspoons baking soda
- 1½ teaspoons salt
- 1 teaspoon cinnamon
- 1 cup chopped dates
- 1 cup chopped pecans

Preheat oven to 350 degrees. Mix pumpkin, eggs, water, sugar, and oil with mixer. Stir together flour, baking soda, salt, and cinnamon. Add to pumpkin mixture. Stir in dates and pecans. Pour into 4 well-greased 1-pound coffee cans, filling ½ full. Bake for 1 hour. Cool a few minutes before removing from cans.

May use 4 small loaf pans instead of coffee cans. Freezes well. Makes wonderful Christmas gifts.

Makes 4 loaves

Lady Jane Vowell

Cranberry Compote

2 medium tart apples, peeled and sliced
1 (12 ounce) package fresh or frozen cranberries
1¼ cups sugar
1 cup golden raisins
¼ cup fresh orange juice
1 teaspoon grated orange peel
½ teaspoon salt
¼ teaspoon ground allspice
¼ teaspoon ground cinnamon
1 (14½ ounce) can sliced peaches, drained
1 (14½ ounce) can apricot halves, drained
½ (3 ounce) package strawberry gelatin

In a large saucepan, combine apples, cranberries, sugar, raisins, orange juice, orange peel, salt, allspice, and cinnamon. Bring to boil. Reduce heat. Simmer, uncovered, 10 minutes or until cranberries pop and apples are tender. Add peaches, apricots, and gelatin. Heat through. Serve warm or chilled. Store in refrigerator.

Serves 8

Nancy Billings

Mother's Bran Muffins

1 cup wheat bran cereal
1 cup boiling water
½ cup butter or margarine, melted
1½ cups sugar
2 eggs, beaten
2 cups buttermilk
2½ cups all-purpose flour
2 teaspoons baking soda
1 teaspoon salt
2 cups wheat bran cereal
¾ cup raisins (optional)
¾ cup pecans, broken in pieces (optional)

Preheat oven to 400 degrees. Put 1 cup cereal into boiling water. Let stand. Mix together butter, sugar, eggs, and buttermilk. Slowly add flour, soda, and salt. Stir in soaked cereal and dry cereal. Add raisins and pecans, if desired. Line muffin tins with paper baking cups. Fill ⅔ full. Bake 20 minutes.

Makes 12 muffins

This batter keeps well for several days in the refrigerator. One-half cup oat bran or wheat bran may be substituted for ½ cup flour to make these muffins even healthier as well as delicious.

Carlene Elrod

Orange Muffins

- 2½ cups all-purpose flour
- 2 teaspoons baking powder
- ½ teaspoon salt
- ¾ cup butter, softened
- 1⅔ cups sugar
- 3 eggs, lightly beaten
- 1 teaspoon vanilla extract
- ½ cup orange juice
- 2 orange rinds, grated
- Confectioners' sugar

Preheat oven to 350 degrees. Sift together flour, baking powder, and salt. In another bowl, cream butter and sugar. Add eggs, vanilla, orange juice, and rind to butter mixture. Combine with dry ingredients. Stir lightly until batter is thoroughly moistened but still lumpy. Grease muffin tins lightly and fill ½ full. Bake about 15 minutes. Remove from oven and sprinkle with confectioners' sugar.

Makes about 3 dozen

Lois Foster

Morning Glory Muffins

(Healthy Version)

- 1½ cups all-purpose flour
- ½ cup whole wheat flour
- 1¼ cups sugar
- 2 teaspoons ground cinnamon
- 1 teaspoon baking powder
- 1 teaspoon baking soda
- ½ teaspoon salt
- 2 cups grated carrots (4 medium)
- 1 cup chopped apples
- 1 cup raisins
- ½ cup chopped pecans
- 2 tablespoons wheat germ, toasted
- 1 large egg, lightly beaten
- 2 large egg whites, lightly beaten
- ½ cup apple butter
- ¼ cup canola oil
- 2 teaspoons vanilla extract

Preheat oven to 375 degrees. Coat 18 muffin cups with vegetable cooking spray. In a large mixing bowl, stir together flours, sugar, cinnamon, baking powder, soda, and salt. Stir in carrots, apples, raisins, pecans, and wheat germ. In a medium-size bowl, whisk together egg, egg whites, apple butter, oil, and vanilla. Add to dry ingredients and stir until moistened. Spoon batter into prepared muffin cups, filling about ¾ full. Bake 15 to 20 minutes or until done.

Makes 18 muffins

Camille Vaughan

Lemon Yogurt Muffins

MUFFINS

3 cups all-purpose flour
¼ teaspoon salt
½ teaspoon baking powder
1 teaspoon baking soda
2-3 tablespoons grated lemon zest
1 cup chopped pecans
1 cup vegetable oil
1¾ cups sugar
3 large eggs
2 cups plain yogurt
¼ cup fresh lemon juice

GLAZE

3 cups sifted confectioners' sugar
Grated zest of 2 lemons
Juice of 1½ lemons

Preheat oven to 350 degrees. Lightly grease muffin pans. Combine flour, salt, baking powder, baking soda, lemon zest, and pecans in a large bowl. Combine oil, sugar, eggs, yogurt, and lemon juice in a separate bowl. Combine flour and egg mixtures, mixing until blended. Pour into muffin cups. Bake 25 to 30 minutes or until muffins are slightly brown at edges. Prepare glaze by combining confectioners' sugar, lemon zest, and lemon juice in a small bowl. Spread glaze on warm muffins. Serve immediately.

Makes 2½ dozen

May be made in mini tins, yielding about 7 dozen. Decrease baking time to 15 to 20 minutes.

Katie Clark

"For where two or three are gathered together in my name, there am I in the midst of them."

Matthew 18:20

Many sermons have been preached from this pulpit and many people have knelt at the altar pictured in the foreground. This pulpit and altar were installed in the renovation of the 1960's.

On December 16, 1979, sixteen chancel kneelers, "Stitches for God," were presented to the glory of God and in loving memory of Billie Scott, for whom the Billie Scott Sunday School Class was named. Mrs. Scott came to Huntsville in 1941 with her husband, Rudolph R. Scott, who was pastor until his death in 1946. Mrs. Scott continued to live in Huntsville and serve the church until her death in 1973.

The kneelers took forty dedicated members nearly four years to create, starting in the spring of 1976 with one year for design and almost three years to stitch. With an average of 196 stitches per square inch, each cushion contains approximately 127,000 stitches and represents a minimum of 350 hours of actual stitching. The entire project comprises over two million stitches. The kneelers are worked in #14 canvas using the finest Persian yarns. Most of the work is done in the basket weave stitch.

The design reflects many hours of research. The symbol of a different Apostle is on each of the twelve large kneelers. Background colors and designs are the same on each. Enclosing the Apostle's symbol is a medallion adapted from the center of the Sanctuary's stained glass windows.

The circular design of the two small corner pillows are derived from a similar one at the top of the windows. The two communion kneelers show the grapes and the wheat sheaves. The altar kneeler was completed in the spring of 1980, and shows the symbols of Alpha and Omega and IHS.

Entrées

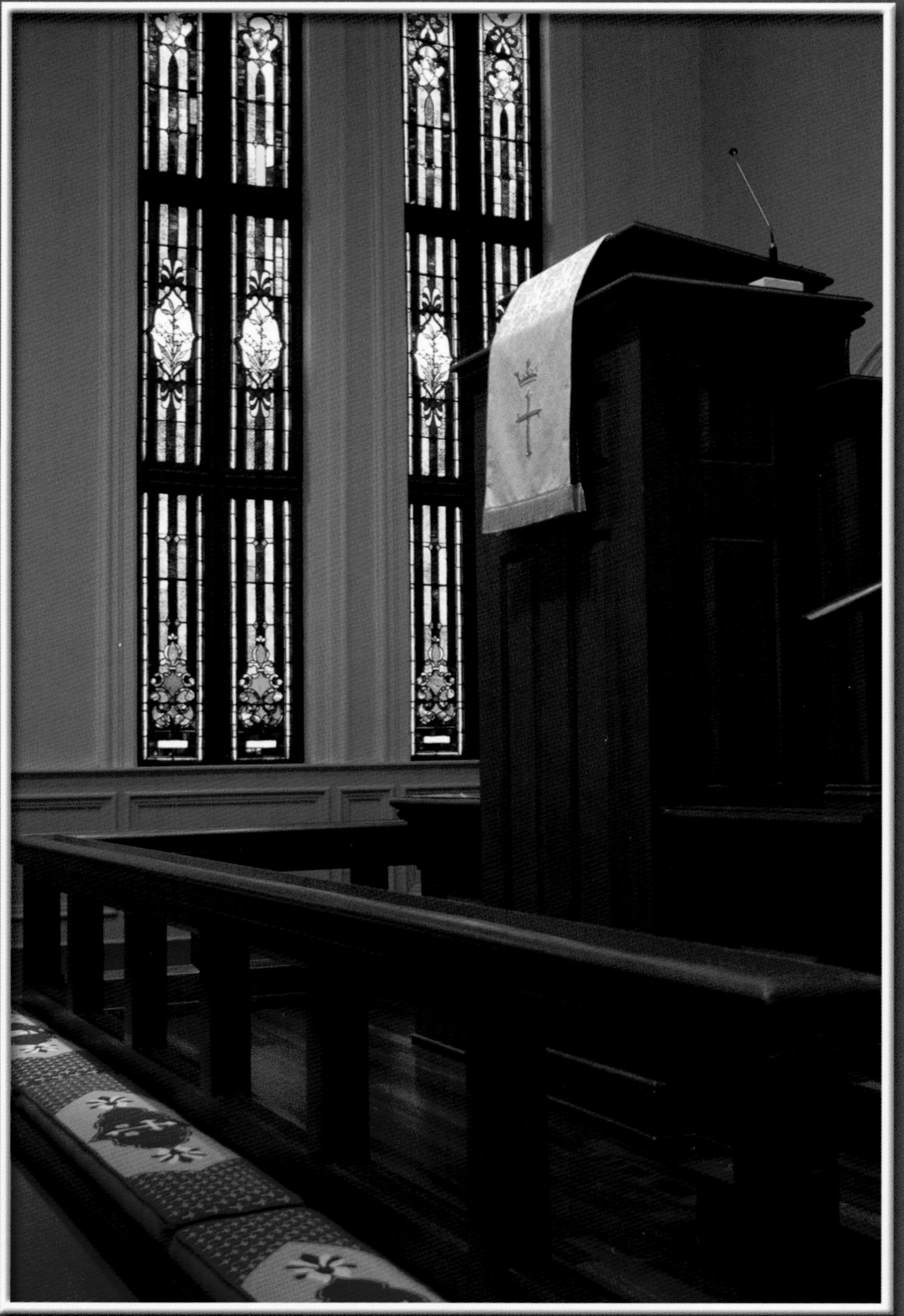

...WHATSOEVER THINGS ARE LOVELY,
... THINK ON THESE THINGS.

PHILIPPIANS 4:8

Noted features of the historic Sanctuary are the stained glass windows. According to Ruth Sykes Ford's *History of the Methodist Church, Huntsville, Alabama, 1808-1958*, the "glass of the original windows was dark amber outlined with blue." The majestic stained glass windows, installed in the late 1890's, embody many Christian symbols and are memorials to pioneering members.

Protective coverings were applied to the exterior of the windows in the 1970's. The covering became discolored and cloudy over the years. In 2007, new coverings created by improved technology were installed. This allows more light and reveals the true beauty of the windows.

Châteaubriand with Roasted Vegetables

- 2 tablespoons grated lemon peel
- 3 tablespoons olive oil
- 2 teaspoons dried thyme leaves
- 1 teaspoon dried marjoram
- 1½ teaspoons salt
- 1 teaspoon pepper
- 1 (4-pound) beef tenderloin roast
- 1 small red bell pepper, cut into 1-inch wedges
- 1 small yellow bell pepper, cut into 1-inch wedges
- 8 green onions, sliced lengthwise
- 2 yellow squash, cut into 1-inch pieces
- Béarnaise or hollandaise sauce

Preheat oven to 425 degrees. Combine lemon peel, oil, thyme, marjoram, salt, and pepper. Rub half the mixture over tenderloin. Toss remaining mixture with vegetables to coat. Place beef in large roasting pan and roast for 40 minutes. Add vegetables to pan and continue cooking another 35 minutes or until thermometer registers 140 degrees for medium rare or 160 degrees for medium doneness. Transfer roast to cutting board. Let rest 5 minutes before slicing. Serve with béarnaise or hollandaise sauce.

Serves 8

Frank Batty

Beef Stroganoff

- 1 pound round steak
- ¼ cup butter or margarine
- 2 cups sliced mushrooms (optional)
- ½-1 cup chopped onion
- 1 (10½ ounce) can beef broth
- 1 (8 ounce) carton sour cream
- 2½ tablespoons all-purpose flour
- Salt
- Pepper
- Cooked noodles or rice

Remove fat from meat and slice diagonally across grain into ¼-inch strips. (Strips should be very thin.) Brown meat quickly in butter and push meat to one side. Add mushrooms and onion and cook until just tender. Stir in broth. Cover and simmer 15 to 20 minutes. Blend sour cream with flour and add to broth. Cook over low heat, stirring until mixture thickens slightly. Add salt and pepper to taste. Serve over buttered noodles or rice.

Serves 4 to 5

Two cups of water and two beef bouillon cubes may be substituted for beef broth.

Harriet Wright

Roast Beef with Blue Cheese Marinade

1 (4 ounce) package blue cheese, crumbled
½ cup lemon juice
3 tablespoons all-purpose flour
1 tablespoon dry mustard
½ teaspoon Worcestershire sauce
4 dashes hot sauce
3 garlic cloves finely chopped
1½ teaspoons salt
1 teaspoon coarsely ground black pepper
1 (4-6 pound) beef roast, any cut of oven roast
1 teaspoon dried green onion
1 cup water

Two days before roast is to be served, combine blue cheese, lemon juice, flour, mustard, Worcestershire sauce, hot sauce, garlic, salt, and pepper to make a paste and smear on meat. Place meat in a glass bowl and cover with plastic wrap. Place in refrigerator. Marinate for 2 days. When ready to cook, preheat oven to 300 degrees. Place roast on rack in roasting pan. Sprinkle dried onion over roast and add 1 cup water to pan. Insert meat thermometer. Bake until roast reaches desired doneness as indicated by thermometer. (Refrigerated cold meat will take approximately 4 hours to reach internal temperature of 160 degrees for medium doneness.) If pan becomes dry during cooking time, add more water. Deglaze roasting pan with a little hot water. Use drippings for gravy.

Serves 8

Carol Hurst

Beef Burgundy for Slow Cooker

- 1 (3-4 pound) beef sirloin roast, cubed
- 2 (10¾ ounce) cans cream of mushroom soup
- 2 (12 ounce) jars beef gravy
- 1 (1.25 ounce) envelope onion soup mix
- 8 ounces canned sliced mushrooms, drained
- 1 (10¾ ounce) soup can red wine
- 1 (16 ounce) package medium or wide noodles, cooked

Mix meat, soup, gravy, soup mix, mushrooms, and wine together in slow cooker. Cover and cook on high 5 to 6 hours. Serve over noodles.

Serves 6

One (10¼ ounce) can of beef broth may be substituted for wine.

Michael Stahl

Variation: May use lean stew meat instead of sirloin roast, substitute 1 can cream of onion soup for onion soup mix and beef gravy, and omit mushrooms. Bake covered with foil at 325 degrees for 3 to 4 hours. Serve over rice.

Janet Walker Davis

Pot Roast

- 1 (3½ pound) chuck roast
- 6 russet potatoes, peeled
- 2 (10¾ ounce) cans cream of mushroom soup
- 1 tablespoon fresh or dried chives
- ½ cup grated sharp Cheddar cheese

Preheat oven to 325 degrees. Place roast in a Dutch oven and bake 1 hour. Remove from oven and arrange potatoes around roast. Pour soup and chives over roast and potatoes. Reduce oven temperature to 300 degrees. Return to oven and cook 2 hours until potatoes are done. Remove from oven and sprinkle roast with cheese. Return to oven until cheese melts.

Serves 5 to 6

Marion Cox

Teriyaki Steak

3 pounds round steak or sirloin
Vegetable oil

MARINADE

1½ cups soy sauce
1½ cups water
2 cloves garlic, sliced
¼-½ cup sugar
Gingerroot or 6 green onions, chopped

Cut steak in thin pieces less than ¼-inch thick. Dip meat in oil. Mix soy sauce, water, garlic, sugar, and gingerroot or onion. Pour marinade over meat and refrigerate 24 hours. Cook quickly in sizzling skillet, turning once. To make gravy from marinade, bring to a boil for at least 10 minutes. Serve immediately and piping hot.

Serves 6

Charlene Lockhart

Corned Beef Cabbage

1 small onion, sliced
1 medium-size cabbage, shredded
2 cups milk
2 tablespoons butter
½ teaspoon salt
1 cup instant potato flakes
1 egg, beaten
½ cup shredded Swiss cheese
¼ teaspoon dried tarragon
¼ teaspoon dried thyme
Pepper
1 (12 ounce) can corned beef
1½ cups shredded Swiss cheese
1 tablespoon butter, melted
¼ cup Italian breadcrumbs

Preheat oven to 350 degrees. Boil onion and cabbage in water for 5 minutes. Drain well and set aside. In a large pan, combine milk, butter, and salt and bring to boil. Remove from heat and stir in potato flakes. Return to heat and bring to boil. Remove from heat and let stand 30 seconds until liquid is absorbed then whip with a fork. Add egg, ½ cup cheese, tarragon, thyme, and pepper to taste. Mix well. Flake corned beef into small pieces. In a greased 2-quart baking dish, layer half the potato mixture, half the corned beef, half the cabbage mixture and half the cheese. Repeat layers. Combine melted butter and breadcrumbs and sprinkle on top. Bake 20 minutes, uncovered.

Serves 4

Marie Fuqua

Barbeque Brisket

DAY 1

1 (5-pound) brisket
2½ ounces liquid smoke
½ cup brown sugar
1 teaspoon celery salt
Salt
Pepper
1 onion, sliced in rings

Place brisket in a 9x13-inch baking dish. Combine liquid smoke, brown sugar, celery salt, and salt and pepper to taste. Pour mixture over brisket. Place onion rings on top. Cover and marinate overnight in refrigerator.

DAY 2

1 cup barbeque sauce
½ cup brown sugar
¼ cup vinegar
¼ cup water
3 tablespoons liquid smoke

Preheat oven to 250 degrees. Bake brisket 4 to 6 hours until tender. Pour off liquid. Remove meat to cutting board. Let stand 15 minutes before slicing. Increase oven temperature to 325 degrees. Return sliced meat to baking dish. To prepare sauce, combine barbeque sauce, brown sugar, vinegar, water, and liquid smoke. Pour sauce over sliced meat and heat in oven until hot.

Serves 12 to 14

Nancy Billings

No Peek Stew

2 pounds stew meat
1 (1 ounce) envelope dry onion soup mix
1 (10¾ ounce) can cream of mushroom soup
1 (6 ounce) jar mushrooms with juice
1 cup red wine
Cooked rice or noodles

Preheat oven to 300 degrees. Combine meat, soup mix, soup, mushrooms, and wine. Pour into a 2½ to 3-quart baking dish with cover. Bake covered for 3 hours and "don't peek." Serve over rice or noodles.

Serves 4 to 6

Tine Purdy

Shepherd's Pie

1 (5½ ounce) package instant potato flakes or 2 potatoes, cooked and whipped
¼ cup fresh chopped parsley
1½ pounds lean cubed steak, cut in pieces
¼ cup olive oil or canola oil
1 (14 ounce) can low fat beef broth
3 carrots, chopped
1 medium onion, chopped
2 cloves garlic, minced
1½ teaspoons dried thyme
Salt
Pepper
2 tablespoons cornstarch

Preheat oven to 350 degrees. Prepare potatoes according to package directions. Add parsley and set aside. In a large skillet, brown meat in oil over medium to medium-high heat until well done. Pour off all but 2 tablespoons fat. Reduce heat and add half the can of beef broth, carrots, onion, garlic, thyme, and salt and pepper, to taste. Mix cornstarch with remaining broth. Add to meat mixture. Cook approximately 5 minutes or until gravy is thick and glossy. Pour mixture into a 2-quart baking dish coated with cooking spray. Top evenly with whipped potato mixture and bake 30 to 35 minutes or until browned.

Serves 6

Variation: Omit whipped potatoes. Add 1 peeled and chopped potato and cook with other ingredients. Using 2 deep-dish pie crusts, place cooked mixture into one crust and cover with the other, sealing edges and making air slits in top crust. Bake 45 to 60 minutes at 350 degrees until both crusts are brown.

Mary Jo Deaver

Italian Meatloaf

- **1 tablespoon extra virgin olive oil**
- **1 red bell pepper, diced**
- **1 onion, diced**
- **2 teaspoons chopped garlic**
- **1 pound ground beef**
- **2 eggs**
- **¾ cup breadcrumbs**
- **1 cup grated Parmesan cheese**
- **1 tablespoon Worcestershire sauce**
- **1 tablespoon balsamic vinegar**
- **1 tablespoon extra virgin olive oil**
- **2 tablespoons chopped fresh basil**
- **1 tablespoon chopped fresh parsley**
- **1 teaspoon salt**
- **½ teaspoon pepper**
- **1 cup marinara sauce**

Preheat oven to 350 degrees. Heat 1 tablespoon of olive oil in a medium sauté pan over medium heat. Add red pepper, onion, and garlic. Sauté until just soft. Remove from pan and cool. When pepper and onion are cool, combine with ground beef, eggs, breadcrumbs, Parmesan cheese, Worcestershire sauce, vinegar, 1 tablespoon olive oil, basil, parsley, salt, and pepper. Pack meat in lightly greased 8-inch loaf pan. If you do not have a loaf pan, form into a loaf shape in a lightly greased baking dish. Spread marinara sauce evenly over top of meatloaf. Bake approximately 50 to 60 minutes or until a meat thermometer inserted into middle of meatloaf registers 160 degrees. Remove from oven and let rest for 5 minutes. Slice and serve.

Serves 4

Frank Batty

French Spaghetti

- **1 pound ground beef**
- **3 medium onions, chopped**
- **1/4 cup olive oil**
- **2 large green bell peppers, seeded and chopped**
- **1 (28 ounce) can tomatoes, drained**
- **1 (14½ ounce) can tomatoes, drained**
- **1 (4½ ounce) jar sliced mushrooms, drained**
- **1 (4 ounce) can chopped black olives, drained**
- **Garlic salt**
- **Salt**
- **Pepper**
- **1 (12 ounce) package spaghetti**
- **1 pound mozzarella cheese, grated**

Brown meat in a large skillet. Drain and set aside. Sauté onion in olive oil until tender. Add peppers and sauté until peppers lose green color. Add meat, tomatoes, mushrooms, olives, garlic salt to taste, and salt and pepper to taste. Cover and simmer 10 to 15 minutes. Cook spaghetti according to package directions. Drain and fold into meat mixture. Heat until bubbly. Add cheese and simmer 15 minutes.

Serves 10

Terry T. Lewis

Barley and Beef Stuffed Bell Peppers

- 4 large bell peppers
- 1 pound lean ground beef
- ¼ cup sliced green onion
- 1 cup cooked barley
- 1 cup chunky salsa
- ⅓ cup shredded carrot
- ¼ teaspoon cumin
- 1 cup grated Monterey Jack cheese, divided

Preheat oven to 350 degrees. Cook peppers in salted water for 3 to 5 minutes. Cut off tops of peppers, remove seeds, and drain. Brown meat and onion in a large skillet. Add barley, salsa, carrot, cumin, and ¾ cup of cheese to beef mixture. Spoon into peppers. Place on cookie sheet or in casserole dish and bake uncovered for 20 to 25 minutes. Top with remaining cheese and cook 5 minutes longer. Freezes well.

Serves 4

Linda Vest

Submitted by Glenda Bragg

Yankee Doodle Hamburger Delight

- 2½ pounds hamburger meat
- 1 large onion, chopped
- 1 (16 ounce) box elbow macaroni
- 2 (28 ounce) cans chopped tomatoes, with juice
- 5 cups shredded Cheddar cheese
- Salt
- Pepper
- Shredded Cheddar cheese

In a large pot, cook meat and onion. Drain and return to pot. Cook macaroni according to package directions. Drain. To meat, add macaroni, tomatoes, 5 cups cheese, and salt and pepper to taste. Mix and heat thoroughly. Top with shredded cheese just before serving.

Serves 10

Laura Jackson Anderson

Spicy Meatloaf or Sandwiches

MEATLOAF

- **2 eggs, beaten**
- **⅔ cup seasoned fine dry breadcrumbs**
- **1 cup finely chopped onion**
- **2 medium tomatoes, seeded and chopped**
- **½ cup raisins**
- **¼ teaspoon ground cloves**
- **½ teaspoon salt**
- **⅛ teaspoon ground black pepper**
- **1½-2 pounds lean ground beef**

TOPPING

- **⅓ cup ketchup**
- **3 tablespoons packed brown sugar**
- **1 tablespoon hot pepper sauce**

SANDWICH

- **⅓ cup mayonnaise**
- **1 tablespoon prepared horseradish**
- **12 slices potato bread**

Preheat oven to 350 degrees. In a bowl, combine eggs, breadcrumbs, onion, tomatoes, raisins, cloves, salt, and pepper. Add meat and mix well. Place meat mixture in a lightly greased 9x5-inch loaf pan and bake1 hour to 1 hour 15 minutes until internal temperature reaches 160 degrees. Drain fat. In a bowl, blend ketchup, brown sugar, and hot sauce for topping. Spread over meat and bake an additional 5 minutes. Remove from oven and let rest 15 minutes before slicing. Mix mayonnaise and horseradish to use as spread on potato bread. Use bread and sliced meatloaf to build a sandwich.

Serves 6 to 8

Connie Cook

Cavatini

- 1 pound ground beef
- 1 pound mild ground pork sausage
- 1 medium onion, chopped
- 1 medium green pepper, chopped
- 1 (3½ ounce) package pepperoni slices, chopped
- 1 (28 ounce) can crushed tomatoes
- 1 (26 ounce) jar regular spaghetti sauce
- 1 (16 ounce) jar mild salsa
- 1 (4 ounce) can sliced mushrooms, drained
- 1 (10 ounce) jar pepperoncini salad peppers, drained and sliced
- 1 (16 ounce) package cooked shell macaroni
- ½ cup grated Parmesan cheese
- 2 cups shredded mozzarella cheese

TOPPING

- ½ cup grated Parmesan cheese
- 2 cups shredded mozzarella cheese

Preheat oven to 350 degrees. Cook ground beef, sausage, onion, and green pepper in a large skillet over medium heat, stirring until meat browns and crumbles. Drain well and set aside. Combine pepperoni, tomatoes, spaghetti sauce, salsa, mushrooms, and salad peppers in a large bowl. Stir in meat mixture and pasta shells. Spoon ¼ of mixture into each of 2 lightly greased 7x11-inch baking dishes. Sprinkle with ½ cup Parmesan and 2 cups mozzarella cheese. Top with remaining pasta mixture. Bake 30 minutes until well heated. Top with remaining cheeses and bake an additional 5 minutes.

Serves 16

May use 4 lightly greased 9x9-inch baking dishes. Unbaked casseroles may be frozen up to 3 months. (Freeze topping cheeses separately.)

Helen Middleton

Meaty Ziti Casserole

- **¾ pound ground beef, cooked and drained**
- **1 (32 ounce) can marinara sauce**
- **1 clove garlic, crushed**
- **1 teaspoon dried oregano**
- **1 teaspoon dried basil**
- **Dash of cayenne pepper**
- **Salt**
- **Pepper**
- **1 (8 ounce) package ziti pasta, cooked al dente**
- **1 (9 ounce) package frozen creamed spinach (REAL cream), thawed**
- **1 cup shredded mozzarella cheese**
- **1 cup shredded Provolone cheese**

Preheat oven to 375 degrees. In saucepan, combine cooked beef, marinara sauce, garlic, oregano, basil, and cayenne. Season with salt and pepper to taste. Spoon 1 cup of sauce on bottom of lightly greased 3-quart glass or ceramic baking dish. Arrange cooked ziti on top. Pour remaining sauce over ziti. Spread creamed spinach evenly on top. Cover tightly with aluminum foil and bake 30 minutes until bubbly. Remove foil and scatter mozzarella and Provolone cheeses on top. Return to oven uncovered, until cheese melts, about 3 to 5 minutes.

Serves 6

One teaspoon bottled chopped garlic may be substituted for fresh garlic; 3 teaspoons fresh basil and 3 teaspoons fresh chopped oregano may be substituted for dried basil and oregano.

Karen Cruze

Lenora's Easy Lasagna

- 1 pound lean ground beef
- 1 tablespoon Italian seasoning
- 1 (32 ounce) jar thick spaghetti sauce
- 1½ cups water
- 1 (16 ounce) carton ricotta cheese or small curd cottage cheese
- 3 cups grated mozzarella cheese
- ½ cup grated Parmesan cheese
- 2 eggs, slightly whipped
- ¼ cup chopped parsley or parsley flakes
- 1 teaspoon salt
- ¼ teaspoon pepper
- 8 ounces uncooked lasagna noodles

Preheat oven to 350 degrees. Brown ground beef in large saucepan and drain off excess grease. Add Italian seasoning, spaghetti sauce, and water. Simmer about 10 minutes. Combine cheeses, eggs, parsley, salt, and pepper in mixing bowl. Mix well. Pour 1 cup of meat sauce into bottom of a lightly greased 9x13-inch baking dish. Place 3 lasagna noodles on top of sauce and cover with 1½ cups of meat sauce. Spread half of cheese mixture over sauce. Repeat layers of noodles, meat sauce, and cheese. Top with a layer of noodles and remaining sauce. Cover with aluminum foil and bake for 55 to 60 minutes. Remove foil and bake for another 10 minutes.

Serves 8 to 10

Lenora Grumbles

Submitted by Sarah Lauren Kattos

Microwave Lasagna

1 pound ground beef
1 (28 ounce) jar spaghetti sauce
½ cup water
2 cups small curd cottage cheese
1 large egg, beaten
1½ teaspoons pepper
8 uncooked lasagna noodles
2 (10 ounce) packages frozen chopped spinach, thawed
2 cups shredded mozzarella cheese
½ cup grated Parmesan cheese

Crumble beef into 2-quart microwave safe bowl. Microwave on high 4 minutes or until meat is browned, stirring once. Drain. Stir in spaghetti sauce and water. Set aside. Combine cottage cheese, egg, and pepper. In a 9x13-inch baking dish, spread ½ cup meat sauce. Top with half of each: noodles, cottage cheese mixture, spinach, meat sauce, and mozzarella cheese. Repeat layers. Cover with heavy-duty plastic wrap. Microwave on high 8 minutes. Microwave on medium 30 to 32 minutes or until noodles are tender, turning dish occasionally. Remove from microwave. Sprinkle with Parmesan cheese. Cover and let stand 15 minutes.

Serves 12

Betty Peeler

Nancy's Enchilada Casserole

1 pound ground beef
1 onion, chopped
1 (15 ounce) can enchilada sauce
¼ cup water
1½ cups shredded sharp Cheddar cheese
½ (1.25 ounce) package taco seasoning mix
6-8 (8 to 9-inch) soft tortillas
Sharp Cheddar cheese for topping

Preheat oven to 350 degrees. Brown ground beef and onion. Drain. Add half of enchilada sauce, water, cheese, and half of taco seasoning mix. Stir and mix well. Spoon mixture onto each tortilla. Roll and place in a 9x13-inch baking pan. Pour remaining half of sauce over enchiladas. Sprinkle with cheese and bake 15 minutes.

Serves 6 to 8

Serve with lettuce, sour cream, and diced fresh tomatoes to dress it up; refried beans and Mexican rice.

Gina Martin Johnston

Karen's Lasagna

- 1 pound ground beef
- 1 (14½ ounce) can diced tomatoes, undrained
- 2 (6 ounce) cans tomato paste
- 1 cup water
- 1 tablespoon crushed dried basil
- 1½ teaspoons salt
- Garlic powder
- 1 (10 ounce) package lasagna noodles
- 2 eggs, beaten
- 1 (24 ounce) carton cottage cheese
- ½ cup grated Parmesan cheese
- 2 tablespoons dried parsley
- Salt
- Pepper
- 1 (16 ounce) package sliced mozzarella cheese

Preheat oven to 375 degrees. In a skillet, brown meat and drain well. Add tomatoes, tomato paste, water, basil, salt, and garlic powder to taste. Simmer covered for at least 15 minutes, stirring occasionally. Cook noodles according to package directions and drain. In a bowl, combine eggs and cottage cheese. Add Parmesan cheese, parsley, and salt and pepper to taste. In a greased 9x13-inch baking dish, layer half of each: noodles, cottage cheese mixture, meat sauce, and mozzarella cheese. Repeat layers. Bake 30 minutes. Remove from oven and let rest about 10 minutes.

Serves 8 to 10

Patricia Everitt

Jezebel Sauce

- 1¼ cups pineapple preserves
- 1¼ cups apple jelly
- ½-¾ cup horseradish (from dairy case)
- 3 tablespoons dry mustard
- 1 teaspoon ground black pepper

Mix all ingredients together and store in refrigerator. This is a very hot sauce. You may want to start with ½ cup of the horseradish and increase the amount if it's not hot enough for your taste. Serve sauce cold with beef, pork, or chicken. May also be served over a block of cream cheese with crackers as an appetizer.

Makes 3 cups

Barbara Chappell

Baked Pork Chops

- **1/4 cup butter**
- **1 cup round buttery cracker crumbs**
- **3 tablespoons Parmesan cheese**
- **1/2 teaspoon salt**
- **1/8 teaspoon pepper**
- **1 egg**
- **2 tablespoons milk**
- **6 pork chops**

Preheat oven to 350 degrees. Melt butter in a 9x13-inch baking dish in the oven. Combine cracker crumbs, cheese, salt, and pepper. Set aside. In a shallow bowl, blend egg and milk. Coat pork chops in crumb mixture then dip into egg mixture and again in crumbs. Place in baking dish with melted butter. Bake 30 minutes. Carefully turn chops and bake an additional 30 minutes or until done.

Serves 6

Kay Brotherton

Marinated Pork Chops

- **8 thick-cut pork chops**
- **3/4 cup vegetable oil**
- **2 tablespoons dry mustard**
- **3/4 cup soy sauce**
- **1/2 cup Worcestershire sauce**
- **1/3 cup lemon juice**
- **1 1/2 tablespoons dry parsley**
- **2 teaspoons salt**
- **1 tablespoon pepper**

Place pork chops in a large pan. In a bowl, slowly add oil to dry mustard and mix until smooth. Add soy sauce, Worcestershire, lemon juice, parsley, salt, and pepper. Mix well. Pour over chops, cover, and marinate overnight. Heat grill. Grill chops approximately 8 to 10 minutes on each side or until done.

Serves 8

Linda Finnell

Pork Chops and Spicy Peaches

- **6 (¾-inch thick) pork chops**
- **1 teaspoon salt**
- **½ teaspoon pepper**
- **1 (29 ounce) can peach halves in syrup**
- **¼ cup reserved peach syrup**
- **½ cup light corn syrup**
- **1 teaspoon fresh lemon juice**
- **¼ teaspoon cinnamon**
- **¼ teaspoon ginger**
- **⅛ teaspoon ground cloves**
- **2 teaspoons all-purpose flour**
- **¼ cup water**

Brown pork chops on both sides in skillet over medium heat. Pour off excess fat. Sprinkle chops with salt and pepper. Drain peaches, reserving ¼ cup syrup. Combine reserved peach syrup, corn syrup, lemon juice, cinnamon, ginger, and cloves. Pour over chops and cook over low heat until pork is cooked, about 45 minutes. Add peaches. When peaches are hot, remove chops and peaches to serving platter and keep warm. Blend flour and water. Add to liquid in skillet, stirring constantly, until it comes to a boil. Spoon over chops or serve in a bowl on the side. Serve immediately.

Serves 6

Jerry Laurine

Barbeque Pork Chops

- **4 (½-inch thick) pork chops**
- **½ cup chopped onion**
- **¼ cup packed brown sugar**
- **¼ cup ketchup**
- **¼ cup vinegar**
- **¼ cup water**
- **1 tablespoon Worcestershire sauce**
- **1 teaspoon paprika**
- **1 teaspoon salt**
- **1 teaspoon pepper**

Preheat oven to 300 degrees. Place pork chops in a lightly greased 9x9-inch baking dish. Combine onion, brown sugar, ketchup, vinegar, water, Worcestershire sauce, paprika, salt, and pepper. Mix well and pour over chops. Bake for 1 hour.

Serves 4

Kay Brotherton

Slow Cooker Barbeque Pork

- **1 (3-4 pound) Boston butt pork roast**
- **1 (18 ounce) bottle barbeque sauce**
- **1 (12 ounce) can cola-flavored carbonated beverage**

Place roast in a 6-quart slow cooker. Pour barbeque sauce and cola over roast. Cover and cook on high 8 hours or until meat is tender and shreds easily.

Serves 6

To reduce fat but not flavor, prepare a day ahead of serving. Cool and refrigerate overnight. Remove and discard any solidified fat before reheating.

Gina Martin Johnston

Mexican Pork Roast

- **1 (4-pound) pork loin roast**
- **2 teaspoons salt**
- **½ teaspoon freshly ground black pepper**
- **2 cloves garlic, minced**
- **3 tomatoes, diced**
- **¾ cup chopped onion**
- **2 cups beef broth**
- **6 Spanish or Italian sausages, sliced**
- **3 tablespoons olive oil**
- **4 green chile peppers, thinly sliced lengthwise**
- **1 cup sliced onion**

Preheat oven to 450 degrees. Rub pork loin with mixture of salt, pepper, and garlic. Place on rack in roasting pan and bake for 30 minutes. Pour off fat and remove rack. Add tomatoes, chopped onion, and broth. Reduce heat to 350 degrees and roast for 1 to 1½ hours. Baste frequently. Brown sliced sausages in skillet. Drain and add to pork. Roast an additional 15 minutes or until instant-read meat thermometer reaches 160 to 170 degrees. Heat olive oil in skillet and sauté sliced peppers and onion for 10 minutes. Carve roast. Skim fat from gravy and pour over pork. Cover with the sautéed pepper and onion.

Serves 12

Canned tomatoes may be used instead of fresh tomatoes.

Mac Wright

Submitted by Mary Richardson

Sweet 'n Sour Pork

- 2 pounds lean pork cut into 2x2-inch pieces
- 2 tablespoons vegetable shortening
- ⅓ cup water
- 2 tablespoons cornstarch
- 1 cup pineapple juice
- 2 tablespoons soy sauce
- ⅓ cup wine vinegar
- ½ cup brown sugar
- ½ teaspoon salt
- 2 tablespoons sesame seed
- ½ cup green bell pepper, cut in strips
- ½ cup thickly sliced onion
- 1 (15¼ ounce) can pineapple tidbits
- 1 cup sliced water chestnuts
- 1 cup sautéed mushrooms, fresh or canned
- Hot cooked rice

Brown pork in shortening. Add water and cook slowly for 1 hour. In a sauce pan, combine cornstarch, pineapple juice, soy sauce, vinegar, brown sugar, and salt. Cook until thick, stirring constantly. Add to meat and let stand about 15 minutes. Add sesame seed, bell pepper, onion, pineapple, water chestnuts, and sautéed mushrooms to meat mixture. Let stand over low heat for 3 minutes. Remove from heat. Vegetables must stay crisp. Serve over hot rice.

Serves 6 to 8

Blanched almonds may be substituted for water chestnuts.

Lola Northington

Grilled Slow Cooker Ribs

3-4 pounds pork loin back ribs
3 cloves garlic, finely chopped
¼ cup packed brown sugar
1 teaspoon salt
½ teaspoon black pepper
3-4 tablespoons liquid smoke
1 medium onion, sliced
½ cup cola-flavored carbonated beverage
1⅔ cups barbeque sauce or Sweet-Sour Sauce for Pork (recipe follows)

Coat 4 to 5-quart slow cooker with cooking spray. Remove inner skin from ribs. Combine garlic, brown sugar, salt, pepper, and liquid smoke. Rub into ribs. Cut ribs into 4-inch pieces. Layer ribs and onion in slow cooker and pour carbonated beverage over ribs. Cover and cook on low setting 8 to 9 hours. Heat grill. Remove ribs from slow cooker. Drain and discard liquid. Place ribs in a grill basket to prevent ribs from falling apart. Brush ribs with barbeque sauce. Secure grill basket. Place ribs on grill over medium heat. Cover grill and cook 15 minutes.

Serves 6

Sweet-Sour Sauce for Pork

1 cup pineapple preserves
1 cup white vinegar
1 cup chili sauce
1 cup water or cola-flavored carbonated beverage

Mix all ingredients together in a saucepan. Cook over low heat until thick and bubbly, about 1 hour. Sauce will thicken more when cooled. Store in refrigerator.

Makes 2 cups

Syble Park

Sausage Casserole

- ½ pound hot sausage
- ½ pound mild sausage
- 1 small onion, chopped
- 1 cup chopped celery
- 1 (10¾ ounce) can cream of mushroom soup
- 1 (10¾ ounce) can chicken and rice soup
- 1 cup uncooked instant rice
- 1 (12 ounce) can evaporated milk
- ¼ teaspoon marjoram
- ¼ teaspoon thyme
- ¼ teaspoon oregano
- 2 cups grated Cheddar cheese

Preheat oven to 350 degrees. Brown sausage and drain. Reserve drippings. Sauté onion and celery in drippings and drain. In a large bowl, combine sausage, onion, celery, soups, rice, milk, marjoram, thyme, and oregano. Place in a greased 2-quart baking dish. Bake 35 minutes. Remove from oven and sprinkle with cheese. Return to oven for 2 to 3 minutes until cheese melts.

Serves 8

Martha Dotzheimer

Sausage and Beef Casserole

- 1 pound pork sausage
- 1 pound ground beef
- 1 onion, chopped
- 2 (6 ounce) boxes long grain and wild rice with seasoning packet
- 3 tablespoons soy sauce
- 1 (4½ ounce) can mushrooms, drained
- 1 (8 ounce) can sliced water chestnuts, drained
- 1 (3 ounce) package sliced almonds

Preheat oven to 300 degrees. In a skillet, cook sausage and ground beef. Drain and return to skillet. Add onion and sauté with meat mixture. While meat is cooking, cook rice according to package directions. Add soy sauce, mushrooms, and water chestnuts to rice and combine with meat. Place in a lightly greased 9x13-inch baking dish. Top with almonds and bake 25 to 30 minutes or until thoroughly heated.

Serves 8

Best when assembled one day, refrigerated, and baked the next day. Remove from refrigerator 1 hour before baking.

Mary Evelyn French

Mango Chicken

DAY 1

8 boneless, skinless chicken breasts
2 cups mango juice
½ cup vegetable oil

Combine juice and oil. Pour over chicken and refrigerate for 12 to 24 hours.

DAY 2

Salt
Pepper
1½ tablespoons cornstarch
1½ tablespoons cold water
¼ cup sugar
¼ cup lemon juice
1 cup mango juice
2 fresh sliced mangoes
4 tablespoons coconut for garnish
8 maraschino cherries for garnish

Preheat oven to 375 degrees. Line a 9x13-inch baking pan with foil and coat with cooking spray. Remove chicken from marinade and season with salt and pepper to taste. Place chicken in baking pan. Cover and bake 30 minutes. While chicken is baking, make sauce by combining cornstarch and water in a small saucepan. Add sugar, lemon juice, and mango juice. Cook and stir over medium heat until mixture thickens and boils. Set aside. Remove chicken from oven. Top each breast with mango slices and 2 ounces of sauce. Garnish with coconut and cherries. Return to oven, uncovered, for 10 to 15 minutes until glazed.

Serves 8

Sallie Colwick

Joy's Chicken

DAY 1

12 boneless, skinless chicken breast halves
2 cups sour cream
¼ cup fresh lemon juice
4 teaspoons Worcestershire sauce
2 teaspoons celery salt
2 teaspoons paprika
½ teaspoon garlic salt
1 tablespoon salt
1 teaspoon pepper

Wash chicken and pat dry. Combine sour cream, lemon juice, Worcestershire, celery salt, paprika, garlic salt, salt, and pepper. Coat chicken with mixture and marinate 24 hours in refrigerator.

DAY 2

1½ cups round buttery cracker crumbs
1½ cups saltine cracker crumbs
1 cup butter or margarine, melted

Preheat oven to 300 degrees. Combine buttery cracker crumbs and saltine cracker crumbs. Roll chicken in crumbs and place in a 10x15-inch baking pan coated with cooking spray. Pour melted butter over chicken. Bake 1½ hours.

Serves 12

Linda Finnell

Chicken Nicholas

8 boneless chicken breasts
3 eggs, beaten
Italian style breadcrumbs
Salt
Pepper
¼ cup butter, melted

Pound chicken until thin and soak in eggs about 30 minutes. Coat with breadcrumbs. Season with salt and pepper to taste. In a skillet, sauté chicken in melted butter until golden brown. Serve hot.

Serves 8 to 16

Chicken breasts become large when pounded. May be cut in half for serving.

Kids and husbands love this dish!

Sue Day

Easy Artichoke Chicken

- 8-10 chicken breasts
- Butter
- 1 (6 ounce) bottle artichoke hearts, chopped
- ½ cup thinly sliced onion
- ⅓ cup all-purpose flour
- 1½ teaspoons rosemary or seasoned salt
- 1½ teaspoons salt
- ¼ teaspoon pepper
- 1 cup chicken broth
- 1 cup dry sherry
- 1 (16 ounce) can sliced mushrooms, drained
- Cooked rice

Preheat oven to 375 degrees. In a skillet, brown chicken in butter. Transfer chicken to a lightly greased 9x13-inch baking dish. Arrange artichokes and onion over chicken. In a saucepan, combine flour, rosemary, salt, and pepper. Add chicken broth and sherry. Cook over medium heat until thickened. Add mushrooms to mixture and pour over chicken. Bake 1 hour. Serve over rice.

Serves 8 to 10

Ferne Leonard

Chicken and Wild Rice Casserole

- 1 (6 ounce) box long grain and wild rice with seasoning packet
- 1 (10¾ ounce) can cream of chicken soup
- 1 (8 ounce) carton sour cream
- 3 chicken breasts, cooked and cut into small pieces
- 1 sleeve round buttery crackers, crushed
- ½ cup margarine, melted

Preheat oven to 350 degrees. Cook rice according to package directions. Place rice in an ungreased 2-quart baking dish. Mix soup and sour cream. Combine with chicken. Pour chicken mixture over rice. Mix crackers with melted margarine and sprinkle on top. Bake 30 minutes.

Serves 6

Carolyn Spearman

Chicken Broccoli Casserole

- 2 (10 ounce) packages frozen chopped broccoli
- 6 chicken breast halves, cooked and cubed
- 2 (10¾ ounce) cans cream of chicken soup
- 2 tablespoons lemon juice
- 1 cup mayonnaise
- 1 cup grated Cheddar cheese
- 3-4 tablespoons butter, melted
- 1½ cups fine breadcrumbs

Preheat oven to 350 degrees. Cook broccoli according to package directions and drain well. Place broccoli in a lightly greased 9x13-inch baking dish. Place chicken on top of broccoli. Combine soup, lemon juice, and mayonnaise. Pour mixture over chicken and broccoli. Sprinkle with cheese. Mix melted butter with breadcrumbs and sprinkle over top of casserole. Bake 20 to 30 minutes.

Serves 8 to 10

Debbie Packard

Chicken Pie

- 1 (15 ounce) package refrigerated pie crust
- 3 chicken breasts, cooked and cut into bite-size pieces (reserve broth)
- 4 potatoes, peeled, cubed, and cooked
- 2 carrots, peeled, sliced, and cooked
- 1 (10¾ ounce) can cream of chicken soup
- ½ cup half-and-half
- ¼ cup chicken broth
- 2 tablespoons chopped fresh parsley
- Salt
- Pepper

Preheat oven to 400 degrees. Line a 9-inch pie pan with 1 crust. Place chicken, potatoes, and carrots over crust. In a medium-size bowl, whisk together soup, half-and-half, and broth. Additional broth may be added to sauce to reach desired consistency. Stir in parsley. Add salt and pepper to taste. Pour sauce over chicken and vegetables. Cover with second pie crust. Overlap top crust and fold underneath the edge of bottom crust. Crimp to seal. Cut a few vent holes in top crust. Bake 40 to 50 minutes or until golden brown.

Serves 4 to 6

Doni Harrison

Sweet and Sour Chicken

(Kiyoko Saito)

CHICKEN

2 pounds chicken wings, legs, or breasts
Garlic salt
Pepper
2 eggs, beaten
Cornstarch
Cooking oil

SAUCE

½ cup sugar
3 tablespoons ketchup
1 teaspoon salt
¼ cup vinegar
1 tablespoon soy sauce
¼ cup chicken broth

Preheat oven to 350 degrees. Season chicken with garlic salt and pepper to taste. Dip chicken in beaten eggs then roll in cornstarch. Fry in oil until brown. Place chicken in a 9x13-inch baking pan. Mix sauce ingredients in a saucepan and bring to a boil. Pour sauce over chicken and bake 30 minutes, turning every 10 minutes.

Serves 4

Pork or shrimp may be substituted for chicken.

Sandy Housley

This is a recipe from Brazil that my mother shared with me while she and my father lived in Taubate, Brazil for 2 years. It has become an all-time family favorite.

Chicken Pot Pie

- 1 (11 ounce) box pie crust mix
- 3 whole chicken breasts, skinned and boned
- 4 hard-boiled eggs, sliced
- ½ cup butter
- 8 tablespoons all-purpose flour
- 1 teaspoon salt
- ⅛ teaspoon pepper
- 4 cups chicken stock
- Butter

Make pie crust dough according to directions on box and chill. Cook chicken in water until tender. Reserve stock. Cut chicken into large pieces. Cover bottom of a lightly greased oblong casserole dish with chicken. Top with egg slices. Preheat oven to 350 degrees. To make sauce, melt butter in a medium saucepan. Stir in flour, salt, and pepper. Slowly add chicken stock and cook until thickened. Pour over chicken. Roll out chilled dough to cover top of casserole dish. Dot crust with butter and bake for 30 minutes.

Serves 4 to 6

Sarah Purdy

Submitted by Tine Purdy

Orange Marinated Chicken

- 2 whole chicken breasts, split
- ½ cup orange juice
- ¼ teaspoon dried marjoram
- ¼ teaspoon dried basil
- ½ teaspoon garlic salt
- ½ teaspoon salt
- ¼ teaspoon pepper

Wash chicken and dry well with absorbent towels. Place chicken in a lightly greased 9x13-inch baking dish. Combine orange juice, marjoram, basil, garlic salt, salt, and pepper. Pour over chicken and refrigerate 1 hour. Preheat oven to 350 degrees. Bake uncovered 45 to 55 minutes, basting occasionally.

Serves 4

Joan Dedrick

Jamie's Chicken and Sausage Jambalaya

- 2 pounds smoked sausage, cut in pieces
- 1 large bell pepper, chopped
- 1 large onion, chopped
- 1 rotisserie chicken, deboned
- 4 cups chicken broth
- 2 cups uncooked long-grain rice
- 1 (10 ounce) can original tomatoes with chiles, undrained
- 1 bunch green onions, chopped
- 1 tablespoon Creole seasoning
- Salt
- Browning seasoning

Brown sausage in a Dutch oven over medium heat. Add bell pepper and onion and sauté about 3 to 4 minutes. Add chicken, broth, rice, tomatoes, green onion, Creole seasoning, and salt to taste. Stir to blend. Add browning seasoning to darken gravy. Taste and add more salt if needed. Gravy should be a little salty. Stir, bring to boil, then reduce heat to simmer until water is almost cooked out. Cover and lower heat to steam rice, about 20 minutes. Enjoy!

Serves 10

Phil Bueche

French Chicken

- 6-8 skinless chicken breasts, boneless or with bones
- Salt
- Pepper
- 6-8 slices Swiss cheese
- 1 (10¾ ounce) can cream of mushroom, chicken, or celery soup
- ⅓-½ cup white wine
- 1 cup canned breadcrumbs
- ½ cup butter, melted

Preheat oven to 350 degrees. Pierce chicken with a fork and lightly salt and pepper to taste. Place chicken in a 9x13-inch baking dish and top each piece with cheese. In a bowl, combine soup and wine. Pour evenly over chicken. Sprinkle breadcrumbs on top to cover well. Drizzle butter over breadcrumbs. Bake 1 hour.

Serves 6 to 8

Chris Riley

Lauren's Chicken Chili Lasagna

2 (3 ounce) packages cream cheese, softened
1 medium onion, chopped
1½ cups shredded Mexican cheese
2 cloves garlic, minced
¼ teaspoon cumin
3 cups shredded, cooked chicken
¼ cup butter
¼ cup all-purpose flour
1½ cups chicken broth
1 cup shredded Monterey Jack cheese
1 (8 ounce) carton sour cream
1 (4 ounce) can green chiles
⅛ teaspoon salt
⅛ teaspoon pepper
½ teaspoon cumin
12 (6 to 7-inch) flour tortillas, cut in half
½ cup shredded Mexican cheese
8 green onions, tops only, chopped

Preheat oven to 350 degrees. In a large mixing bowl, combine cream cheese, onion, 1½ cups Mexican cheese, garlic, and ¼ teaspoon cumin. Add cooked chicken. Set aside. Melt butter in a saucepan. Stir in flour until smooth. Gradually add chicken broth. Bring to a boil and cook, stirring until thickened. Remove from heat and stir in Monterey Jack cheese, sour cream, chiles, salt, pepper, and ½ teaspoon cumin. Grease bottom of a 9x13-inch baking dish. Layer ½ cup cheese sauce, 6 tortilla halves, ⅓ chicken mixture, and ¼ of remaining cheese sauce. Repeat layers of tortilla, chicken, and cheese sauce twice. Top with remaining tortilla halves and cheese sauce. Sprinkle with ½ cup Mexican cheese and green onion. Cover and bake 30 minutes. Uncover and bake another 10 minutes.

Serves 12

Linda Finnell

Aunt Ruth's Southwest Chicken Casserole

1 cup uncooked rice
2 cups chicken broth (reserved after cooking chicken)
2 cups cooked chicken breast, cut into strips
1 medium onion, chopped
1 teaspoon chili powder
1 (10¾ ounce) can cream of chicken soup
1 (8 ounce) carton sour cream
1 (16 ounce) package shredded Cheddar cheese
1 (10 ounce) can tomatoes and green chiles, undrained

Preheat oven to 350 degrees. Cook rice according to package directions, substituting reserved broth for water. Pour cooked rice into a 9x13-inch baking dish lightly coated with cooking spray. Mix chicken, onion, chili powder, soup, sour cream, and cheese. Spoon on top of rice. Top with tomatoes and chiles. Bake 45 minutes or until bubbly.

Serves 8

Canned chicken broth may be substituted for reserved broth.

Pat Martin

Grandmother's Chicken Tetrazzini

3-4 chicken breast halves
12 ounces vermicelli, broken in pieces
½ cup butter
⅓ cup all-purpose flour
¼ cup chopped onion
1 clove garlic, minced
2 cups reserved chicken stock
1 (28 ounce) can diced or petite diced tomatoes
1 (10 ounce) can tomatoes and green chiles, chopped
1 (4½ ounce) jar sliced mushrooms, drained
Salt
Pepper
¾ pound processed cheese loaf, cubed

Preheat oven to 400 degrees. Cook chicken in large stockpot in boiling water until done, about 20 minutes. Remove chicken from pot. Reserve 2 cups of chicken stock for later use. Cook vermicelli in remaining stock until done, adding water if needed. Drain and set aside. While vermicelli is cooking, remove skin from chicken and cut into cubes. Set aside. In another large pot, melt butter over medium heat. Add flour and stir until blended. Cook for a few minutes. Add onion and garlic. Sauté about 5 minutes, stirring constantly. Slowly add reserved chicken stock. Stir until sauce thickens. Add chicken, tomatoes, tomatoes and green chiles, mushrooms, and salt and pepper to taste. Add cheese and stir CONSTANTLY until cheese is melted. Add vermicelli and mix well. Pour mixture into a lightly greased 9x13-inch or 3-quart baking dish and fill almost to the top (there may be some left over). Cover with aluminum foil and bake 15 to 20 minutes. Remove cover and bake an additional 15 to 30 minutes or until hot and bubbly.

Serves 8 to 10

May be made a day ahead or frozen. If frozen, defrost completely and bring to room temperature before baking as directed.

Judy McLaurine

Chicken Piccata

- **2 whole boneless, skinless chicken breasts, cut in half**
- **1 tablespoon all-purpose flour**
- **Salt**
- **Pepper**
- **¼ cup unsalted butter**
- **2 tablespoons vegetable oil**
- **4 thin slices of lemon, peeled and seeded**
- **2 tablespoons small capers, drained**
- **½ cup dry white wine**
- **Salt**
- **Pepper**

Flatten chicken breasts between sheets of moistened wax paper until they are ¼ inch thick. Season flour with salt and pepper. Dredge chicken in seasoned flour. Shake off excess. In a large heavy skillet, heat butter and oil over moderate heat until foam subsides. Add chicken. Cook 3 to 4 minutes or until golden, turning once. Transfer chicken to warm plate. Add lemon, capers, and wine to drippings in skillet. Cook mixture over moderate heat, swirling skillet until sauce is thickened slightly. Add salt and pepper to taste. Spoon sauce over chicken.

Serves 4

Glenda Bragg and Lenda Woody

Creamed Chicken and Biscuits

- **1½ teaspoons butter**
- **½ large white onion, chopped**
- **4 cups chopped cooked chicken**
- **1 (10¾ ounce) can cream of chicken soup**
- **1 (8 ounce) carton sour cream**
- **½ cup milk**
- **½ cup chopped pimiento (optional)**
- **1 cup shredded mild Cheddar cheese**
- **6 frozen biscuits, thawed**

Preheat oven to 350 degrees. Grease sides and bottom of a 7x11-inch baking dish. Melt butter in a small non-stick skillet over medium-high heat. Stir in onion and sauté until tender. In a medium bowl, combine onion, chicken, soup, sour cream, milk, and pimiento and mix well. Spoon mixture into prepared baking dish and bake 15 minutes. Remove from oven. Sprinkle half of cheese over the top. Arrange biscuits over top and sprinkle with remaining cheese. Bake 20 minutes or until biscuits are brown and sauce is bubbly.

Serves 6

Shawna Schmitz

Chicken Alfredo

- **1/3 cup olive oil**
- **2 boneless, skinless chicken breasts**
- **1/2 cup Italian seasoned breadcrumbs**
- **2 tablespoons dry garlic seasoning blend**
- **1/2 cup butter, melted**
- **1 cup heavy cream**
- **3/4 cup freshly grated Parmesan cheese**
- **1/4 teaspoon freshly ground pepper**
- **Salt**
- **2 cups cooked rotini pasta, drained**
- **Nutmeg (optional)**
- **Parsley (optional)**

Heat oil to 350 degrees in electric skillet. Cut chicken into 1 to 1½-inch pieces. Mix breadcrumbs and garlic seasoning in a zip-top bag. Add chicken to breadcrumb mixture and shake to coat. Sauté chicken in oil until golden brown, turning on all sides, about 6 to 8 minutes depending on thickness of chicken. In a small saucepan, combine butter, cream, Parmesan cheese, pepper, and salt to taste. Heat over medium-low setting until cheese is melted, stirring frequently. To serve, layer chicken over pasta and top with sauce. Sprinkle lightly with nutmeg and garnish with parsley, if desired.

Serves 4

Variation: Cook chicken on a nonstick griddle with olive oil flavored cooking spray or 3 tablespoons olive oil. Commercial Alfredo sauce in jars is available and quite good. Any small pasta such as shells, penne, bowtie, or rigatoni will work in this dish. Boneless pork loin or chops may be substituted for chicken.

Nancy Barnett Darnall

Chicken Spectacular

- **1 (6 ounce) package long grain and wild rice with seasonings**
- **3 cups cubed cooked chicken**
- **1 (8 ounce) can sliced water chestnuts, drained**
- **1 (10¾ ounce) can cream of celery soup**
- **1 (2 ounce) jar diced pimiento**
- **1 medium onion, chopped**
- **1 (14½ ounce) can French style green beans, drained**
- **1 cup mayonnaise**
- **1 cup grated Cheddar cheese**

TOPPING

- **½ cup grated Cheddar cheese**
- **Grated almonds**

Preheat oven to 350 degrees. Cook rice according to package directions. Combine rice, chicken, water chestnuts, soup, pimiento, onion, beans, mayonnaise, and 1 cup cheese. Place in a lightly greased 9x13-inch baking dish. Bake 20 minutes. Remove from oven and top with ½ cup cheese and almonds to cover. Return to oven and bake an additional 10 minutes.

Serves 8 to 10

Wanda Eppes

Variation: Substitute Parmesan cheese for Cheddar cheese. May be made ahead and refrigerated. Bring to room temperature and bake.

Paula Sanders

Poulet de Normandy

DAY 1

1 (16 ounce) package seasoned stuffing mix
1 cup hot water
½ cup butter, melted
¼ cup chopped green onion
½ cup diced celery
½ cup mayonnaise
¾ teaspoon salt
2½ cups cubed cooked chicken breasts
2 eggs, beaten
1½ cups milk

Combine stuffing mix with hot water and butter. Set aside. Mix onion, celery, mayonnaise, salt, and chicken. Set aside. In a lightly greased 9x13-inch baking dish, spread half the stuffing mixture. Spread all the chicken mixture over stuffing, then spread remaining half of stuffing mixture over chicken. Combine beaten eggs and milk and beat again. Pour egg mixture over chicken and stuffing. Cover and refrigerate overnight.

DAY 2

1 (10¾ ounce) can cream of chicken soup
1 cup grated Cheddar cheese

Remove from refrigerator 30 minutes before baking and spread soup on top. Preheat oven to 425 degrees. Bake 30 to 40 minutes or until heated thoroughly. Remove from oven and sprinkle cheese on top. Return to oven and bake an additional 10 minutes.

Serves 10 to 12

Pat Martin

Cranberry Orange Marmalade

1 package fresh cranberries
6 jelly jars with lids
2 (16 ounce) jars orange marmalade

Wash and sort cranberries discarding any soft or shriveled berries. Drain on paper towels. Wash jars and lids and drain. In 3-quart microwave safe bowl, empty one jar of orange marmalade and set aside. Place half of cranberries in a food processor and pulse 4 to 6 times until coarsely chopped. Pour on top of orange marmalade. Repeat process with remaining cranberries and add to marmalade mixture. Add remaining jar of orange marmalade. Stir until marmalade and cranberries are well mixed. Cover with lid and place in microwave. Cook on high 2 minutes. Remove from microwave and stir. Continue this process at 2 minute intervals for a total of 6 minutes. Spoon mixture into jars and seal with lids. Cool completely before refrigerating. Place labels on lids.

Makes 5 or 6 jars

Serve on biscuits, rolls, or turkey sandwiches. Bake on ham steaks or whole ham. Good with pork or poultry dishes. May be served on crackers with a slice of ham or turkey as an appetizer. Will keep in refrigerator for 1 year. If sugary, return to microwave for 2 minutes on high.

Lois Bruce

Chicken and Cornbread

3 cups crumbled cornbread
1 tablespoon poultry seasoning
1 teaspoon sage
½ cup butter, melted
3½ cups chopped cooked chicken
1½ cups chicken stock
1 cup sour cream
½ cup mayonnaise
1 (4½ ounce) can sliced mushrooms, with juice
½ cup chopped onion
½ cup chopped celery
Salt

Preheat oven to 325 degrees. Combine cornbread, poultry seasoning, and sage in a bowl. Pour butter over cornbread mixture and stir. Cover bottom of a 9x13-inch glass baking dish with half of crumb mixture. In a separate mixing bowl, combine chicken, chicken stock, sour cream, mayonnaise, mushrooms, onion, and celery. Salt to taste. Spread chicken mixture on top of crumbs. Top with remaining crumb mixture. Bake 30 to 35 minutes.

Serves 8 to 10

May also be topped with cheese.

Mary Elizabeth Mills

Submitted by Beverly McCulloch

Hot Chicken Salad

4-5 cups diced cooked chicken
1½ cups chopped celery
¾ cup slivered almonds, toasted
2 tablespoons diced pimiento
¼ cup chopped green bell pepper
¼ cup chopped onion
2 hard-boiled eggs, chopped
1 (10¾ ounce) can cream of chicken soup
½ cup mayonnaise
2 tablespoons lemon juice
½ teaspoon salt
White pepper
Crushed potato chips

Preheat oven to 350 degrees. Combine chicken, celery, almonds, pimiento, bell pepper, onion, egg, soup, mayonnaise, lemon juice, salt, and white pepper to taste. Pour into a lightly greased 2-quart baking dish. Top with crushed potato chips. Bake 30 minutes.

Serves 8 to 10

Dee Gibson

Grilled Dove Breasts

Dove breasts
Bacon
Jane's Krazy Mixed-Up Salt
Lemon pepper seasoning
Worcestershire sauce or powder

Wrap each dove breast with a slice of bacon and secure with a toothpick. Season with Mixed-Up Salt and lemon pepper. Sprinkle with Worcestershire sauce or Worcestershire powder, if available. Grill over charcoal until done.

Dr. Robert Sammons

Submitted by Susan Sullins

Dr. Robert Sammons was "chef-in-charge" of grilling the doves that were served to hunters on opening day of dove season at Joe Fleming's farm in Tennessee. Several hundred dove were prepared this way and were the highlight of the meal per Camille Fleming Vaughan.

Susan Sullins' Pasta Shrimp Casserole

2 large eggs
1 cup evaporated milk
1 cup plain yogurt
12 ounces feta cheese, crumbled
8 ounces shredded Swiss cheese
⅓ cup chopped fresh parsley
1½ teaspoons dried basil
1½ teaspoons dried oregano
4 cloves garlic, minced
8 ounces angel hair pasta, cooked
1 (16 ounce) jar mild chunky salsa
1½ pounds medium-size shrimp, uncooked, peeled and deveined
8 ounces shredded mozzarella cheese

Preheat oven to 350 degrees. In a large mixing bowl, blend eggs, milk, yogurt, feta and Swiss cheeses, parsley, basil, oregano, and garlic. Cook pasta according to package directions and drain. Spread half of pasta over bottom of a 9x13-inch lightly greased baking dish. Cover with salsa. Cover with half the shrimp. Spread remaining pasta over shrimp. Pour and spread egg mixture over pasta. Cover with remaining shrimp and top with mozzarella cheese. Bake 30 minutes. Remove from oven and let stand 10 minutes before serving.

Serves 14 to 16

Helen Middleton

Low Country Shrimp Boil

2 large onions, quartered
3 lemons, quartered
4-5 pounds very small new potatoes
4 heaping tablespoons salt
6-10 ears corn, halved
2-2½ pounds hot smoked link sausage
Seafood seasoning
4-6 pounds large or extra-large shrimp, unpeeled

Fill a large pot (a really BIG pot) half full of water. Quarter onions and lemons. Place in the water and bring to a rolling boil. At this point, add new potatoes (the smaller the better). Oh yeah, also add about 4 heaping tablespoons of salt. Yep, you read correctly — 4 heaping tablespoons. Boil approximately 10 minutes. Check potatoes with fork to insure done. Into boiling water, add corn and hot smoked link sausage. Boil 5 to 6 minutes. Add a good amount (read "a lot") of seafood seasoning. Any really good seasoning will do. After about 1 minute, add shrimp. Bring mixture back to near boil. Turn off heat and allow to sit for no longer than 5 minutes. Drain and serve.

Serves 12 to 14

Connie Cook

Spicy Baked Shrimp

½ cup olive oil
2 tablespoons Cajun or Creole seasoning
2 tablespoons fresh lemon juice
2 tablespoons chopped fresh parsley
1 tablespoon honey
1 tablespoon soy sauce
Pinch of cayenne pepper
1 pound large uncooked shrimp, peeled and deveined
Lemon wedges for garnish

In a 9x13-inch baking dish, combine olive oil, seasoning, juice, parsley, honey, soy sauce, and pepper. Add shrimp and toss to coat. Refrigerate 1 hour. Preheat oven to 450 degrees. Bake until shrimp are cooked through, stirring occasionally, about 10 minutes. Garnish with lemon wedges. Serve with French bread.

Serves 4

Willie Williams

Shrimp and Linguini

2 pounds uncooked shrimp, peeled and deveined
2 lemons, juiced
½ cup butter
1 (8 ounce) package cream cheese
3 ounces blue cheese
1 (8 ounce) package linguini

Preheat oven to 400 degrees. Place shrimp in an 8x10-inch glass or ceramic baking dish and sprinkle with juice. Melt butter, cream cheese, and blue cheese in a bowl in microwave on 50 percent power. Stir to blend. Pour mixture over shrimp. Bake 20 minutes. Meanwhile, cook linguini according to package directions. Drain. Serve shrimp over linguini.

Serves 4 to 6

Juice of 2 limes or juice of 1 lemon and 1 lime may be substituted for juice of 2 lemons.

Karen Cruze

Barbeque Shrimp

3-5 pounds large shrimp, unpeeled
1 (1 ounce) envelope Italian dressing mix
1 (10 ounce) bottle Worcestershire sauce
¾ cup butter
1 teaspoon garlic powder
1 teaspoon lemon pepper
1 teaspoon black pepper
½ teaspoon cayenne pepper

Preheat oven to 300 degrees. Allow ½ pound shrimp per serving. Place shrimp in a 9x13-inch baking dish or roaster pan. Sprinkle dressing mix, Worcestershire sauce, butter, garlic powder, lemon pepper, black pepper, and cayenne pepper over shrimp. Bake uncovered about 40 minutes or until shrimp is pink, stirring often. Do not overcook.

Serves 6 to 10

For an informal supper, use newspaper to make a tablecloth and allow guests to put the shrimp shells on the table as they eat. For a yummy flavor, dip French bread in the sauce. Have a stack of napkins handy!

Glenda Bragg

Shrimp and Grits

1 pound fresh shrimp, peeled and deveined
6 slices bacon
Peanut oil
2 cups sliced fresh mushrooms
1 cup sliced scallions
1 clove garlic, pressed or crushed
4 teaspoons lemon juice
Hot sauce
Salt
Pepper
Cheese Grits (recipe follows)
Parsley for garnish

Wash shrimp, cut in half, and pat dry. Dice and cook bacon until just crisp in a large skillet. Reserve grease. Drain bacon and set aside. Add enough peanut oil to the bacon grease to make a thin layer. When grease is hot, add shrimp. Stir and add mushrooms when shrimp begin to turn pink. Add scallions and garlic. Season to taste with lemon juice, hot sauce, salt, and pepper. Divide cheese grits among 4 warm plates. Spoon shrimp over grits. Sprinkle with bacon and parsley. Serve immediately.

Cheese Grits

4 cups water
1 cup grits
½ teaspoon salt
¼ cup butter
1 cup grated sharp Cheddar cheese
½ cup grated Parmesan cheese
Pinch of white pepper
Pinch of cayenne pepper

Bring water to a boil. Slowly stir in grits. Reduce heat and continue cooking, stirring frequently, for 20 to 30 minutes until grits are thick and tender. Stir in salt, butter, cheeses, white pepper, and cayenne pepper.

Serves 4

This is best cooked, served, and eaten without delay!

Liz Herrin

Cajun Shrimp

- 1 (46 ounce) can tomato juice
- 1 (6 ounce) can tomato paste
- 1 teaspoon salt
- 1 tablespoon hot sauce
- 1 teaspoon Cajun seasoning, or to taste
- ½ teaspoon thyme
- ½ teaspoon garlic powder
- ½ teaspoon onion powder
- 1 pound shrimp, peeled and deveined
- Cooked rice

In a large saucepan or skillet, combine tomato juice, tomato paste, salt, hot sauce, Cajun seasoning, thyme, garlic powder, and onion powder. Cook over medium heat until sauce begins to get thick, about 15 minutes. Add shrimp and cook until shrimp are done, about 3 minutes. Serve over rice.

Serves 5

Pat McCrory

Catfish Parmesan

- 1 cup grated Parmesan cheese
- ½ cup all-purpose flour
- 1 teaspoon paprika
- ½ teaspoon seasoned salt
- ¼ teaspoon black pepper
- 1 egg, beaten
- ½ cup milk
- 6 catfish fillets
- ¼ cup margarine, melted
- Paprika
- Black pepper

Preheat oven to 350 degrees. Combine cheese, flour, paprika, salt, and pepper. Mix well and set aside. Combine egg and milk and stir well. Dip fillets in egg mixture, then dredge in flour mixture. Place fillets in a lightly greased 9x13-inch baking dish and drizzle with margarine. Top with light coating of paprika and pepper. Bake 40 minutes or until fish flakes.

Serves 6

Barbara McWilliams

Shrimp and Oyster Creole

- **2 pounds fresh shrimp**
- **1 tablespoon margarine or butter**
- **4 dozen shucked oysters**
- **½ cup margarine or butter**
- **1 cup chopped celery**
- **2 cups chopped onion**
- **1½ cups diced green bell pepper**
- **2 (8 ounce) packages sliced fresh mushrooms**
- **2 (28 ounce) cans diced tomatoes**
- **1 bay leaf**
- **1 teaspoon tarragon vinegar**
- **1 cup oyster liquid**
- **3 dashes hot pepper sauce**
- **3 cloves garlic, crushed**
- **1 teaspoon sugar**
- **4 teaspoons salt**
- **¼ teaspoon black pepper**
- **Pinch of cayenne pepper**
- **Hot cooked rice**

Cook, shell, and devein shrimp. Set aside. In a large skillet, melt 1 tablespoon margarine. Add oysters and heat about 5 minutes or until edges curl. Drain oysters, reserve liquid, and set aside. In the same skillet, heat ½ cup margarine and sauté celery, onion, bell pepper, and mushrooms until tender. Add tomatoes, bay leaf, vinegar, oyster liquid, pepper sauce, garlic, sugar, salt, black pepper, and cayenne pepper. Simmer 20 minutes. Remove bay leaf. Add cooked shrimp and oysters and heat quickly. Serve immediately with hot cooked rice.

Serves 12

Lola Northington

Grilled Marinated Fish

- **4 tablespoons lemon juice**
- **2 tablespoons soy sauce**
- **½ teaspoon hot pepper sauce**
- **½ teaspoon garlic powder**
- **½ teaspoon pepper**
- **4 tablespoons olive oil**
- **2½ pounds ½-inch thick mahi-mahi, wahoo, amberjack, or grouper fillets**

In blender, combine lemon juice, soy sauce, pepper sauce, garlic powder, and pepper. Blend 15 seconds. Add olive oil and blend another 15 seconds. Place fish in zip-top plastic bag, add marinade, and seal bag. Marinate at least 4 hours. Grill over medium heat 5 minutes per side.

Serves 4

Frank Batty

Salmon with Zucchini, Dill and Cream

- **4 (6 ounce) center-cut salmon fillets with skin (1¼-inches thick), pin bones removed**
- **¼ teaspoon salt**
- **¼ teaspoon pepper**
- **1 teaspoon olive oil**
- **½ cup finely chopped shallots**
- **1 green zucchini, sliced**
- **1 yellow squash, sliced**
- **⅓ cup dry white wine**
- **1 cup heavy cream**
- **½ teaspoon salt**
- **¼ teaspoon black pepper**
- **2 tablespoons chopped fresh dill**
- **1 tablespoon fresh lemon juice**

Preheat broiler. Line rack of broiler pan with aluminum foil and lightly oil. Rinse salmon and pat dry. Place on broiler pan, skin side down. Sprinkle with salt and pepper. Broil 4 to 5 inches from heat until almost cooked through, about 6 minutes. Loosely cover with foil and keep warm. Meanwhile, in a 12-inch heavy skillet, heat oil over moderately high heat and sauté shallots, stirring 1 minute. Add zucchini and squash and sauté 3 to 4 minutes. Add wine, cream, salt, and pepper and boil, stirring occasionally, until liquid is thickened and reduced by half. Stir in dill and lemon juice. Spoon zucchini and squash mixture over salmon to serve.

Serves 4

Sylvia Bruens

Salmon Roasted with Tomatoes and Olives

- 2 pounds ripe tomatoes, cut into thin wedges
- ½ medium onion, sliced
- 2 strips orange zest, cut into thin slivers
- 2 cloves garlic, minced
- 1 tablespoon olive oil
- ⅓ cup kalamata olives, pitted and coarsely chopped
- 1 tablespoon chopped fresh rosemary
- ¼ teaspoon salt
- Pepper
- 1¼ pounds salmon fillet, skin removed, cut into 4 portions

Preheat oven to 400 degrees. Combine tomatoes, onion, orange zest, and garlic in large roasting pan. Drizzle with oil and toss to coat. Roast uncovered, stirring occasionally until tender and beginning to brown on edges, about 45 minutes. Remove pan from oven. Increase oven temperature to 450 degrees. Add olives, rosemary, salt, and pepper to taste. Clear 4 spaces in pan and place 1 portion of salmon in each. Spoon tomato mixture over salmon. Roast until salmon is opaque in the center, 10 to 15 minutes depending on thickness.

Serves 4

Ellen Marks

Baked Salmon

- 1 whole fillet of salmon
- 1 teaspoon seasoned salt
- 1 teaspoon dried dill

Preheat oven to 350 degrees. Line a 7x11-inch baking pan with aluminum foil and lightly grease with olive oil. Place salmon in pan and sprinkle with salt and dill. Thin tail part of fish can be folded under to keep from overcooking. Bake 20 minutes or until fish flakes easily.

Serves 2 to 3

Jo Ann Braam

Salmon Cakes

- 1/3 cup crushed saltine crackers
- 1/3 cup breadcrumbs
- 2 (7½ ounce) cans salmon, drained and flaked
- 2 eggs, beaten
- 1/4 cup finely chopped onion
- 1/4 cup chopped bell pepper
- 1 teaspoon lemon juice
- 1/4 teaspoon black pepper
- 1 teaspoon seafood seasoning
- 2 tablespoons sweet pickle relish (optional)
- 2-3 tablespoons vegetable oil

Combine crushed crackers and breadcrumbs. Reserve a small amount to coat patties. Combine cracker mixture with salmon, eggs, onion, bell pepper, juice, pepper, seasoning, and sweet relish. Shape into 1-inch thick patties. Coat patties with cracker mixture. Place on waxed paper and chill 20 minutes. In a heavy skillet, heat oil over medium heat. Add patties and cook 4 to 5 minutes on each side until brown. Drain on paper towels.

Serves 3 to 4

This is my emergency dinner when I forget to go to the store. I can always pull out 2 cans of salmon and have dinner.

Diana Finley

Marinade for Grilled Salmon, Lamb, Pork Tenderloin

- 1 cup orange juice
- 1/3 cup olive oil
- 4 tablespoons fresh rosemary, chopped
- 1/4 cup soy sauce
- 4 garlic cloves, minced
- 1/4 cup honey
- Kosher salt
- Fresh cracked pepper

Combine all ingredients and pour over meat or fish. Marinate fish for 30 to 60 minutes; lamb or pork for 2 hours. Grill fish or meat to desired doneness.

Makes about 1¾ cups

Camille Vaughan

Cheesy Broiled Tilapia

- 2 pounds tilapia fillets
- 2 tablespoons lemon juice
- ¼ cup butter, melted
- ½ cup grated Parmesan cheese
- 3 tablespoons mayonnaise
- 3 green onions, chopped
- Dash of hot sauce

Set oven to broil. Brush both sides of fillets with lemon juice. Combine butter, cheese, mayonnaise, onion, and hot sauce. Mix well and set aside. Broil tilapia 4 to 6 minutes or until done. Remove from oven and spread with cheese sauce. Return to oven and broil 30 to 40 seconds or until cheese sauce is lightly brown and bubbly.

Serves 4

Frank Batty

Eggplant Parmesan

- 1 medium eggplant
- 8 ounces uncooked pasta
- ½ cup dry breadcrumbs
- ¼ cup grated Parmesan cheese
- ½ teaspoon garlic powder
- ¼ teaspoon salt
- 1-2 tablespoons olive oil
- 1 (24 ounce) jar pasta sauce
- 8 ounces fresh mozzarella cheese

Preheat oven to 425 degrees. Peel and slice eggplant into ¼-inch slices. Cook pasta according to package directions. Drain and keep warm. Combine breadcrumbs, Parmesan cheese, garlic powder, and salt in a shallow bowl. Place olive oil in a separate bowl. Lightly coat each eggplant slice with oil, then coat evenly with breadcrumb mixture. Arrange eggplant slices on a large baking sheet and bake about 12 minutes. Remove from oven. Pour pasta sauce over eggplant and top with mozzarella. Return to oven and bake until cheese melts. Serve over cooked pasta.

Serves 4

For a healthier version, use whole wheat pasta and part-skim mozzarella cheese.

Mary Alice Brinkley

Fettuccine à la Carbonara

- 4 eggs
- ¼ cup whipping cream
- ¼ cup butter or margarine
- ½ pound bacon, cut up
- 1 (12 ounce) package fettuccine
- 1 cup grated Parmesan cheese
- ¼ cup chopped parsley
- Freshly ground pepper

Let eggs, cream, and butter stand at room temperature 2 to 3 hours. Fry bacon until brown. Drain on paper towels. Beat eggs and cream together just till blended. Cook pasta according to package directions. Drain and return to warm cooking pot. Add butter to pasta and toss. Add egg mixture and toss till pasta is well coated. (The hot pasta will cook the eggs.) Add bacon, Parmesan cheese, and parsley. Toss to mix. Season to taste with freshly ground pepper. Serve immediately.

Serves 4 as main dish or 8 as side dish

Carol Hurst

Penne with Sun-Dried Tomatoes and Goat Cheese

- 20 sun-dried tomatoes, oil-packed
- 3 tablespoons olive oil
- 4 cloves garlic, chopped
- ¼ teaspoon salt
- ⅛ teaspoon pepper
- Italian herbs
- 1 (16 ounce) package penne pasta
- 5 ounces fresh goat cheese, crumbled

Drain tomatoes and cut into strips. In a large bowl, combine olive oil, garlic, salt, pepper, and herbs to taste. Add tomato strips and set aside. Cook pasta according to package directions. Drain pasta and add to olive oil mixture. Toss until pasta is well coated. Add goat cheese. Toss well and serve.

Serves 6 to 8

Carol Hurst

Pasta Primavera

- **1 cup sliced zucchini**
- **1½ cups broccoli florets**
- **1½ cups snow peas**
- **1 cup baby green peas**
- **6-8 spears fresh asparagus, sliced**
- **1 (16 ounce) package spaghetti or fettuccine**
- **12 cherry tomatoes, cut in half**
- **2 teaspoons minced fresh garlic**
- **2 cups sliced mushrooms**
- **2 tablespoons olive oil**
- **¼ cup chopped flat leaf parsley**
- **Salt**
- **Freshly ground black pepper**
- **⅓ cup pine nuts**
- **1 tablespoon olive oil**
- **⅓ cup butter**
- **½ cup freshly grated Parmesan cheese**
- **1 cup heavy cream**
- **⅓ cup chopped fresh basil**
- **⅓ cup pasta water**

Blanch zucchini, broccoli, snow peas, green peas, and asparagus in boiling salted water, 1 to 2 minutes each, until crisp and tender. Drain and refresh under cold water. Set aside. In a large pan, cook pasta in boiling salted water until al dente, about 8 to 11 minutes. Reserve ⅓ cup pasta water. Drain pasta. In a skillet, sauté tomatoes, garlic, and mushrooms in 2 tablespoons oil. Add parsley and salt and pepper to taste. Remove from skillet and set aside. Sauté pine nuts in 1 tablespoon oil until brown. In a large pan, melt butter over medium heat and add cheese, cream, and basil, stirring to blend until cheese is melted. Add pasta, zucchini, broccoli, snow peas, green peas, asparagus, tomato mixture, and pine nuts. Toss to coat. Heat mixture until good and hot, being careful not to scorch. Check seasonings to taste. If mixture becomes too thick, add pasta water to thin. Garnish with fresh basil ribbons, cherry tomatoes, and more Parmesan cheese, if desired.

Serves 6 to 8

Camille Vaughan

...HE BREATHED ON THEM, AND SAITH UNTO THEM,
"RECEIVE YE THE HOLY GHOST."

JOHN 20:22

"NEW SONG, NEW HOPE, NEW LIFE," a resurrection cross, consecrated on October 14, 2001, is the worship symbol for the New Song worship service. The artist Dennis Brickell of Cullman, Alabama, had been creating sculpture professionally over fifteen years. The worship symbol was his first commission for a church.

The African mahogany cross is fifty inches wide and nine feet tall, crafted from one board. Mr. Brickell selected the materials of stone, bronze, steel, mahogany and maple. White Italian alabaster doves flying from the cross indicate the purity of Christ; the bronze vines symbolize sin and the world; the steel rods and maple triangles in threes are the trinity and light emitting from the cross; and a bronze ring binds the piece in unity. The title was inspired by the beauty of the New Song Sanctuary.

Vegetables & Sides

And he hath put a new song in my mouth, even praise unto our God: many shall see it, and fear, and trust in the Lord.

Psalms 40:3

When the Rev. Cheryl Blankenship started the "New Song" Worship Service in 1997, little did anyone know that it would become so meaningful and so popular with the First United Methodist congregation.

When construction was begun for the 2000 church renovations and the new building, initial plans were for building the Wesley Worship Center to seat up to 250 worshippers. Since attendance had grown so much, the building committee unanimously voted to expand seating to accommodate 450 worshippers.

The Center is equipped with audio, video, and projection technology for speakers, singers, musicians, and on-screen presentations. To the right is the cross and to the left is the Pentecost banner, dedicated on December 2, 2001. The banner was designed by artist and Church member Maggie Little. Funded by the Memorial Committee, it was constructed by ten dedicated women members who spent twelve weeks and approximately 360 hours in its creation.

Elizabeth's Cranberry Apple Casserole

- **3 cups chopped unpeeled red or green cooking apples**
- **2 cups whole fresh cranberries**
- **1¼ cups sugar**
- **1½ cups oats**
- **½ cup brown sugar**
- **⅓ cup all-purpose flour**
- **½ cup chopped pecans**
- **½ cup butter, melted**

Preheat oven to 350 degrees. In a large bowl, mix apples, cranberries, and sugar. Pour into a greased 2-quart baking dish. In another bowl, mix oats, brown sugar, flour, pecans, and butter. Mix until crumbly. Sprinkle over apples and cranberries. Bake 1 hour.

Serves 6 to 8

Peggy Christian

Scalloped Apples

- **4-6 cups peeled, sliced, and cooked apples or canned apples**
- **1½ cups sugar**
- **1 cup butter**
- **1½ cups self-rising flour**
- **1 pound cubed processed cheese loaf**
- **2 cups crushed round buttery crackers**
- **½ cup butter**

Preheat oven to 350 degrees. In a large mixing bowl, cream sugar and 1 cup butter until fluffy. Add flour and cubed cheese. Mix well. Spread half of apples in bottom of a 9x13-inch baking dish. Crumble dough mixture over apples. Place remaining half of apples over dough. Sprinkle crushed crackers over apples. Melt ½ cup butter and drizzle over crackers. Bake 30 to 40 minutes or until bubbly.

Serves 12

Laura Mae Hereford Wilbourn

Submitted by Laura Jo Hamilton

Nana's Cornbread Dressing

- 3 **tablespoons bacon grease**
- 2 **cups plain cornmeal**
- ½ **cup flour**
- 2½ **teaspoons baking powder**
- 1 **teaspoon salt**
- 1 **tablespoon sugar**
- 2 **jumbo eggs**
- 2 **cups buttermilk**
- 8 **hamburger buns**
- ½ **cup margarine**
- 3 **medium onions, coarsely chopped**
- 2 **ribs celery, coarsely chopped**
- 6 **cups chicken stock or broth**
- **Salt**
- **Pepper**
- 4 **jumbo eggs**

Preheat oven to 400 degrees. In an iron skillet, melt bacon grease in hot oven. In a large bowl, whisk together cornmeal, flour, baking powder, salt, and sugar. Add 2 eggs and buttermilk. Stir. DO NOT BEAT. Pour hot bacon grease into mixture. Stir. Pour mixture into hot skillet and bake approximately 20 minutes. Remove cornbread from oven and let cool completely. Reduce oven temperature to 375 degrees. Process cornbread in batches in a blender or food processor to form crumbs. Place crumbs in a large mixing bowl. Process hamburger buns to form crumbs. Add to cornbread crumbs and set aside. Melt margarine in a skillet. Sauté onions and celery until clear. Add to crumbs. Add chicken stock and stir well. Add salt and pepper to taste. Add 4 eggs and stir well. The mixture should be the consistency of cornmeal batter. Pour into a lightly greased 9x13-inch baking dish and bake for 30 minutes.

Serves 12

Hailey Williams

Garlic-Roasted Asparagus

- 1½ **pounds fresh asparagus**
- 2-3 **cloves garlic, thinly sliced**
- 2-3 **tablespoons olive oil**
- ¼ **teaspoon salt**
- ¼ **teaspoon ground black pepper**

Preheat oven to 450 degrees. Snap off and discard woody bases from asparagus. Place asparagus and garlic in a 15x10x1-inch baking pan. Drizzle with oil and sprinkle with salt and pepper. Toss to coat. Roast 10 to 15 minutes or until asparagus is crisp-tender, stirring once halfway through roasting. Serve immediately.

Serves 6

Connie Cook

Pesto Pine-Nut Asparagus

2½ pounds fresh asparagus
½ cup pine nuts
3 tablespoons unsalted butter
¾ cup pesto sauce, pre-packaged in jar
½ cup fresh shredded Parmesan cheese

Wash asparagus, breaking stems to eliminate woody part. Steam or boil asparagus until nearly done. Sauté pine nuts in butter until lightly browned. Watch carefully to avoid over-browning. Add pesto sauce, just to warm. Turn on oven broiler to preheat. Drain asparagus and lay into a baking dish. Spread pine nut-pesto mixture over asparagus. Top with shredded cheese. Place under broiler until cheese melts.

Serves 8 to 12

Variation: To cook on the grill, combine asparagus, pine nuts, 1 tablespoon butter, and pesto sauce in a foil packet. Place on hot grill 8 to 10 minutes. Turn onto warmed platter or casserole. Top with Parmesan cheese, if desired.

Nancy Barnett Darnall

Asparagus-Mushroom Casserole

¼ cup margarine
1 (2¼ ounce) package sliced almonds
1 cup cooked rice
1 (10¾ ounce) can cream of mushroom soup
½ cup milk
1 (15 ounce) can asparagus spears, drained
½ cup grated sharp Cheddar cheese
1 cup crisp rice cereal

Preheat oven to 300 degrees. Melt margarine in a 2-quart casserole dish. Add almonds and toast lightly in oven. Add rice and mix well. Mix soup with milk and pour over rice. Do not stir. Layer asparagus on top and gently press down into soup. Top with cheese and rice cereal. Bake 20 minutes or until bubbly.

Serves 6

Gloria Pennington

Submitted by Mary Richardson

Cowboy Beans

- **4 slices bacon, chopped**
- **6 green onions, chopped**
- **1 green bell pepper, chopped**
- **1 small jalapeño pepper, seeded and chopped (optional)**
- **2 (15½ ounce) cans pork and beans**
- **1 (16 ounce) can kidney beans, drained**
- **1 (15½ ounce) can lima beans, drained**
- **1 (15 ounce) can pinto beans, drained (optional)**
- **½ cup brown sugar**
- **1 cup ketchup**
- **½ teaspoon salt**
- **1 teaspoon pepper**

Preheat oven to 325 degrees. In a frying pan, sauté bacon, onion, and peppers for 5 minutes or until soft. In a 10x14-inch baking dish, combine bacon mixture, pork and beans, kidney beans, lima beans, pinto beans, sugar, ketchup, salt, and pepper. Mix well. Bake 1 to 1½ hours.

Serves 12 to 16

Judy McLaurine

Basil Green Beans

- **3 (14½ ounce) cans whole green beans**
- **2 cloves garlic**
- **½ small onion**
- **1½ teaspoons salt**
- **1 teaspoon freshly ground pepper**
- **¼ cup red wine vinegar**
- **2 tablespoons Dijon mustard**
- **1 tablespoon sugar**
- **¾ cup canola oil**
- **15-20 fresh basil leaves or 2 teaspoons dried basil**

Rinse and drain beans. In a food processor, mince garlic and onion. Add salt, pepper, vinegar, mustard, and sugar. Add oil slowly through tube of food processor. If using fresh basil, slice into fine shreds and combine with the green beans. If using dried basil, add to the marinade. Pour marinade over green beans and chill several hours or overnight.

Serves 6 to 8

Doni Harrison

Beans and Greens Under Cornbread

FILLING

- 1 large onion, cut into thin wedges
- 1 tablespoon vegetable oil
- 2 (15 ounce) cans great Northern beans, drained and rinsed
- 1 (10 ounce) package frozen chopped turnip greens or collards, thawed and drained
- 1 (14½ ounce) can diced tomatoes, undrained
- ½ cup cooked and chopped country or sugar-cured ham

CRUST

- 1 egg, beaten
- ¼ cup vegetable oil
- ½ cup milk
- 1 cup self-rising cornmeal mix

Preheat oven to 425 degrees. In a 12-inch cast iron skillet, cook onion in oil about 5 minutes or until tender. Stir in beans, greens, tomatoes, and ham. Cook 2 to 3 minutes. In a medium bowl, combine crust ingredients stirring until smooth. Spoon batter around edges of filling in skillet. Bake 25 to 30 minutes or until golden.

Serves 6 to 8

Virginia Laux

Green Bean Relish

- 2 (14½ ounce) cans French cut green beans, drained
- 3 dill pickles, sliced thinly
- 1 (4 ounce) jar pimientos, thinly sliced
- 1 medium onion, thinly sliced
- 1 cup brown sugar
- 1 cup vinegar

Mix together green beans, pickles, pimientos, and onion. Combine vinegar and brown sugar in a small saucepan. Boil for l minute. Cool. Pour over green bean mixture and refrigerate. Let stand for several hours.

Makes 4 cups

Lola Northington

Green Bean and Corn Casserole

CASSEROLE

2 (14½ ounce) cans French cut green beans
1 (11 ounce) can shoepeg corn
½ cup chopped celery (optional)
¾ cup chopped onion
1 (8 ounce) carton sour cream
¾ cup grated Cheddar cheese
1 (8 ounce) can sliced water chestnuts
Salt
Pepper

TOPPING

2 cups crushed round buttery crackers
¼ cup butter, melted

Preheat oven to 350 degrees. Mix casserole ingredients well and pour into a greased 2-quart casserole dish. Mix topping ingredients together and add to top of casserole. Bake approximately 40 to 45 minutes.

Serves 8 to 10

May be made the day before without the topping and refrigerated. Let warm to room temperature and add topping just before baking.

Elizabeth Geron

Submitted by Paula Sanders

Bundle of Beans

3 (14½ ounce) cans cut green beans
1 onion, sliced
1 cup brown sugar
½ cup vinegar
½ teaspoon dry mustard
1 teaspoon seasoned salt
4 slices bacon

Preheat oven to 350 degrees. Drain beans, rinse in cold water, and drain well. Put beans in a 9x13-inch casserole. Place onion on top of beans. Mix brown sugar, vinegar, dry mustard, and salt. Pour over beans. Cut bacon slices in half and place on beans. Bake uncovered 30 minutes. Cover and bake an additional 30 minutes.

Serves 8

Virginia Laux

Laura's Garlic "Spider" Beans

- 2 (14½ ounce) cans whole green beans
- 1 tablespoon brown sugar
- 1 pound bacon slices, cut in half
- 6 cloves garlic, minced

Preheat oven to 350 degrees. Drain beans, reserving liquid from 1 can. Dissolve brown sugar in reserved liquid. Set aside. Coat a 9x13-inch baking dish with cooking spray. Wrap small bundles of beans with bacon slices and place in prepared dish. Sprinkle with minced garlic. Pour liquid mixture over beans. Bake 30 minutes or until bacon is done.

Serves 8

Ashley Sparks

These got their name when my mom accidentally overcooked them and the beans curled up like spider legs.

Curried Cauliflower

- 1 large head cauliflower
- 1 (10¾ ounce) can cream of chicken soup
- 1 cup shredded Cheddar cheese
- ⅓ cup mayonnaise
- ½ teaspoon curry powder
- ¼ cup dried breadcrumbs
- 2 tablespoons butter, melted

Preheat oven to 350 degrees. Cut or break cauliflower into small florets. Microwave or steam cauliflower 5 minutes. Stir soup, cheese, mayonnaise, and curry in a lightly greased 2-quart casserole dish. Add cauliflower and mix well. Toss breadcrumbs in butter and sprinkle on top of cauliflower mixture. Bake uncovered 40 minutes.

Serves 8 to 10

Amount of curry can vary from ¼ to 1 teaspoon. One teaspoon is VERY spicy. Any mixture of vegetables may be used in this recipe to total 4 to 5 cups. Broccoli, carrots, and cauliflower make a colorful dish. To freeze, prepare all but crumbs. When ready to cook, thaw in refrigerator all day, add crumbs, and bake as directed.

Nancy Barnett Darnall

Sweet and Sour Green Beans

- **2 (14½ ounce) cans French cut green beans**
- **3 onions, thinly sliced**
- **½ cup sugar**
- **½ cup vinegar**
- **½ cup vegetable oil**
- **8 slices bacon, or 1 (3 ounce) bottle bacon bits**

Drain beans. Layer beans and onions alternately in a casserole dish. Whisk together sugar, vinegar, and oil. Pour over beans and onions. Cover and refrigerate overnight. When ready to cook, preheat oven to 325 degrees. Fry bacon until crisp. Drain, crumble, and set aside. Pour liquid from beans and onions. Cover casserole and bake 1 hour or until onions are tender. Sprinkle bacon over beans before serving.

Serves 6

Betty Burkett

Carrot Soufflé

- **3 pounds carrots, sliced**
- **1½ cups butter or margarine**
- **6 large eggs**
- **½ cup all-purpose flour**
- **1 tablespoon baking powder**
- **3 cups sugar**
- **¼ teaspoon ground cinnamon**

The day before serving, cook carrots in boiling water to cover 15 minutes or until tender. Drain well and chill overnight. The next day when ready to bake, preheat oven to 350 degrees. Process carrots and remaining ingredients in a food processor until smooth, stopping once to scrape down sides. Spoon into 2 lightly greased 1½-quart soufflé or baking dishes. Bake 1 hour or until set and lightly browned. Serve immediately.

Serves 12

Syble Park

When we lived in Izhevsk, Russia, we could not get sweet potatoes so we used carrots instead. Not only did we enjoy it, but shared it with our Russian friends and taught them how to prepare it.

Corn Casserole

- 2 (10 ounce) packages frozen corn, thawed and drained
- 1 (16 ounce) carton sour cream
- 1 tablespoon finely chopped onion
- ½ teaspoon salt
- 1 cup butter, melted
- 2 stacks crushed round buttery crackers

Preheat oven to 350 degrees. Mix corn with sour cream, onion, and salt. Mix butter and cracker crumbs. Add half the butter and cracker crumb mixture to corn and blend well. Set aside remaining crumb mixture to use later as a topping. Spoon corn and crumb mixture into a buttered 9x13-inch casserole dish. Cover and bake about 30 minutes. Remove cover and sprinkle remaining crumb mixture on top. Return to oven uncovered until lightly browned.

Serves 10

Jean Hinson

Variation: Top casserole with 2 to 4 slices of cooked and crumbled bacon instead of cracker crumbs before baking.

Carol Hurst

Sue's Jalapeño Corn Casserole

- 12 ounces cream cheese
- ½ cup milk
- 4 tablespoons butter
- ¼ teaspoon black pepper
- 1 teaspoon garlic salt or powder
- 3-4 fresh jalapeños, seeded and chopped
- 4 (15¼ ounce) cans whole kernel corn, drained

Preheat oven to 350 degrees. In a saucepan over low heat, cook cream cheese, milk, butter, pepper, and garlic salt or powder, stirring until mixture is melted and forms a sauce. Remove from heat and add jalapeños and corn. Mix well. Pour into a greased 9x13-inch baking dish. Bake 30 minutes.

Serves 8 to 10

Wear gloves when seeding and chopping fresh jalapeños. You may substitute 4 tablespoons canned or bottled seeded, chopped jalapeños.

Sue Day

Scalloped Eggplant

- 1 medium eggplant
- Salt
- Pepper
- 1 egg, beaten
- 2 tablespoons butter, melted
- 1 small onion, finely chopped
- 1 cup dry breadcrumbs
- ½ cup buttered breadcrumbs or cracker crumbs

Preheat oven to 375 degrees. Pare eggplant and cut in 1-inch cubes. Cook in water until tender. Drain thoroughly. Add salt and pepper to taste. Add egg, butter, onion, and breadcrumbs. Mix thoroughly and place in a greased 1-quart baking dish. Cover with buttered crumbs and bake about 30 minutes.

Serves 6

Mabry B. Miller

Baked Eggplant Slices

- 1 eggplant
- 1 tablespoon dried onion
- ½ teaspoon salt
- ⅓ cup dry breadcrumbs
- ⅓ cup Parmesan cheese
- ½ teaspoon dried Italian seasoning
- ½ cup mayonnaise

Preheat oven to 400 degrees. Wash and peel eggplant. Slice ¼-inch thick. Mix dried onion, salt, breadcrumbs, cheese, and seasoning well. Place on wax paper. Brush eggplant slices on each side with mayonnaise and dip in dry ingredients. Place on a greased cookie sheet. Bake 15 minutes, turning over once.

Serves 4 to 6

Imogene Davis

Easy Baked Mac and Cheese

1½ cups macaroni
Salt
1 cup sour cream
8 ounces shredded Cheddar cheese
⅔ cup milk

Preheat oven to 350 degrees. Cook macaroni in boiling salted water until barely tender. Drain well. Place half of macaroni in a greased 1½-quart casserole. Spread with half of sour cream and sprinkle with half of cheese. Repeat layers, ending with cheese. Pour milk over cheese. Bake 25 to 30 minutes.

Serves 6

Glenda Goldfinger

Mackie's Macaroni

1 (16 ounce) box elbow macaroni
1 (10¾ ounce) can cream of mushroom soup
1 cup mayonnaise
1 (2 ounce) jar chopped pimiento, drained
¼ cup chopped onion
8 ounces grated sharp Cheddar cheese
1 (4 ounce) can sliced mushrooms, drained
⅛ teaspoon pepper
Round buttery crackers
3 tablespoons butter

Preheat oven to 300 degrees. Cook macaroni in salted water according to package directions. Drain. In a large bowl, mix macaroni, mushroom soup, mayonnaise, pimiento, onion, cheese, mushrooms, and pepper. Pour into a greased 9x13-inch baking dish. Crumble crackers on top and dot with butter. Bake 25 minutes.

Serves 12

Linda Finnell

Glorified Green Peas

½ green bell pepper, chopped
2 tablespoons butter
1 (10¾ ounce) can cream of mushroom soup
½ cup grated Cheddar cheese
1 (2 ounce) jar chopped pimiento
1 (15 ounce) can green peas, drained

Preheat oven to 350 degrees. Melt butter in a saucepan. Add green pepper and cook until tender. Add soup, cheese, and pimiento to mixture. Cook over moderate heat until a smooth sauce has formed. Add drained peas and continue cooking slowly until hot. Pour into a greased 8x8-inch baking dish. Bake 10 to 15 minutes.

Serves 8

Betty Smith

Pineapple Casserole

2 (20 ounce) cans chunk pineapple with heavy syrup
¾ cup sugar
6 tablespoons all-purpose flour
½ cup butter, melted
2 cups grated sharp Cheddar cheese
1 cup round buttery or whole wheat cracker crumbs

Preheat oven to 350 degrees. Drain pineapple reserving 6 tablespoons of juice. Combine sugar and flour and stir in pineapple juice. Add butter, cheese, and pineapple. Pour into a lightly greased 2-quart casserole dish. Bake uncovered 20 minutes. Add cracker crumbs on top and bake 5 to 10 minutes or until lightly browned.

Serves 8

Felicia Downs

Orzo with Roasted Peppers

- 1 cup grape tomatoes
- 1 small eggplant, cut in ¾-inch cubes
- 1 red bell pepper, cut in 1-inch chunks
- 1 yellow bell pepper, cut in 1-inch chunks
- 2 cloves garlic, minced
- ⅓ cup extra virgin olive oil
- 1½ teaspoons kosher salt
- ½ teaspoon pepper
- 8 ounces orzo
- ⅓ cup fresh lemon juice
- ¼ teaspoon grated lemon zest
- ⅓ cup extra virgin olive oil
- 1 teaspoon kosher salt
- ½ teaspoon cracked pepper
- ¼ cup toasted pine nuts
- 12 ounces crumbled feta cheese
- 8-10 basil leaves, chiffonade cut

Preheat oven to 425 degrees. Mix tomatoes, eggplant, peppers, garlic, olive oil, 1½ teaspoons salt, and ½ teaspoon pepper in a large bowl. Spread on a foil-lined cookie sheet. Roast 30 to 40 minutes. While vegetables roast, cook orzo in salted water in a large pot 7 to 9 minutes or until al dente. Combine lemon juice, lemon zest, olive oil, 1 teaspoon salt, and cracked pepper for dressing. Toss orzo with roasted vegetables. Pour dressing over this mixture. Before serving, add pine nuts, feta cheese, and basil. Toss again. Correct seasoning and serve.

Serves 6 to 8

To make a chiffonade cut for the basil, stack the leaves, roll them up, and slice in narrow strips.

Fleming Sharp

Vidalia Onion Bake

- 4 Vidalia onions, quartered
- ¼ cup butter, cut into 5 pieces
- ¼ cup brown sugar
- ½ cup Parmesan cheese

Preheat oven to 350 degrees. Grease a 9x13-inch casserole dish. Break apart quartered onions into single pieces and place in casserole dish. Place butter on top of onions. Cover with aluminum foil and bake 45 minutes. Remove casserole from oven and uncover. Sprinkle brown sugar and Parmesan cheese evenly over onions. Cover and bake an additional 45 minutes.

Serves 4 to 6

Natasha McCrary

Louisiana Smashed Potatoes

- **5 pounds small red potatoes, unpeeled**
- **2 tablespoons salt**
- **4-5 tablespoons liquid crab boil**
- **½ cup margarine, cut into pieces**
- **1 (16 ounce) carton sour cream**
- **1 (3 ounce) bottle real bacon bits**
- **2 cups shredded Cheddar cheese**
- **1 bunch green onions, chopped**
- **Salt**
- **Milk**

Wash potatoes. Cut in half if large. Place potatoes in a large pot and cover with water. Add salt and crab boil. Boil on medium high heat until potatoes are very tender. Drain and return to pot. Smash with a potato masher or large fork. Add margarine, sour cream, bacon bits, cheese, and green onion. Mix well. Salt to taste. Add milk until consistency is perfect. Serve in casserole dish.

Serves 12 to 15

Judy Bueche

Easy Potato Onion Bake

- **6 medium potatoes, unpeeled**
- **6 medium onions**
- **½ cup butter or margarine, melted**
- **1 clove garlic, minced**
- **½ teaspoon salt**
- **¼ teaspoon pepper**
- **¼ teaspoon celery seeds**
- **¼ teaspoon paprika**

Preheat oven to 400 degrees. Cut potatoes and onions into ¼-inch slices. Alternate potato and onion slices, slightly overlapping in a single layer in a 9x13-inch baking dish. Drizzle with melted butter or margarine. Sprinkle with garlic, salt, pepper and celery seeds. Cover and bake 40 minutes. Remove from oven, uncover, and sprinkle with paprika. Bake uncovered an additional 20 minutes.

Serves 8

Alice Ozier

Marinated Potatoes

14-15 red potatoes
1 purple onion, cut in rings
1 green bell pepper, cut in rings
1 yellow bell pepper, cut in rings
1 cup olive oil
½ cup tarragon vinegar
3 cloves garlic, minced
1 teaspoon salt
½ teaspoon dry mustard
1 tablespoon sugar
1 tablespoon Worcestershire sauce

Boil whole potatoes in water to cover until tender. Drain and cool. Peel potatoes and cut in slices. Layer potatoes, onion, and peppers in a bowl. Whisk together olive oil, vinegar, garlic, salt, dry mustard, sugar, and Worcestershire. Pour over potatoes, onion, and peppers. Cover and allow to stand all day or overnight. DO NOT refrigerate. Potatoes must marinate at least 4 hours. Stir frequently.

Serves 10 to 12

This is great for holidays when there is not a lot of refrigerator space. Also good for picnics.

Robbie Burlison

Corn and Rice Casserole

1 (5 ounce) bag saffron yellow rice
2 (11 ounce) cans corn with peppers
1 (2 ounce) jar pimiento, drained
1 (10¾ ounce) can cream of chicken soup
1 cup grated Cheddar cheese

Preheat oven to 350 degrees. Cook rice according to directions on bag. Combine rice, corn, pimiento, soup, and cheese. Pour into a greased 2-quart baking dish. Bake 30 minutes.

Serves 8 to 10

Joan Jackson

Variation: Add ¼ cup butter to cooked rice. Use 1 can corn with peppers, 2 cups grated cheese, and salt and pepper to taste.

Laura R. Edwards

Potato Pie

1 (16 ounce) carton small curd cottage cheese
2 cups boiled, mashed potatoes, about 3 to 4 potatoes
½ cup sour cream
2 eggs
¼ teaspoon salt
⅛ teaspoon cayenne pepper
2-3 shallots, finely minced and lightly sautéed
¼ cup sliced green onion tops
1 10-inch unbaked pastry shell
3 tablespoons grated Parmesan cheese

Preheat oven to 425 degrees. Pulse cottage cheese in food processor 2 to 3 times to make it smooth. Beat mashed potatoes into cottage cheese. Beat in sour cream, eggs, salt, and cayenne pepper. Stir in shallots and green onion tops. Spoon into pastry shell. Sprinkle with Parmesan cheese. Bake for about 50 minutes until golden.

Serves 8

Dottye Montgomery

This is a favorite in the French provinces where it is usually served hot the first day and cold the next. It is a good side dish to steak and prime rib.

Chile Cheesy Rice

1½ cups uncooked instant rice
1 (16 ounce) carton sour cream
1 (10¾ ounce) can cream of celery soup
2 (4 ounce) cans chopped green chiles, undrained
Salt
1 cup shredded sharp Cheddar cheese
1 cup shredded American cheese

Preheat oven to 350 degrees. Cook rice according to package directions. Combine rice, sour cream, soup, chiles, and salt to taste. Stir to blend. Butter a 9x13-inch casserole and pour in half the rice mixture. Combine cheeses and sprinkle half over rice. Repeat layers. Cover and bake 50 minutes.

Serves 8

Virginia Laux

Golden Potato Casserole

6 large white potatoes, about 4 pounds
¼ cup margarine, melted
1 (16 ounce) carton sour cream
1½ cups shredded mild Cheddar cheese
1 ($10\frac{3}{4}$ ounce) can cream of chicken soup
6-8 green onions, chopped
Crushed corn flakes
2 tablespoons butter

Preheat oven to 350 degrees. Cook potatoes in boiling water to cover until tender. Cool, peel, and slice potatoes. Blend together butter, sour cream, cheese, soup, and onion. Carefully fold potatoes into sour cream mixture. Pour into a greased 9x13-inch baking dish. Sprinkle crushed corn flakes over potatoes and dot with butter. Bake 40 to 45 minutes.

Serves 8 to 10

May be prepared the night before it is to be baked. As an option, you may layer potatoes and sour cream mixture alternately in the baking dish.

Sandy Housley

Variation: Coarsely grate potatoes instead of slicing. Omit cream of chicken soup and corn flakes. Use salt and pepper to taste. Bake at 350 degrees for 25 minutes.

Cindy McCullough

Blue Cheese Crusted Onions

3-4 medium sweet onions, thinly sliced
6 ounces blue cheese, crumbled
6 tablespoons butter, softened
2 teaspoons Worcestershire sauce
2 teaspoons fresh dill
1 teaspoon black pepper

Preheat oven to 425 degrees. Spread onions in a 9x13-inch greased baking dish. Mix cheese, butter, Worcestershire, dill, and pepper. Spread over onions. Bake 20 minutes, then broil until brown.

Serves 8

Judy McLaurine

Company Rice

- 1 cup uncooked rice
- ½ cup butter or margarine
- 1 cup chopped onion
- ½ cup chopped celery
- ½ cup raisins
- ½ cup chopped peanuts
- 2 (10¾ ounce) cans beef consommé
- 1 (4½ ounce) jar sliced mushrooms

Preheat oven to 350 degrees. Sauté rice and onion in butter in a heavy pan on medium heat 10 minutes or until lightly browned, stirring frequently. Add celery, raisins, peanuts, consommé, and mushrooms. Stir and pour into a greased 8x11-inch baking dish. Bake uncovered 50 to 60 minutes.

Serves 6 to 8

One and one-half times the recipe made in a 9x13-inch baking dish serves 12. Bake 50 to 60 minutes.

Virginia Walker Jennings

Holiday Rice

- 1 cup uncooked rice
- 2 cups chicken broth
- ½ cup butter
- 4 cloves garlic, chopped
- 1 cup broken nested vermicelli
- ½ green bell pepper, cut in large pieces
- ½ red bell pepper, cut in large pieces
- 1 small onion, chopped
- 1 (8 ounce) can sliced mushrooms
- 1 (8 ounce) can ripe olives, halved
- 1 (8 ounce) can sliced water chestnuts
- Salt
- Pepper

Preheat oven to 350 degrees. Wash rice until water runs clear. Placed washed rice in a casserole dish and cover with chicken broth. Melt butter in a skillet and cook garlic until golden brown. Remove garlic and discard. Add vermicelli to butter and cook until dark brown. Add to rice mixture. Stir in bell pepper, onion, mushrooms, olives, and water chestnuts. Add salt and pepper to taste. Mix well. Cover and bake approximately 1 hour or until all liquid is absorbed.

Serves 8

Glenda Goldfinger

Dirty Rice with Hoppin' John

This is a very easy dish to prepare. It has three parts: marinated onions, dirty rice, and black-eyed peas. The marinated onions must be made in advance and chilled.

- **1 large onion, diced**
- **⅓ cup white vinegar**
- **1 tablespoon sugar**
- **⅓ teaspoon ground black pepper**
- **1 (16 ounce) package frozen black-eyed peas**
- **4 cups chicken broth**
- **2 cups water**
- **½ teaspoon seasoned pepper**
- **½ teaspoon salt**
- **1 pound hot or mild ground pork sausage**
- **2 (8 ounce) packages dirty rice mix**
- **5 cups water**
- **1 small jar prepared pepper relish**

Dice onion and cover it with vinegar in a jar with a lid. Add sugar and black pepper. Shake to dissolve sugar and put in refrigerator for at least 4 hours to marinate. Put black-eyed peas in a large saucepan. Cover with chicken broth and enough water to generously cover peas. Add seasoned pepper and salt. Bring to a boil. Turn to medium low and partially cover, simmering 30 to 40 minutes or until peas are tender. Drain peas and set aside. Brown sausage in a Dutch oven. Drain excess fat. Add dirty rice mix and 5 cups of water. Bring to a boil. Cover and simmer on low heat 25 minutes or until liquid is absorbed. Add black-eyed peas to rice and sausage mixture. Taste before adjusting salt, since the amount of salt in the broth, rice mixes, and sausage can vary. Serve in soup bowls and top with a generous portion of marinated onions and 1 to 2 teaspoons of pepper relish.

Serves 6 to 8

Serve with cornbread and pass the hot sauce. Great for New Year's Day, game day, or cold weather meal.

Amanda Vaughan

Sweet Potato Dream

- **3 cups mashed cooked sweet potatoes**
- **¼ cup margarine, melted or softened**
- **2 eggs**
- **½ cup sugar**
- **½ cup milk**
- **½ teaspoon salt**
- **½ teaspoon vanilla extract**

TOPPING

- **½ cup butter**
- **1 cup brown sugar**
- **⅓ cup all-purpose flour**
- **1 cup pecan pieces**

Preheat oven to 350 degrees. Mix sweet potatoes, margarine, eggs, sugar, milk, salt, and vanilla. Pour into a greased 9x9-inch baking dish. For topping, melt butter in a small saucepan. Combine brown sugar, flour, and pecans. Add to butter in saucepan and cook 3 minutes. Pour over potato mixture. Bake 35 minutes.

Serves 8 to 10

Eulie Ballard

Submitted by Linda Steed

Black Jack Sweet Potatoes

- **3 (29 ounce) cans sweet potatoes**
- **1 cup sugar**
- **⅓ cup good whiskey**
- **½ cup butter, melted**
- **½ teaspoon vanilla extract**
- **2 cups miniature marshmallows**

Preheat oven to 350 degrees. Cook sweet potatoes in a large saucepan until thoroughly heated. Drain off some of the liquid and mash potatoes. Add sugar, whiskey, butter, and vanilla. Mix well. Pour into a lightly greased 9x13-inch baking dish. Sprinkle marshmallows on top. Bake uncovered 30 minutes or until marshmallows are golden.

Serves 15

Sibyl Wilkinson

Florence Sweet Potato Pudding

- **¾ cup sugar**
- **2 eggs, well beaten**
- **4 tablespoons butter, melted**
- **1½ cups milk**
- **½ teaspoon nutmeg**
- **2 cups grated sweet potatoes**

Preheat oven to 350 degrees. Mix sugar, eggs, butter, milk, and nutmeg. Add potatoes and stir well. Bake in a small, shallow, buttered baking dish until brown, about 30 minutes. Serve immediately.

Serves 8

This is wonderful, but has a tendency to water if not served hot from the oven.

Mary Evelyn French

Sweet Potato Casserole

- **4 cups cooked sweet potatoes (about 4 medium potatoes)**
- **1 cup sugar**
- **½ cup brown sugar**
- **3 eggs**
- **½ cup margarine, softened**

TOPPING

- **½ cup margarine, melted**
- **3 cups crushed corn flakes**
- **1 cup chopped pecans**

Preheat oven to 350 degrees. Mash cooked potatoes and add sugars, eggs, and margarine. Mix well. Pour into a lightly greased 9x13-inch baking dish. Combine melted margarine, corn flakes, and pecans for topping. Spoon over potato mixture and bake 20 to 30 minutes or until topping is golden brown.

Serves 8 to 10

Louise Fain

Submitted by Laura Zeek

Squash and Green Chile Casserole

4-5 pounds fresh yellow squash
1 medium onion
1 cup crushed saltine crackers
2 eggs, beaten
Salt
Pepper
2 (4½ ounce) cans chopped green chiles
1 cup shredded Cheddar cheese
1 cup shredded mozzarella cheese

Preheat oven to 350 degrees. Slice squash and onion. Combine and cook in a small amount of salted water. Drain well. Mash together slightly. Add eggs, cracker crumbs, and salt and pepper to taste. In a greased 9x13-inch casserole, layer half of squash, half of green chiles, and half of cheeses. Repeat layers. Bake covered 25 to 30 minutes or until bubbly. Uncover and cook until brown, about 10 minutes.

Serves 8

Glenda Bragg

Squash and Sausage Casserole

3 pounds squash, thinly sliced
½ pound ground hot pork sausage
1 large onion, chopped
½ cup butter, melted
3 eggs, slightly beaten
¼ cup sugar
½ cup milk
½ cup mayonnaise
1 cup grated Cheddar cheese
½ teaspoon salt
2 hamburger buns, crumbled

Preheat oven to 350 degrees. Cook squash in water to cover until tender. Drain and set aside. Cook sausage and onion together until sausage is browned. Drain. Add sausage mixture to squash. Add butter, eggs, sugar, milk, mayonnaise, cheese, salt, and hamburger buns. Mix well. Pour into a greased 3-quart casserole dish and bake 30 minutes or until well done.

Serves 10 to 12

This is a hit with people who don't even like squash! Mixture may be divided into 5 small casseroles for freezing. The recipe came from Camp Jackson (Boy Scout Camp).

Mackie Bethay

Fiesta Zucchini

1 pound zucchini (about 3)
2 tablespoons olive oil
3 cloves garlic, minced
¼ teaspoon dried oregano
½ cup purchased medium salsa
½ cup shredded Monterey Jack cheese

Quarter zucchini lengthwise, cut crosswise into ½-inch wide pieces. Heat olive oil in a heavy skillet over medium-low heat. Add zucchini, garlic, and oregano. Sauté until garlic is just golden, about 2 minutes. Add salsa and simmer until zucchini is tender, about 6 minutes. Reduce heat to low. Sprinkle cheese over zucchini. Cover and cook until cheese melts, about 2 minutes.

Serves 4

Frank Batty

Squash Casserole

6-8 yellow squash, cut into pieces
1 medium onion, chopped
2 eggs, slightly beaten
½ cup milk
¼ cup margarine
1 cup grated Cheddar cheese
1 sleeve crushed saltine crackers

Preheat oven to 350 degrees. Cook squash and onion in water until tender. Drain well. Combine with eggs and milk. Melt margarine and combine with cheese and crushed crackers. Mix well. Add half of cracker mixture to squash mixture. Pour into a greased 2-quart baking dish. Top with remaining cracker mixture. Bake 30 minutes.

Serves 6 to 8

Joan Rice

Variation: Add 1 teaspoon sugar and ½ teaspoon salt to water while cooking squash and onion. Substitute round buttery crackers or boxed stuffing mix for saltines.

Jo Johnson

Fire and Ice

(Marinated Tomatoes)

6 tomatoes, peeled and quartered
1 large Vidalia onion, sliced, separated into rings
1 green bell pepper, cut in strips

MARINADE

3/4 cup vinegar
1/4 cup cold water
1 1/2 teaspoons celery salt
1 1/2 teaspoons mustard seed
1 1/2 teaspoons salt
4 1/2 teaspoons sugar
1/8 teaspoon cayenne pepper
1/8 teaspoon pepper

Layer tomatoes, onion rings, and pepper strips in a 9x13-inch glass dish. Combine all marinade ingredients in a small saucepan, heat to boiling, and boil for 1 minute. Pour over tomato mixture immediately and refrigerate. Serve chilled.

Serves 6 to 8

This will keep up to 1 week in refrigerator.

Linda Steed

Green Tomato Bake

5 large green tomatoes, unpeeled and sliced thin (1/4 inch)
Salt
1/2 cup butter, cut into small pieces
2 cups grated sharp Cheddar cheese
Round buttery crackers, crumbled
Paprika

Preheat oven to 350 degrees. Coat a 9x13-inch casserole dish with vegetable spray. Layer half of tomatoes in casserole. Salt tomatoes to taste. Place half of butter on tomatoes. Sprinkle with half of cheese and half of crackers. Repeat layers. Sprinkle with paprika. Cover casserole with foil and bake 45 minutes. Uncover and bake an additional 10 minutes.

Serves 8 to 10

These ingredients are easily adjusted to suit number to be served.

Virginia Laux

Tomato Delight

4 ripe tomatoes
Salt
1 red bell pepper, diced
1 small onion, diced
2 tablespoons butter, melted
½ cup cooked rice
1 egg, well beaten
⅛ teaspoon oregano
⅛ teaspoon ground basil
¼ teaspoon salt
½ cup shredded Cheddar cheese
2 slices bacon, cooked and crumbled

Preheat oven to 350 degrees. Cut tops off tomatoes and scoop out pulp. Chop pulp and set aside. Sprinkle inside of tomato shell lightly with salt, invert to drain. Sauté pepper and onion in butter. Add tomato pulp, rice, egg, oregano, basil, and salt. Mix well. Stir in cheese and bacon, reserving a small amount of each. Fill tomatoes with rice mixture. Sprinkle top with reserved cheese and bacon. Place tomatoes in a greased shallow baking dish. Add a small amount of water and bake 25 to 30 minutes.

Serves 4

Frank Batty

Tomato Basil Pie

1 deep-dish pie crust
½ cup shredded mozzarella cheese
4 tomatoes, sliced
1 cup chopped fresh basil
4 cloves garlic, minced
1 cup shredded mozzarella cheese
½-1 cup mayonnaise
¼ cup shredded Parmesan cheese
⅛ teaspoon white pepper

Preheat oven to 400 degrees. Bake pie crust for 9 minutes. Remove from oven and reduce heat to 350 degrees. Sprinkle hot crust with ½ cup mozzarella cheese and let cool. Layer tomatoes in cooled crust. Combine basil and garlic in a small bowl and layer over tomatoes. Combine 1 cup mozzarella, mayonnaise, Parmesan, and pepper in a separate bowl. Mixture will be sticky. Use enough mayonnaise to make spreadable. Spread over basil and garlic layer, spreading with fingers if necessary. Bake 30 to 40 minutes.

Serves 6 to 8

Chris Bragg

Tomato Pie

2 (9 inch) pie shells
6 tomatoes
Salt
6 slices bacon
2 cups mayonnaise
1 bunch green onions, chopped
8 ounces shredded mozzarella cheese
6-8 basil leaves, chopped

Bake pie shells according to package directions. Set aside to cool. Preheat oven to 375 degrees. Peel and slice tomatoes. Drain on paper towels and sprinkle with salt. Fry bacon, drain on paper towels, and crumble. Set aside. Mix mayonnaise, green onions, and mozzarella cheese together. Set aside. Place tomatoes in cooled pie shells and sprinkle with basil and bacon. Top with mayonnaise mixture and bake 30 minutes.

Serves 8

Good as a side dish or entrée.

Sarah Mullins

Turnip Green Casserole

4-5 cups cornbread crumbs
1 (27 ounce) can turnip greens
1 onion, chopped
1 (10¾ ounce) can cream of chicken soup

Preheat oven to 350 degrees. Butter a 2½-quart baking dish and sprinkle ⅓ of cornbread crumbs in bottom. Mix turnip greens and chopped onion together and spread ½ on top of crumbs. Spoon ½ of soup over turnip greens. Repeat the layers of breadcrumbs, turnip greens, and soup. Top with remaining ⅓ of breadcrumbs. Bake 30 minutes.

Serves 8

May substitute cooked fresh or frozen turnip greens seasoned to your taste.

Jane Graham

Submitted by Marie Fuqua

Vegetable Confetti

- 3 medium baking potatoes, unpeeled
- 5 medium zucchini, unpeeled
- 4 medium fresh tomatoes
- 2-3 purple onions
- ¼ cup olive oil
- Seasoned salt
- Black pepper
- 8 basil leaves, chopped

Preheat oven to 400 degrees. Thinly slice potatoes, zucchini, tomatoes, and onions. Arrange in a lightly greased 9x13-inch casserole dish. Alternate vegetable slices. Drizzle with olive oil and bake 30 to 40 minutes or until potatoes are done. Sprinkle with seasoned salt, pepper, and basil leaves. Serve hot.

Serves 10

Barbara McWilliams

Cheese Vegetable Medley

- 1 (16 ounce) bag frozen mixed vegetables
- 1 (10¾ ounce) can cream of mushroom soup
- ½ cup shredded Cheddar cheese
- ⅓ cup sour cream
- ¼ teaspoon pepper
- 1 (4 ounce) jar diced pimiento, drained
- ½ cup canned French fried onions
- ½ cup shredded Cheddar cheese
- 1 cup canned French fried onions

Preheat oven to 350 degrees. Combine vegetables, mushroom soup, ½ cup cheese, sour cream, pepper, pimiento, and ½ cup fried onions. Pour into a shallow, 1-quart casserole dish. Bake uncovered 30 minutes or until vegetables are done. Top with ½ cup cheese and 1 cup fried onions. Return to oven and bake 5 minutes or until golden brown.

Serves 6

Sally Garrard

Vegetable Casserole with Creole Sauce

- 1 (15¼ ounce) can baby limas
- 1 (15 ounce) can English peas
- 1 (14½ ounce) can French cut green beans
- Butter
- Salt
- Pepper
- 2 hard-cooked eggs, grated
- 1 teaspoon prepared mustard
- 1 teaspoon Worcestershire sauce
- 1 cup mayonnaise
- ½ medium onion, grated
- 4 tablespoons vegetable oil
- Dash of hot sauce
- 1 (6 ounce) can fried onions

Preheat oven to 350 degrees. Separately cook lima beans, peas, and green beans with a little butter, salt, and pepper. Drain each vegetable and set aside. Make sauce by combining eggs, mustard, Worcestershire, mayonnaise, onion, oil, and hot sauce. In a greased 8x8-inch dish, put layers of lima beans, sauce, peas, sauce, green beans, and sauce. Bake 20 to 30 minutes or until bubbly. Remove from oven and add fried onions. Return to oven for 5 minutes.

Serves 6 to 8

Lynn Walker Lewis

Chili Relish

- 18 large tomatoes
- 6 large onions
- 12 long hot banana peppers
- 3 cups white vinegar
- 2 cups sugar
- 3 tablespoons salt
- 1 teaspoon ground cloves
- 1 teaspoon allspice
- 1 teaspoon cinnamon

Cut tomatoes into small pieces and dice onions and peppers. Combine in a large pot. Add vinegar, sugar, salt, cloves, allspice, and cinnamon. Bring to a boil. Reduce heat and simmer 3 to 4 hours, stirring occasionally, until very little liquid remains. Put in jars and seal.

Makes 7 to 8 pints

This is great on vegetables.

Eunice Williamson

Submitted by Edna Stone

"I am Alpha and Omega, the beginning and the ending," saith the Lord, which is, and which was, and which is to come, the Almighty.

Revelation 1:8

Since 1972, a Chrismon Tree has enhanced Advent worship in the Sanctuary. Originally a live tree was used, with the trunk of this tree reused at Easter for the Resurrection Cross.

The Chrismon Tree originated in the Lutheran Church of the Ascension, Danville, Virginia, in 1957 to honor Christ. Chrismon is derived from two words, Christ and Monogram, and is just that, a monogram of Christ. Research found these monograms in many places.

More than three hundred ornaments decorate this tree. Members make all the ornaments by hand. The ongoing necessity to repair and replace the ornaments offers many members the opportunity to participate in this inspiring worship. Only gold and white, the liturgical colors for Christmas, are used. A crown at the top proclaims the Kingship of our Lord Jesus Christ. Two large circles, the Christian Year Series, are predominant on the tree.

A second Chrismon Tree graces the entrance to the Wesley Worship Center each year. These symbols serve to connect the congregation with Christ's earliest followers and continue to inspire all worshippers.

Desserts

O come O come Emmanuel and ransom captive Israel that mourns in lonely exile here until the Son of God appear
This, this is Christ the King whom shepherds guard and angels sing haste haste to bring him laud the babe the son of Mary
And His name shall be called wonderful counselor the mighty God the everlasting Father the prince of peace

For unto you is born this day in the city of David a Saviour, which is Christ the Lord.

Luke 2:11

These beautiful Advent Banners have been used continuously in every Advent Season since 1993. The five banners represent each of the four Sundays in Advent plus Christmas Day: the Promise, the Annunciation, the Trip to Bethlehem, Shepherds in the Field, and the Manger Scene. Each banner is eleven feet tall and four feet wide.

At the request of the Rev. Robert Archibald, artist John White, long-time art teacher, designed the banners matching the Romanesque Revival architecture of the church. He wanted the banners to look like they had been in a closet for 200 years. The first one is the darkest and they get lighter each week of Advent. John and his wife, Cora, went to northern Greece for a family wedding in August of 1993. While there, they purchased the banner bells. John chose each one for its melodious tone.

The style of lettering over the Chapel door was a particular favorite of John's. He commissioned Ginny Dixon, a local calligrapher, to design similar lettering for the banners. Church women cut out and hand-stitched every piece of material from satins and silk to tapestry and velvet. The Committee on Memorials funded the project. Over 2400 hundred hours, two dozen volunteers, and limitless patience yielded this glorious artistry while providing a unique bonding among the workers. Several church men designed and constructed the standards while others devised the special lighting. When the task was completed, the church had five wonderful banners and John White had joined the First United Methodist Church.

Mary Spencer's Sugar Plum Cake

2 cups self-rising flour
2 cups sugar
1 cup vegetable oil
3 eggs
1 teaspoon ground cinnamon
1 teaspoon ground cloves
1 cup chopped pecans or walnuts
2 (4 ounce) jars plum baby food

Preheat oven to 325 degrees. Grease Bundt pan and coat heavily with sugar. Blend all ingredients and pour into prepared pan. Bake about 1 hour.

Serves 10 to 12

Betty Jones

Submitted by Carolyn Blue

Our unseen guest O'Master dear, help us to feel your presence here, be with us now and bless our food, and fill our hearts with gratitude. In Jesus name, Amen.

Blessing used by Betty Jones at dinner parties.

Kim's Chocolate Cake

1 (18.25 ounce) box butter cake mix
1 (3.9 ounce) package chocolate instant pudding mix
1 cup vegetable oil
¼ cup water
4 jumbo eggs, room temperature
1 teaspoon vanilla extract
8 ounces sour cream
6 ounces semi-sweet chocolate chips

Preheat oven to 350 degrees. Mix all ingredients except chocolate chips. Fold in chocolate chips. Bake 1 hour in greased Bundt pan.

Serves 12 to 16

Lakshmi Nallamala

Date Nut Upside Down Cake

- 1½ cups brown sugar
- 1½ cups water
- ½ cup butter
- 1 cup all-purpose flour
- 1 cup sugar
- 1 cup milk
- ¼ teaspoon salt
- 1 teaspoon baking powder
- ½ cup chopped pecans
- ½ cup chopped dates
- Whipping cream (optional)

Preheat oven to 350 degrees. Mix brown sugar, water, and butter in a 10-inch iron skillet and let come to a boil. Mix flour, sugar, milk, salt, baking powder, pecans, and dates. Pour over melted mixture. Bake 45 to 60 minutes. Spoon out. Top with a dollop of whipped cream.

Serves 8

Martha Dotzheimer

Orange Cake

CAKE

- 1 (18.25 ounce) box yellow cake mix
- 1 (3.4 ounce) box instant vanilla pudding
- 4 eggs
- 1 cup orange juice
- ½ cup vegetable oil
- 1 cup pecan pieces

GLAZE

- ½ cup butter
- 1 cup sugar
- ½ cup orange juice

Preheat oven to 350 degrees. Combine cake mix and pudding. Add eggs and mix thoroughly. Add orange juice and vegetable oil. Grease and flour a Bundt pan. Put pecan pieces in bottom of pan. Pour batter into pan and bake 50 to 60 minutes. Do not immediately remove cake from pan. For glaze, melt butter in a saucepan. Add sugar and orange juice to pan and boil 2 minutes. Punch holes in top of cake while in pan. Pour or spoon glaze over top of hot cake. Let cake sit 30 minutes before removing from pan.

Serves 12 to 16

Edna Stone

Carrot Cake

CAKE

- 2 cups unsifted all-purpose flour
- 2 cups sugar
- 2 teaspoons cinnamon
- 2 teaspoons baking soda
- 1 teaspoon salt
- 1½ cups vegetable oil
- 4 eggs
- 3 cups grated carrots

ICING

- ½ cup butter or margarine, softened
- 1 (8 ounce) package cream cheese, softened
- 1 (16 ounce) box confectioners' sugar, sifted
- 2 teaspoons pure vanilla extract
- 1 cup chopped nuts or grated coconut

Preheat oven to 350 degrees. Grease and flour three 8 or 9-inch round cake pans. Place wax paper circles in the bottom of each pan. Sift together flour, sugar, cinnamon, soda, and salt. Add oil to sifted mixture. Add eggs, one at a time, beating well after each. Add carrots. Pour batter into pans and bake 30 to 35 minutes. Cool cake in pans 10 minutes before turning layers onto a cooling rack. Cool completely before icing. Prepare icing by creaming together butter and cream cheese. Mix in confectioners' sugar, vanilla, and nuts. Use 1 cup of icing between layers. Frost cake with remaining icing.

Serves 12 to 14

I have used this recipe for years and it makes a good, moist cake. My family always wants me to make this for Thanksgiving and Christmas.

Edith Benton White

Submitted by Virginia Walker Jennings

Sunshine Cake

CAKE

½ cup vegetable oil
4 eggs
1 (11 ounce) can Mandarin oranges, undrained
1 (18.25 ounce) package golden butter cake mix
½ cup chopped pecans

FROSTING

1 (5.1 ounce) package vanilla instant pudding mix
1 (20 ounce) can crushed pineapple, undrained
1 (8 ounce) carton frozen whipped topping, thawed

Preheat oven to 350 degrees. Add oil, eggs, and oranges to cake mix. Blend until moistened. Beat 4 minutes with mixer at medium speed. Blend in pecans. Bake in 3 greased and lightly floured 9-inch round pans 15 minutes. Cool. For frosting, beat pudding mix and pineapple with mixer until thick. Fold in whipped topping. Frost cake and store in refrigerator until ready to serve.

Serves 16 to 18

Elizabeth McDonald

Chocolate Chocolate Chip Cake

1 (18.25 ounce) box devils food cake mix
1 (5.9 ounce) package chocolate instant pudding
1 cup sour cream
1 cup vegetable oil
4 eggs, beaten
½ cup warm water
1 (12 ounce) package semi-sweet chocolate chips

Preheat oven to 350 degrees. In a large bowl, combine cake mix, pudding, sour cream, oil, eggs, and water. Stir in chocolate chips and pour batter into a well-greased 12-cup Bundt pan. Bake 50 to 55 minutes. Serve plain, sprinkle with confectioners' sugar, or drizzle with warm icing.

Serves 14 to 16

Jean Kirby

Cranberry Pound Cake

CAKE

2 cups cranberries, washed and drained
3 cups all-purpose flour, setting aside ¼ cup
1 teaspoon baking powder
½ teaspoon salt
1 cup unsalted butter, softened
2 cups plus 2 tablespoons sugar
4 eggs, room temperature
1½ teaspoons vanilla extract
Grated rind of 1 orange
¼ teaspoon orange extract (optional)

ORANGE GLAZE

¼ cup fresh orange juice
2 cups confectioners' sugar

Preheat oven to 325 degrees. Toss berries with ¼ cup flour and set aside. Sift remaining 2¾ cups flour with baking powder and salt. Set aside. Cream butter and sugar. Add eggs one at a time, beating well after each addition. Add vanilla and beat until fluffy. Add orange rind and orange extract. Fold flour, baking powder, and salt mixture into batter until well blended. Gently stir in cranberries. Turn into a greased and floured 10-inch tube or Bundt pan. Bake about 1 hour and 10 minutes, or until cake tests done. Cool in pan 10 minutes before removing. Mix orange glaze ingredients until smooth. Pour over cake. Allow glaze to harden before serving.

Serves 12 to 16

Celeste Hemby

Donna's Mocha Chip Cake

1 (18.25 ounce) box chocolate cake mix
2 cups sour cream
2 eggs
½ cup coffee-flavored liqueur
1 (3.4 ounce) package French vanilla instant pudding
1 (12 ounce) package semi-sweet chocolate chips
⅓ cup vegetable oil

Preheat oven to 350 degrees. Place cake mix, sour cream, eggs, liqueur, pudding mix, chocolate chips, and oil in a large bowl. Mix by hand. Pour batter into a greased and floured Bundt pan. Bake 45 to 50 minutes or until cake springs back when touched. Cool 20 minutes before removing from pan.

Serves 12 to 16

Debbie Packard

German Chocolate Cake with Coconut Pecan Filling

CAKE

1 (4 ounce) package German sweet chocolate
½ cup boiling water
1 cup butter
2 cups sugar
4 egg yolks
2½ cups cake flour
1 teaspoon baking soda
¼ teaspoon salt
1 cup buttermilk
1 teaspoon vanilla extract
4 egg whites

FILLING

1 cup sugar
1 (12 ounce) can evaporated milk
3 egg yolks
1 cup butter
2 cups chopped pecans
1 (14 ounce) package grated coconut
1 teaspoon vanilla extract

Preheat oven to 350 degrees. Grease and flour three 9-inch layer pans. Melt chocolate in boiling water. Set aside to cool. Cream butter and sugar in mixing bowl. Add egg yolks, one at a time, mixing after each. Mix flour, baking soda, and salt in separate bowl. Combine buttermilk with melted chocolate and add alternately with flour mixture to butter, sugar, and egg mixture. Add vanilla and mix well. Beat egg whites until stiff and gently fold into batter. Pour into pans and bake 30 to 40 minutes or until cake springs to the touch. Remove from pans and place on racks to cool. To make filling, combine sugar, milk, egg yolks, and butter in saucepan. Stir constantly over medium heat for 12 to 15 minutes or until thickened. Remove from heat and add nuts, coconut, and vanilla. Spread between cooled cake layers and on top and sides.

Serves 12 to14

Idelle Tillman

Submitted by Sarah Lauren Kattos

Idelle was my great grandmother. We made 10 of these cakes one Christmas for friends. It is one of the best memories of my childhood. I make this cake at Christmas every year in memory of Idelle.

Chocolate Angel Food Cake

¾ cup sifted all-purpose flour
¼ cup cocoa
¾ cup sugar
1½ cups egg whites, room temperature
½ teaspoon salt
1½ teaspoons cream of tartar
¾ cup sugar

Preheat oven to 350 degrees. Sift flour, cocoa, and ¾ cup sugar 5 times. Set aside. Place egg whites in a large mixing bowl. Add salt and beat on high speed until foamy. Add cream of tartar and continue beating at high speed until peaks form. DO NOT beat until dry. Gradually sprinkle in ¾ cup sugar. Beat on lower speed until blended. Turn mixer to lowest speed. Sprinkle in flour mixture evenly and quickly, scraping bowl often. Pour into an ungreased tube pan. Cut 3 times to remove bubbles. Bake 30 to 35 minutes. Invert pan to cool.

Serves 8 to 10

Do not try this cake on a rainy day.

Betty Lou Jones

Apple Dapple Cake

CAKE

1½ cups vegetable oil
2 cups sugar
3 eggs
1 teaspoon baking soda
1 teaspoon salt
3 cups all-purpose flour
1½ cups chopped nuts
2 cups peeled chopped apples

DAPPLE

1 cup packed brown sugar
¼ cup milk
½ cup butter or margarine

Preheat oven to 350 degrees. Cream oil and sugar together. Add eggs one at a time, beating after each addition. Mix soda and salt with flour and add to egg mixture. Fold in nuts and apples. Bake in a well-greased tube pan 1 hour. For dapple, mix brown sugar, milk, and butter in a saucepan and cook 3 minutes after mixture has melted. Pour over warm cake. Allow cake to cool before removing from pan.

Serves 10 to 12

Norma Colbath

Oatmeal Cake

CAKE

½ cup margarine
1 cup packed light brown sugar
1 cup sugar
2 eggs
1½ cups all-purpose flour
1 teaspoon baking soda
1 teaspoon cinnamon
1 teaspoon vanilla extract
½ teaspoon salt
½ cup chopped pecans
½ cup coconut or ground raisins
1½ cups boiling water
1 cup quick-cooking oats

TOPPING

6 tablespoons margarine
1½ cups brown sugar
½ cup evaporated milk
1 cup flake coconut
1 cup chopped pecans

Preheat oven to 350 degrees. In a large mixing bowl, cream margarine, brown sugar, and sugar. Add eggs, flour, soda, cinnamon, vanilla, salt, pecans, coconut (or ground raisins), and water. Mix together and stir in oats. Pour batter into a greased 9x13-inch pan and bake 25 minutes. Prepare topping by combining margarine, brown sugar, and evaporated milk in small saucepan. Bring to a boil and pour over cake. Mix coconut and pecans together and cover top of cake. Return cake to oven and lightly brown under broiler. Watch carefully!

Serves 15 to 18

Ida Emerson Butler

Submitted by Jean Rast

Variation: For cake batter, substitute ½ cup vegetable oil for margarine; omit coconut, raisins, and pecans. For topping, add coconut, pecans and ½ teaspoon vanilla extract to other ingredients before pouring over hot cake. Do not brown under broiler.

Cleo Goddard

Pecan Praline Cake

CAKE

- **1 cup buttermilk**
- **½ cup butter**
- **2 cups light brown sugar**
- **2 eggs**
- **2 cups all-purpose flour**
- **1 teaspoon baking soda**
- **¼ teaspoon salt**
- **1 teaspoon vanilla extract**

ICING

- **½ cup butter**
- **1 cup firmly packed light brown sugar**
- **⅓ cup light cream or evaporated milk**
- **1 cup chopped pecans**
- **Whipped cream**

Preheat oven to 350 degrees. In small saucepan, heat buttermilk and butter until warm, not hot. In a large bowl, combine brown sugar and eggs. Beat well. Combine flour, soda, and salt and sift directly into bowl. Add vanilla. Pour batter into a greased and floured 9x13-inch pan. Bake 25 minutes. Prepare icing by combining butter, brown sugar, cream, and pecans in saucepan until butter melts. Spread mixture over warm cake while still in pan. Turn on broiler. Place cake 4 inches below broiler and cook 1 to 2 minutes until icing bubbles and turns golden. Serve warm. Just before serving, top with whipped cream.

Serves 9 to 12

May prepare ahead and reheat when ready to serve.

Mona Gay Keith

Brown Sugar Pound Cake

- 3 cups all-purpose flour
- ½ teaspoon salt
- 1 teaspoon baking powder
- 1 cup butter, softened
- ½ cup shortening
- 1 (16 ounce) box light brown sugar
- 1 cup sugar
- 6 eggs, room temperature
- 2 teaspoons vanilla extract
- 1 cup milk, room temperature

Preheat oven to 350 degrees. Sift together flour, salt, and baking powder. Set aside. Cream together butter, shortening, brown sugar, and sugar. Beat until fluffy. Add eggs, 1 at a time, beating after each, until just blended. Add vanilla. Stir in about ⅓ of the flour mixture until just blended. Add ½ of the milk, mixing until just blended. Continue alternating flour mixture and milk until all is mixed. Pour batter into a well-greased and floured 10-inch tube pan and bake approximately 1 hour and 15 minutes until toothpick inserted in center comes out clean. Let rest in pan 20 minutes. Turn out on rack and let cool before slicing.

Serves 12 to 14

Susan Clanton

Chocolate Pound Cake

- 1 cup butter
- 2 cups sugar
- 4 eggs
- 3 cups all-purpose flour
- ½ teaspoon baking soda
- 1 teaspoon salt
- 1 cup buttermilk
- 1 (4 ounce) package German sweet chocolate
- ⅓ cup chocolate syrup
- 1 teaspoon vanilla extract

Preheat oven to 300 degrees. Cream butter and sugar together. Add eggs one at a time, beating after each. Beat until fluffy (like whipped cream). Sift together flour, soda, and salt. Add alternately with buttermilk. Melt chocolate and combine with chocolate syrup. Add chocolate mixture to batter and mix. Stir in vanilla. Pour batter into a greased and floured 10-inch tube pan. Bake 1½ hours. Cool in pan a few minutes. Remove to wire rack to cool. Wrap in foil or place in airtight container for 24 hours.

Serves 16 to 18

Mary Rutledge

Mer's Sour Cream Pound Cake

1 cup butter
3 cups sugar
6 eggs
1 teaspoon vanilla extract
½ teaspoon lemon extract
¼ teaspoon almond extract
Dash of ground mace
3 cups all-purpose flour
¼ teaspoon baking soda
8 ounces sour cream

Preheat oven to 325 degrees. Coat a 10-inch tube pan with cooking spray and swirl a little sugar around to coat inside of pan. Set aside. Cream butter and sugar together. Add eggs, 1 at a time, beating after each. Add vanilla, lemon, and almond extracts and mace. Add flour and soda alternately with sour cream and mix well. Bake 1 hour and 15 minutes or until done. Cool 15 minutes before removing from pan.

Serves 14 to 16

Gladys Craft

Submitted by Don Craft and Janie Byers

Variation: May omit mace and substitute ½ teaspoon orange, lemon, or almond extract for lemon and almond extracts.

Imogene Davis

Shelia's Cream Cheese Pound Cake

1½ cups butter
1 (8 ounce) package cream cheese
3 cups sugar
6 eggs
1 teaspoon vanilla extract
3 cups cake flour, sifted

Preheat oven to 300 degrees. Line tube pan with parchment paper and grease with shortening. Beat butter and cream cheese together. Beat in sugar. Add eggs 1 at a time, beating well after each. Add vanilla. Add flour and beat on medium speed 1½ to 2 minutes. Pour batter into pan and bake 1 hour and 45 minutes. Cool in pan 5 to10 minutes. Turn out onto parchment paper in order to turn cake right side up easily. Cool on rack.

Serves 14 to 18

Freezes well in chunks (not slices). Stays moist more than 1 week without refrigeration.

Carole Rogers Booher

Virginia's Amaretto Cheesecake

CRUST

- **1½ cups graham cracker crumbs**
- **2 tablespoons sugar**
- **1 teaspoon cinnamon**
- **6 tablespoons butter, melted**

FILLING

- **3 (8 ounce) packages cream cheese, softened**
- **1 cup sugar**
- **4 eggs**
- **⅓ cup amaretto liqueur**

TOPPING

- **1 (8 ounce) carton sour cream**
- **4 teaspoons sugar**
- **1 tablespoon amaretto liqueur**
- **¼ cup sliced almonds**
- **1 (1.55 ounce) chocolate bar, grated**

Preheat oven to 375 degrees. Combine graham cracker crumbs, 2 tablespoons sugar, cinnamon, and butter. Mix well. Firmly press mixture onto bottom and ½ inch up sides of a 9-inch springform pan. For filling, beat cream cheese with electric mixer until light and fluffy. Gradually add 1 cup sugar, mixing well. Add eggs, 1 at a time, beating well after each addition. Stir in ⅓ cup amaretto and pour into prepared pan. Bake 45 minutes or until set. Increase oven temperature to 500 degrees. For topping, combine sour cream, remaining sugar, and amaretto. Stir well and spoon over cheesecake. Bake 5 minutes. Let cool to room temperature. Refrigerate 24 hours or more. Garnish with almonds and grated chocolate.

Serves 12

Peggy Christian

Amy's Blueberry Cheesecake

- 1½ cups graham cracker crumbs
- ½ cup sugar
- ½ cup butter, melted
- 2 (8 ounce) packages cream cheese, softened
- 4 eggs, slightly beaten
- 2 cups sugar
- 2 teaspoons vanilla extract
- 1 (1 pound 6 ounce) can blueberry pie filling
- 1 (8 ounce) carton frozen whipped topping, thawed

Preheat oven to 375 degrees. Combine crumbs, ½ cup sugar, and melted butter. Blend well. Pack mixture firmly in bottom of a 9x13-inch baking dish. Beat cream cheese until smooth. Add eggs, 2 cups sugar, and vanilla. Beat until fluffy. Spread over crumb mixture. Bake 30 minutes. Remove from oven and cool. Spread pie filling over cheesecake. Spread whipped topping over blueberry layer. Cut into squares to serve.

Serves 14

Carol Hurst

Berry Trifle

- 1 (15 ounce) angel food cake
- 1 (8 ounce) package cream cheese, softened
- 1 (12 ounce) carton frozen whipped topping, thawed
- 1 (14 ounce) can sweetened condensed milk
- 1 (16 ounce) package strawberries
- 2 cups blueberries
- 1 (6 ounce) package raspberries

Tear cake into bite-size pieces. Place ⅓ of cake pieces in a trifle bowl. Beat cream cheese with electric mixer. Add whipped topping and condensed milk. Mix well. Spread ⅓ of this mixture over cake pieces. Combine strawberries, blueberries, and raspberries. Add a layer of fruit over cream cheese mixture. Repeat until you have 3 layers of each. Keep in refrigerator until ready to serve.

Serves 8 to 10

Jean Hinson

Favorite Cheesecake

CRUST

2¼ cups crushed graham crackers
½ cup butter, melted
¼ cup sugar

FILLING

2 (8 ounce) packages cream cheese, softened
½ cup sugar
3 eggs
2 teaspoons lemon juice

TOPPING

2 cups sour cream
½ cup sugar
1 teaspoon vanilla extract

Preheat oven to 350 degrees. Mix graham crackers, butter, and sugar. Press into an 8-inch square pan or a springform pan. Bake 5 minutes. For filling, beat cream cheese, sugar, eggs, and lemon juice with an electric mixer until smooth. Pour into crust and bake 15 to 20 minutes. Cool to room temperature. Prepare topping by combining sour cream, sugar, and vanilla with a spoon. Pour over cream cheese layer and bake 10 minutes. Cool completely. Refrigerate 24 hours before serving.

Serves 8 to10

Julia Parker

Walnut Fudge Pie

3 eggs, beaten
½ cup firmly packed brown sugar
¼ cup all-purpose flour
¼ cup butter, melted
1 teaspoon vanilla extract
1 (12 ounce) package semi-sweet chocolate morsels, melted
1½ cups walnut or pecan pieces
1 (9-inch) unbaked pie crust
Coffee ice cream

Preheat oven to 375 degrees. Stir together eggs, brown sugar, flour, butter, and vanilla. Stir in melted chocolate morsels and nuts. Spoon filling into pie crust and bake 30 minutes. Cool. Serve with coffee ice cream.

Diana Finley

Chocolate Pie

PIE

- 2 (1 ounce) squares unsweetened chocolate
- 2 tablespoons butter
- ⅓ cup all-purpose flour
- 1 cup sugar
- ¼ teaspoon salt
- 2½ cups milk, scalded
- 3 egg yolks
- ¾ teaspoon vanilla extract
- 1 (9-inch) baked pie crust

MERINGUE

- 3 egg whites
- ⅓ cup sugar
- Chopped nuts

Preheat oven to 350 degrees. Melt chocolate and butter in top of a double boiler. Mix flour, sugar, and salt into chocolate. Add milk slowly and stir until thickened, about 15 minutes. In a separate bowl, beat egg yolks well. Stir a small amount of chocolate mixture into egg yolks. Add to chocolate in top of double boiler. Continue cooking 2 minutes, stirring constantly. Remove from heat. Cool slightly. Add vanilla and pour into pie crust. To make meringue, beat egg whites, adding sugar gradually, until whites are stiff. Spread on top of pie and swirl. Sprinkle with nuts. Bake 12 to 15 minutes until slightly golden. Cool before serving.

Serves 6 to 8

Betty Houston

Submitted by Charles Houston

Easy Lemon Pie

- 1 (14 ounce) can sweetened condensed milk
- ⅓ cup fresh lemon juice
- 1 tablespoon grated lemon rind
- ¼ teaspoon salt
- 1 (9-inch) baked pie shell
- Whipped cream (optional)

Combine condensed milk, lemon juice, lemon rind, and salt in bowl. Stir until well mixed and thickened. Pour into pie crust and refrigerate at least 2 hours. Top with whipped cream, if desired.

Serves 6 to 8

Geneva Kilgore

Fudge Pie

- ½ **cup butter or margarine**
- ⅓ **cup cocoa**
- 1 **cup sugar**
- 1 **teaspoon vanilla extract**
- 2 **eggs, beaten**
- ½ **cup all-purpose flour**
- ½ **cup chopped walnuts**
- ½ **cup semi-sweet chocolate chips**
- **Whipped cream (optional)**
- **Ice cream (optional)**

Preheat oven to 350 degrees. Spray deep pie pan with vegetable cooking spray. DO NOT use disposable type pan. Melt butter in medium saucepan over low heat. Add cocoa, sugar, vanilla, and eggs, stirring well after each ingredient. Add flour, walnuts, and chocolate chips. Spread into pan and bake for 20 minutes. Do not overcook. Pie will be moist inside. Slice and top with whipped cream, or serve warm with ice cream.

Serves 12

Mary Summerlin

Amazing Coconut Pie

- 1¾ **cups sugar**
- ¼ **cup butter, softened**
- 4 **eggs, well beaten**
- 2 **cups whole milk**
- 1 **teaspoon vanilla extract**
- ½ **cup self-rising flour**
- 1 **(3½ ounce) can flake coconut**

Preheat oven to 350 degrees. Cream together sugar and butter. Mix eggs with milk and vanilla. Add flour and milk mixture alternately to sugar mixture, beating well. Add coconut. Pour into 2 well-greased 8-inch pie plates and bake 30 to 40 minutes until golden brown. Crust will form as it bakes.

Makes 2 pies

Katherine Robertson

Peanut Butter Yum Yum

CRUST

- 1/4 cup light corn syrup
- 1/3 cup sugar
- 1/4 cup plus 2 teaspoons water
- 6 tablespoons butter, melted
- 2 cups plus 3 tablespoons crisp rice cereal

PEANUT BUTTER LAYER

- 2/3 cup coarsely chopped milk chocolate
- 3/4 cup peanut butter

GANACHE LAYER

- 1/3 cup coarsely chopped bittersweet dark chocolate (61% cacoa)
- 1/4 cup coarsely chopped extra bittersweet dark chocolate (72% cacao)
- 1/2 cup heavy cream
- 4 teaspoons light corn syrup
- 1/4 cup butter, softened
- 1 cup chopped salted peanuts

Combine corn syrup, sugar, and water. Cook over medium heat 10 to 15 minutes or until mixture is a light caramel. Pour melted butter into syrup mixture and add cereal. Mix well and press into a 9-inch pie pan to form the crust. For peanut butter layer, melt milk chocolate in microwave on 50 percent power 20 seconds at a time or over a double boiler. Once chocolate is melted, allow it to cool to 90 degrees. After cooled, combine chocolate and peanut butter and pour into pie crust. To make ganache layer, place both dark chocolates in a small bowl and set aside. Combine cream and syrup in a small saucepan and cook over medium heat. Once cream comes to a boil, pour cream over chocolate. Stir until combined. When this chocolate mixture reaches 90 degrees, stir in butter until smooth. Spread mixture on top of peanut butter layer. Garnish with chopped peanuts. Refrigerate.

Serves 10 to 12

For a really elegant dessert, add a layer of meringue over the ganache. Using a butane torch, lightly scorch meringue and sprinkle additional chopped salted peanuts on top. DO NOT brown under broiler, ganache will melt.

Andrew Shotts

Drew Shotts, a life-long member of FUMC and the son of deceased members Sue and Don Shotts, is an award-winning pastry chef and the owner of Garrison Confections in Providence, RI.

Patterson's Favorite Chess Pie

- 2 cups sugar
- 2 tablespoons cornmeal
- 1 tablespoon vinegar
- ½ cup butter, melted
- 1 tablespoon milk
- 1 teaspoon vanilla extract
- 4 eggs
- 1 (9-inch) unbaked pie shell

Preheat oven to 350 degrees. Mix together sugar, cornmeal, vinegar, and melted butter. Add milk, vanilla, and eggs. Mix well. Pour into pie shell and bake 50 minutes or until inserted knife comes out clean.

Serves 6 to 8

Mildred Patterson

Submitted by Gerald Patterson

Lemon Chess Pie

- 2 cups sugar
- 1 tablespoon all-purpose flour
- 1 tablespoon cornmeal
- 4 eggs, beaten
- ¼ cup butter, melted
- ¼ cup milk
- ¼ cup lemon juice
- 3 teaspoons grated lemon peel
- 1 (9-inch) pie shell, unbaked

Preheat oven to 450 degrees. In large bowl, toss sugar, flour, and cornmeal with fork. Add eggs, butter, milk, lemon juice, and grated lemon peel. Mix well. Pour into pie shell and bake 10 minutes. Reduce heat to 350 degrees and bake an additional 30 minutes. Check after 15 minutes to see if crust is brown. If so, cover pie with a sheet of aluminum foil.

Serves 6

Geneva Kilgore

Apple Pie

Pastry for double crust for 10-inch pie
¼ cup all-purpose flour
¾ cup sugar
½ teaspoon cinnamon
6 cups peeled and sliced Granny Smith apples
1 tablespoon butter

Preheat oven to 400 degrees. Place bottom pastry in pie plate. Mix flour, sugar, and cinnamon. Combine with apples and put in pie crust. Dot with butter. Moisten edges of bottom crust and add top crust. Fold edge under bottom crust and crinkle. Slit center of pie for steam to escape. Bake 50 minutes.

Serves 6 to 8

Jo Ann Braam

Youngs' Fresh Blueberry Pie

Pastry for double crust for 9-inch pie
½ cup sugar
⅓ cup all-purpose flour
1 teaspoon ground cinnamon
4 cups fresh blueberries
1 tablespoon lemon juice
2 tablespoons margarine or butter

Preheat oven to 425 degrees. Place bottom pastry in pie pan. Mix sugar, flour, and cinnamon. Stir in blueberries. Turn into pastry-lined pie pan. Sprinkle with lemon juice and dot with margarine. Cover with top crust. Cut slits in crust, seal to bottom crust, and flute. Cover edge of crust with strips of aluminum foil to prevent excessive browning. Remove foil during last 15 minutes of baking. Bake 35 to 45 minutes until crust is brown and juice begins to bubble through slits in crust.

Serves 8

DO NOT use frozen blueberries.

Debbie and John Youngs

Strawberry Pie

1 (9-inch) baked pastry shell
1 quart fresh ripe strawberries, stems removed
1 cup sugar
2 tablespoons cornstarch
1 cup whipping cream, whipped

Select enough large berries to cover bottom of pastry shell, placing stem end down. Crush remaining berries. Add sugar and cornstarch to crushed berries and place mixture in top of a double boiler. Cook over simmering water until thick. Cool. Pour over berries in pastry shell. Place in refrigerator to set. Serve topped with whipped cream.

Serves 6 to 8

Marguerite Simpson

Mother's Summer Pie

1 (5 ounce) can evaporated milk
1 cup unsweetened pineapple juice
⅔ cup sugar
1 (6 ounce) package strawberry flavored gelatin
1 graham cracker or vanilla wafer crust
Fresh strawberries (optional)

Place can of evaporated milk in freezer and chill about 1 hour until crystals form. Chill beaters of electric mixer and large mixing bowl. Combine pineapple juice, sugar, and gelatin in saucepan and bring to boil. Chill mixture to room temperature. Use prepared graham cracker crust, or layer vanilla wafers in bottom of a 9 or 10-inch pie pan. Whip chilled milk until light and fluffy. Fold in gelatin mixture. Pour into crust and chill until firm, about 2 hours. Garnish with fresh strawberries, if desired.

Serves 8 to 10

Any flavor gelatin or sugar-free gelatin may be used. Two 8-inch pie crusts may be used.

Wanda Groome

Strawberry Yogurt Pie

1 (8 ounce) container frozen whipped topping, thawed
2 (8 ounce) cartons strawberry yogurt
½ (10 ounce) package frozen strawberries, thawed
1 graham cracker pie crust
Fresh strawberries

Mix whipped topping, yogurt, and strawberries together well. Pour into pie crust. Freeze for several hours. Garnish with fresh strawberries before serving.

Serves 6 to 8

Peaches and peach yogurt may be used instead of strawberry.

Gwen Riley

Pumpkin Chiffon Pie

1½ cups gingersnap crumbs
4 tablespoons melted butter
1 (.25 ounce) envelope unflavored gelatin
⅓ cup sugar
½ teaspoon salt
½ teaspoon cinnamon
½ teaspoon allspice
¼ teaspoon ginger
¼ teaspoon nutmeg
½ cup milk
3 egg yolks
1 cup canned pumpkin
3 egg whites
¼ cup sugar
1 cup whipping cream
¼ cup confectioners' sugar, sifted
½ teaspoon vanilla extract
¼ teaspoon cinnamon
Grated or ground pecans for garnish (optional)

Preheat oven to 375 degrees. Combine crumbs and melted butter. Press into a 9-inch buttered pie plate. Bake 8 minutes. Cool. In a saucepan, combine gelatin, sugar, salt, cinnamon, allspice, ginger, and nutmeg. Stir in milk, egg yolks, and pumpkin. Cook and stir over medium heat until mixture boils and gelatin dissolves. Remove from heat and chill until partially set. Beat egg whites until soft peaks form. Gradually add remaining sugar and beat to stiff peaks. Fold mixtures together and put into crust. Beat whipping cream, confectioners' sugar, vanilla, and cinnamon to stiff peaks. Refrigerate before spreading over pie. Top with grated pecans. Chill until firm.

Serves 8

Annette Cox

Frosty Peanut Butter Pie

4 ounces cream cheese, softened
¼ cup peanut butter, creamy or crunchy
¼ cup sugar
1 teaspoon vanilla extract
1 (8 ounce) container frozen whipped topping, thawed
1 (8-inch) chocolate crumb crust
2 teaspoons chocolate syrup

Beat cream cheese, peanut butter, sugar, and vanilla until smooth. Fold in whipped topping. Spoon into crust and drizzle with chocolate syrup. Cover and freeze 4 hours or until set. Remove from freezer 30 minutes before serving.

Serves 6

Sylvia Bruens

Delicious Pecan Pie

3 eggs, slightly beaten
1 cup dark corn syrup
1 cup sugar
2 tablespoons butter or margarine, melted
1 teaspoon vanilla extract
1½ cups pecan halves
1 (9-inch) unbaked deep dish pie shell

Preheat oven to 375 degrees. In a large bowl, stir together eggs, corn syrup, sugar, butter, and vanilla. Blend well and add pecan halves. Pour into pie shell. Bake 50 to 55 minutes or until knife inserted in center and edge comes out clean. Cool before serving.

Serves 6 to 8

Mildred Patterson

Submitted by Gerald Patterson

Derby Pie

- ½ cup margarine or butter
- 1 cup sugar
- ½ cup all-purpose flour
- 2 eggs, beaten
- 1 teaspoon vanilla extract
- 1 cup chopped pecans
- ¾ cup semi-sweet chocolate chips
- 1 (9-inch) unbaked pie shell

Preheat oven to 350 degrees. Melt margarine or butter and cool. Add sugar, flour, eggs, vanilla, and pecans. Add chocolate chips last so they will not melt. Pour into pie shell and bake 30 to 40 minutes.

Serves 6 to 8

Julia Parker

Toasted Coconut Chocolate Chunk Pecan Pie

- 1 cup sweetened flake coconut
- 1 (15 ounce) package refrigerated pie crusts
- ⅓ cup butter, melted
- 1 cup sugar
- 1 cup light corn syrup
- 4 large eggs, slightly beaten
- 1 teaspoon vanilla extract
- ¼ teaspoon salt
- 1½ cups pecan halves
- ¼ cup semi-sweet chocolate chunks or morsels
- Vanilla ice cream

Preheat oven to 300 degrees. Place coconut on a baking sheet and roast 5 to 8 minutes or until golden. Set aside to cool. Increase oven temperature to 325 degrees. Unroll 1 pie crust and place on lightly floured surface. Lightly brush top of crust with water. Unroll remaining crust and place over bottom crust. Gently roll into a 10-inch circle. Fit into a 9-inch pie plate. Fold edges under and crimp together. Set aside. Stir together butter, sugar, corn syrup, eggs, vanilla, and salt. Stir in pecans, coconut, and chocolate chunks. Pour filling into pie crust. Bake 1 hour and 15 minutes or until filling is set. Shield crust after 45 minutes with aluminum foil, if necessary. Cool completely on a wire rack. Top each slice with vanilla ice cream, if desired.

Serves 8 to 10

Syble Park

Cracker Pie (Mock Apple Pie)

4 egg whites
1 cup sugar
1 teaspoon baking powder
1 teaspoon almond extract
20 crushed round buttery crackers
½ cup chopped pecans
Whipped cream (optional)

Preheat oven to 350 degrees. Beat egg whites until they peak. Add sugar, baking powder, almond extract, crushed crackers, and pecans. Bake in a greased 9-inch pie pan 30 minutes. Serve with whipped cream.

Serves 8

Jane Monroe

Variation: Use vanilla extract instead of almond extract in pie. Mix almond extract with whipped cream for topping.

Tine Purdy

Apple Dumplings

½-¾ cup butter
1-1¼ cups sugar
1 teaspoon cinnamon
2 cans crescent rolls
2 large Granny Smith apples, peeled or unpeeled
1 (12 ounce) can lemon-lime soda

Preheat oven to 350 degrees. In a saucepan, combine butter, sugar, and cinnamon. Heat until butter melts. Separate crescent rolls into triangles. Cut apples into 8 slices each. Roll 1 apple slice in each piece of dough. Place in a 9x13-inch baking dish coated with cooking spray. Pour butter mixture over the rolled apples. Dumplings can be made ahead to this point and refrigerated until ready to bake. Pour soda over all. Bake uncovered 45 minutes.

Makes 16 dumplings

May use ½ cup butter, 1 cup sugar, reduced-fat rolls, and diet lemon-lime soda and it still tastes delicious.

Joyce Bagwell

Apple Crumble

- **4 cups peeled and sliced apples**
- **½ cup water**
- **1 teaspoon cinnamon**
- **¾ cup all-purpose flour**
- **½ cup shortening or margarine**
- **¾ cup plus 2 tablespoons sugar**
- **Vanilla ice cream**

Preheat oven to 350 degrees. Place apples, water, and cinnamon in a greased 8x8-inch baking dish. Mix flour, shortening, and sugar together until crumbly. Spread over apples and bake 40 minutes. Serve warm with ice cream.

Serves 6

This is a quick and easy dessert.

Mary Payne

Submitted by Wynn Rodgers

Country Fruit Cobbler

- **2 cups peeled and sliced fresh fruit**
- **½ cup sugar**
- **6 tablespoons butter**
- **¾ cup all-purpose flour**
- **1 cup sugar**
- **2 teaspoons baking powder**
- **½ teaspoon salt**
- **¾ cup milk**

Preheat oven to 350 degrees. Stir sugar into fruit and set aside. Melt butter in an 8x8-inch baking pan. Sift together flour, sugar, baking powder, and salt. Add milk and mix well. Pour batter into pan of melted butter. DO NOT mix. Pour fruit over batter. Bake 50 minutes.

Serves 8

To double recipe, use a 9x13-inch pan.

Virginia Walker Jennings

Peach Cobbler

- **6 tablespoons butter**
- **1 (29 ounce) can sliced peaches, undrained**
- **⅔ cup sugar**
- **¾ cup self-rising flour**
- **⅔ cup sugar**
- **1 cup milk**

Preheat oven to 350 degrees. Melt butter in a 9x13-inch baking dish. Mix peaches and ⅔ cup sugar. Set aside. In a separate bowl, mix flour, remaining sugar, and milk. Pour flour mixture in dish with melted butter. Spoon in peaches. Bake 1 hour.

Serves 6

JoJo Campbell

Quick Peach Cobbler

- **3 cups peeled and sliced fresh peaches**
- **Sugar**
- **1 tablespoon lemon juice**
- **1 cup sifted all-purpose flour**
- **1 cup sugar**
- **½ teaspoon salt**
- **1 egg, beaten**
- **6 tablespoons melted butter or margarine**
- **Whipped topping or ice cream (optional)**
- **Cinnamon (optional)**

Preheat oven to 375 degrees. Sweeten peaches to taste. Sprinkle lemon juice over peaches. Place peaches in a deep baking dish. Sift flour, sugar, and salt together. Add beaten egg. Mix with a fork until crumbly. Sprinkle evenly over peaches. Pour melted butter or margarine over crumb mixture. Bake 35 to 45 minutes until crusty and brown. Serve warm with whipped topping or ice cream with a touch of cinnamon sprinkled over top.

Serves 6 to 8

Jeanette Watson

Too-Easy Peach Cobbler

6 medium ripe peaches
½ cup butter
5-6 slices white bread, crusts removed
1 cup plus 2 tablespoons sugar, adjusted to sweetness of peaches
2 tablespoons all-purpose flour
1 egg

Preheat oven to 350 degrees. Peel and slice peaches. Melt butter in an 8-inch square baking pan. Pour melted butter into a bowl and set aside. Pan will have enough butter left in it to grease the pan. Add peaches to pan, spreading evenly. Cut each slice of bread into 5 strips. Cover peaches completely with bread strips. Add sugar, flour, and egg to bowl of melted butter. Mix well. Pour and spread this mixture over bread, covering to edges. Bake 35 minutes or until golden brown.

Serves 6

Best served right out of the oven. Doubles easily.

Beverly Fulton

Julia Parker

Variations: Add ½-1 teaspoon cinnamon. May add blueberries, blackberries, or raspberries to peaches. Left over dinner rolls may be substituted for bread.

May be prepared ahead and frozen. Thaw before cooking.

Claudia Davis

Pumpkin Crisp

1 (15 ounce) can pumpkin
1 cup evaporated milk
1 cup sugar
1 teaspoon vanilla extract
½ teaspoon ground cinnamon
1 (18.25 ounce) box yellow butter cake mix
1 cup chopped pecans
1 cup butter, melted
Whipped cream
Ground nutmeg

Preheat oven to 350 degrees. Stir together pumpkin, milk, sugar, vanilla, and cinnamon. Pour into a 9x13-inch casserole dish. Sprinkle cake mix evenly over pumpkin mixture. Sprinkle pecans over cake mix. Drizzle with melted butter. Bake 1 hour or until golden. Let stand 10 minutes. Serve warm with whipped cream. Sprinkle with nutmeg.

Serves 12 to15

Virginia Laux

Blender Pot de Crème

6 ounces semi-sweet chocolate chips
6 ounces milk chocolate chips
¾ cup half-and-half, warmed
3 egg yolks
⅓ cup sugar
Whipped cream

Use blender to mix chocolate chips, half-and-half, egg yolks, and sugar thoroughly. Pour into pot de crème cups, demitasse cups, or small lotus bowls and chill. Serve with a dollop of whipped cream.

Makes 8 small or 5 large servings

12 ounces of all semi-sweet chocolate chips may be used if desired

Variation: Add 2 tablespoons very strong coffee, 1 teaspoon rum extract, or 1 tablespoon orange liqueur.

Len Walker Peeler

Submitted by Betty Peeler

Sugar Plum Pudding

PUDDING

2 cups pitted prunes
1½ cups butter, softened
3 cups sugar
4 cups all-purpose flour
1 teaspoon cinnamon
2½ teaspoons baking soda
4 eggs
2 cups buttermilk

GLAZE

1 cup butter
1 cup buttermilk
2 cups sugar
2 teaspoons vanilla extract

Preheat oven to 350 degrees. Cook prunes according to package directions until tender. Drain and set aside. Use a mixer to cream butter and sugar. Sift together flour, cinnamon, and baking soda. Beat eggs slightly and combine with buttermilk. Alternately add dry ingredients, egg mixture, and prunes to the creamed mixture. Mix well. Pour into a greased 10x15-inch pan and bake until firm, approximately 45 minutes. Prepare glaze by combining butter, buttermilk, and sugar in a saucepan over medium heat. Bring just to a boil and remove from heat immediately. Cool slightly and add vanilla. Pour half the sauce over baked pudding. Reserve the other half to pour over each serving when ready to serve.

Serves 20

Linda Finnell

This recipe has been in our family for more than 50 years and is one we always have at Christmas. It came from the dietician at Tuscaloosa Junior High School in the early 1950's and is one she served to students and teachers. She was a member of FUMC Tuscaloosa and a faithful Sunday School teacher for many years, at whose feet Woolsey and I sat to hear the Bible stories that she lovingly read to us.

Bread Pudding with Bourbon Sauce

PUDDING

- 2 cups hot water
- 1½ cups sugar
- 1 (12 ounce) can evaporated milk
- 4 large eggs
- 1 cup flake coconut
- ½ cup crushed pineapple, drained
- ½ cup raisins
- ⅓ cup butter, melted
- 1 teaspoon vanilla extract
- ½ teaspoon nutmeg
- 9 slices French bread, cut into ½-inch cubes

BOURBON SAUCE

- ½ cup butter
- 1 cup sugar
- 1 egg, beaten
- 3 tablespoons bourbon

Preheat oven to 350 degrees. Combine water and sugar in a large bowl and stir until sugar dissolves. Add milk and eggs. Blend with a wire whisk. Stir in coconut, pineapple, raisins, melted butter, vanilla, and nutmeg. Add bread cubes. Let stand, stirring occasionally, 30 minutes. Pour into a greased 9x13-inch pan. Bake approximately 45 minutes or until a knife inserted comes out clean. Prepare sauce by heating butter and sugar in the top of a double boiler until very hot and sugar is dissolved well. Add egg and whip rapidly to prevent egg from curdling. Let cool, add bourbon to taste, and pour over warm bread pudding.

Serves 12

Julia Parker

Mocha Chip Dessert

- 1 cup sugar
- ½ cup all-purpose flour
- ½ cup butter, melted
- 2 large eggs, slightly beaten
- 3 tablespoons cocoa
- 2 tablespoons finely chopped nuts
- 1 teaspoon instant coffee granules
- ½ teaspoon ground cinnamon
- 1 teaspoon vanilla extract
- Coffee chocolate chip ice cream

Preheat oven to 325 degrees. Combine all ingredients except ice cream and stir until blended. Pour into a greased 8-inch baking dish. Bake uncovered 25 minutes. Serve warm with a scoop of ice cream on top.

Makes 16 (2-inch) squares

Gina Martin Johnston

Pumpkin Bread Pudding with Caramel Sauce

PUDDING

- **2 cups half-and-half**
- **1 (15 ounce) can pure pumpkin**
- **1 cup plus 2 tablespoons packed dark brown sugar**
- **2 large eggs**
- **1½ teaspoons pumpkin pie spice**
- **1½ teaspoons ground cinnamon**
- **1½ teaspoons vanilla extract**
- **10 cups egg bread, cut into ½-inch cubes**
- **½ cup golden raisins**

CARAMEL SAUCE

- **1¼ cups packed dark brown sugar**
- **½ cup unsalted butter**
- **½ cup whipping cream**
- **Sweetened whipped cream**
- **Confectioners' sugar**

Preheat oven to 350 degrees. In a large bowl, whisk together half-and-half, pumpkin, brown sugar, eggs, pie spice, cinnamon, and vanilla. Fold in bread. Stir in raisins. Transfer mixture to lightly sprayed 11x7-inch glass baking dish. Let stand 15 minutes. Bake approximately 40 minutes, or until tester inserted in center comes out clean. To prepare sauce, whisk together brown sugar and butter in a heavy saucepan over medium heat until butter melts. Whisk in whipping cream. Stir until sugar dissolves and sauce is smooth, about 3 minutes. Sift confectioners' sugar over warm bread pudding. Serve with caramel sauce and whipped cream.

Serves 8 to 12

Egg bread is any bread that has egg used in the dough. Other bread may be substituted.

Jan Kelly

Best Banana Pudding Ever

1 (5.1 ounce) box vanilla instant pudding
1 (8 ounce) container frozen whipped topping, thawed
1 (8 ounce) package cream cheese, softened
1 (14 ounce) can sweetened condensed milk
2 teaspoons vanilla extract
8 bananas
1 (12 ounce) box vanilla wafers

Mix pudding according to package directions. Add whipped topping, cream cheese, condensed milk, and vanilla. Using a 9x13-inch dish, layer sliced bananas, wafers, and then pudding mixture. Repeat layers. Cover and refrigerate.

Serves 12

Laura Jackson Anderson

Aunt Hazel's Layered Dessert

1½ cups all-purpose flour
½ cup chopped pecans
¾ cup melted butter
¾ cup sifted confectioners' sugar
1 (8 ounce) package cream cheese, softened
1 cup frozen non-dairy whipped topping, thawed
1 (3.9 ounce) box instant chocolate pudding
1 (3.4 ounce) box instant vanilla pudding
3 cups milk
2-3 cups frozen non-dairy whipped topping, thawed
Chopped pecans

Preheat oven to 375 degrees. Mix flour, nuts, and melted butter. Spread in bottom of a 9x13-inch baking dish and bake 15 minutes or until golden brown. Cool. Beat confectioners' sugar and cream cheese until smooth. Blend in whipped topping and spread over cooled pastry. Combine puddings and milk and beat 2 minutes. Spread over cream cheese layer. Cover with a layer of whipped topping and garnish with chopped pecans. Refrigerate 4 to 5 hours. Slice and serve.

Serves 12

Butterscotch pudding may be substituted for chocolate pudding.

Pat Martin

Chocolate Toffee Ice Cream Cake

2 (3 ounce) packages ladyfingers, cut in half
½ gallon vanilla ice cream, softened
12 ounces toffee chips
1 cup whipping cream, whipped
1 teaspoon vanilla extract
1 tablespoon sugar

HOT CHOCOLATE SAUCE

½ cup butter
⅔ cup sugar
1½ (1 ounce) squares semi-sweet chocolate
1 teaspoon vanilla extract
Dash of salt
⅔ (scant) cup heavy cream

Line sides and bottom of 10-inch springform pan with ladyfinger halves, cut side down. Divide ice cream into 3 equal parts. Spoon ⅓ of ice cream over ladyfingers and top with ⅓ of toffee chips. Repeat these layers 2 more times. Mix together whipped cream, vanilla, and sugar, and spread on top of layers. Freeze. To prepare chocolate sauce, mix butter, sugar, chocolate, vanilla, salt, and cream in saucepan. Cook to boiling point but do not allow to boil. Remove cake from freezer 10 minutes before serving. Remove sides of cake pan and drizzle hot chocolate sauce over cake. Slice and serve.

Serves 12 to16

Mary Ann Barr

Submitted by Betty Peeler

Cinnamon Ice Cream

½ gallon premium vanilla ice cream, softened
1 tablespoon ground cinnamon
3 tablespoons sugar

Place ice cream in large bowl of mixer. Add cinnamon and sugar and mix well at low speed. Do not over mix. Refreeze.

Makes ½ gallon

Delicious served by itself or on pound cake, apple cake, etc.

Judy McLaurine

Peppermint Ice Cream

- 3 eggs, beaten
- 1 cup sugar
- 2 (14 ounce) cans sweetened condensed milk
- 2 cups half-and-half
- 1 cup whipping cream
- 2 tablespoons vanilla extract
- 1 cup crushed peppermint candy
- Peppermint extract
- 2-3 drops red food coloring
- Whole milk

Combine beaten eggs with sugar. Add condensed milk, half-and-half, whipping cream, vanilla, crushed peppermint, a few drops of peppermint extract to taste, and food coloring. Pour in ice cream freezer. Add whole milk to fill line. Chill mixture 3 to 4 hours in refrigerator. Freeze according to freezer manufacturer's instructions.

Makes about 2 quarts

Daphne Reed

Peanut Butter Ice Cream Pie

CRUST

- 1½ cups graham cracker crumbs
- ¼ cup sugar
- ½ cup melted butter

FILLING

- 4 cups homestyle vanilla ice cream, softened
- ½ cup chunky peanut butter
- ½ cup frozen whipped topping, thawed
- Chopped peanuts (optional)
- Graham cracker crumbs (optional)

Combine graham cracker crumbs, sugar, and melted butter and press into a 9-inch pie pan. Chill in refrigerator while preparing filling. Stir together ice cream and peanut butter until thoroughly mixed. Gently fold in whipped topping. Spoon into chilled crust and freeze until firm, about 5 hours. Garnish with chopped peanuts or graham cracker crumbs if desired. Remove from freezer 15 minutes before serving.

Serves 8 to 10

Homestyle vanilla ice cream is best. Vanilla bean and French vanilla ice cream are not recommended. May also be served topped with your favorite chocolate syrup.

Pat Martin

Butterscotch Cookies

1 (11 ounce) package butterscotch chips
⅓ cup peanut butter
6 cups corn flakes cereal

Melt chips and peanut butter in a large saucepan. Remove from heat and stir in corn flakes. Drop by spoonfuls onto wax paper. Allow to cool and harden.

Makes 2 dozen

Easy recipe to make with children.

Keith Dedrick

Submitted by Linda Dedrick

Becky Farmer's Cookies

1¼ cups all-purpose flour
¼ cup sugar
¾ teaspoon maple extract
½ cup margarine, softened
1 teaspoon vanilla extract
⅓ cup finely chopped pecans
¼ cup confectioners' sugar

Preheat oven to 325 degrees. Combine flour, sugar, maple extract, margarine, vanilla, and pecans in bowl. Mix by hand. Shape level tablespoons of dough into 3-inch logs. Place logs on ungreased cookie sheet 2 inches apart. Bake 25 to 30 minutes until light brown. Place cookies on wire rack to cool. Roll cooled cookies in confectioners' sugar.

Makes about 22

Cookies may be rolled into the shape of your choice.

Becky Blundell Farmer

Submitted by Ethel McDonald

Each year on Becky's birthday, September 21, a group of FUMC friends, who were part of Becky's support group during her 15-year battle with Lou Gehrig's disease, bake these cookies in her memory.

Chocolate "Cracked" Cookies

1⅓ cups all-purpose flour
1 cup sugar
⅓ cup firmly packed brown sugar
½ cup cocoa
1 teaspoon baking powder
¼ teaspoon salt
¼ cup butter or margarine, softened
3 large egg whites, lightly beaten
1 teaspoon vanilla extract
⅓ cup confectioners' sugar

Preheat oven to 350 degrees. Spray baking sheet. In a large bowl, combine flour, sugar, brown sugar, cocoa, baking powder, and salt, breaking up any lumps of brown sugar. Stir in margarine or butter until mixture is well combined and crumbly. This can be done in a food processor. Add egg whites and vanilla. Stir by hand until dough holds together. Place confectioners' sugar in a shallow bowl. Roll dough into 1½-inch balls. Roll balls in confectioners' sugar to coat. Place 2 inches apart on baking sheet. Bake 12 minutes. Cookies will be soft in the middle. Cool.

Makes 4 dozen

Julia Sutton

Fruit Cookies

¾ cup shortening
1 cup brown sugar
1 egg
1 teaspoon vanilla extract
1 tablespoon milk
2 cups all-purpose flour
½ teaspoon salt
½ teaspoon baking soda
1 cup chopped pecans
1 (3½ ounce) can flake coconut
8 ounces chopped candied cherries
8 ounces chopped candied pineapple
4 ounces chopped candied citron

Preheat oven to 375 degrees. Blend together shortening, brown sugar, and egg. Add vanilla and milk. Sift together flour, salt, and soda. Toss candied fruit with a small amount of flour mixture. Set aside. Stir remaining flour into shortening mixture. Add pecans, coconut, and fruit and mix well. Drop by small teaspoonfuls on ungreased cookie sheet. Bake 10 to 15 minutes.

Makes 3 dozen

Wilma Gattis

Good Cookies

- 1 cup shortening
- 1 cup brown sugar
- 1 cup sugar
- 2 eggs, beaten
- 1 teaspoon vanilla extract
- 2 cups all-purpose flour
- 1 teaspoon salt
- 1 teaspoon baking soda
- ½ teaspoon baking powder
- 2 cups crisp rice cereal
- 2 cups uncooked oats
- 1 cup grated coconut or chopped nuts

Preheat oven to 350 degrees. Cream shortening, brown sugar, and sugar together. Add eggs and vanilla. Sift flour, salt, soda, and baking powder together and add to mixture. Mix together rice cereal, oats, and coconut or nuts. Add to dough and mix well. Drop by teaspoonfuls onto greased baking sheet. Bake 8 to 10 minutes.

Makes 4 dozen

Jean Kastanakis

Submitted by Edna Stone

Lemon Cookies

COOKIES

- 1 cup butter or margarine
- ⅓ cup confectioners' sugar
- ¾ cup cornstarch
- 1¼ cups all-purpose flour
- ½ cup finely chopped pecans

LEMON FROSTING

- 1 cup confectioners' sugar
- 1 teaspoon (or more) butter, softened
- 1 tablespoon lemon juice

Preheat oven to 350 degrees. Blend butter with sugar. Add cornstarch and mix well. Stir in flour and chill dough until firm. Form dough into 1-inch balls and roll in chopped nuts. Place on greased cookie sheet and flatten with a fork. Bake 7 to 10 minutes. Allow cookies to cool before frosting. For frosting, mix together sugar, butter, and lemon juice until smooth. Spread on cooled cookies.

Frosted cookies may be decorated with a flower or holiday design using tinted frosting.

Makes 3 dozen

Julia Gasson Harless

Submitted by Virginia Harless Cook

Seven Layer Bar Cookies

- ¼ cup butter
- 1 cup graham cracker crumbs
- 1 (3½ ounce) can flake coconut
- 1 (6 ounce) package semi-sweet chocolate chips
- 1 (6 ounce) package butterscotch chips
- 1 (14 ounce) can sweetened condensed milk
- 1 cup chopped pecans

Preheat oven to 325 degrees. Melt butter in a 9x13-inch pan. Add ingredients in order listed, spreading out over pan. Bake 30 minutes. Let cool before cutting.

Serves 12 to 16

May substitute peanut butter chips for butterscotch chips.

Geneva Kilgore

Sweet Dreams "A Different Chocolate Chip Cookie"

- 1 cup butter, slightly softened
- 1½ cups firmly packed brown sugar
- 1 egg
- 1½ teaspoons vanilla extract
- 2¼ cups all-purpose flour
- 1 teaspoon baking soda
- ½ teaspoon salt
- 1 teaspoon cinnamon
- 1 teaspoon ginger
- 1 cup chopped pecans or walnuts
- 1 (12 ounce) package semi-sweet chocolate chips
- Confectioners' sugar

Preheat oven to 375 degrees. Cream butter in mixing bowl. Add brown sugar, egg, and vanilla, mixing well with an electric mixer. Combine flour, baking soda, salt, cinnamon, and ginger, and slowly add to dough mixture. Stir in nuts and chocolate chips. Chill dough several hours. Form into balls about 1 to 1½-inch in size. Roll balls in confectioners' sugar. Place on lightly greased cookie sheet. Bake 8 to 10 minutes.

Makes 6 dozen small cookies

Karen Cruze

Mincemeat Cookies

- ½ cup margarine, softened
- 2 cups brown sugar
- 2 eggs
- 2 cups all-purpose flour
- 2 teaspoons baking powder
- ½ teaspoon salt
- 1 (9 ounce) package condensed mincemeat, crumbled
- ½ cup confectioners' sugar

Preheat oven to 350 degrees. Cream together margarine and brown sugar. Add eggs and beat. Sift together flour, baking powder, and salt and add to margarine mixture. Mix well. Add crumbled mincemeat and combine thoroughly. Press into a greased 9x13-inch glass baking dish and bake 30 to 35 minutes. Dust with sifted confectioners' sugar and cut into small squares.

Makes 2 dozen

This recipe will NOT work with the mincemeat found in jars and used for pies. It must be the condensed mincemeat found in a package.

Virginia Hancock

Submitted by Lynda Sobera

Mary's Dishpan Cookies

- 2 cups brown sugar
- 2 cups sugar
- 2 cups vegetable oil
- 4 eggs
- 1 teaspoon vanilla extract
- 4 cups all-purpose flour
- ½ teaspoon salt
- 2 teaspoons baking soda
- 3 cups semi-sweet chocolate chips
- 2 cups oats
- 4 cups corn flakes
- 1 cup chopped nuts
- 1 cup raisins
- 1 cup dates (optional)

Preheat oven to 350 degrees. Mix all ingredients together in a huge bowl. Form into balls or drop by teaspoonfuls. Bake on ungreased baking sheet 10 to 15 minutes.

Makes 15 dozen

Cookies got their name because recipe makes a dishpan full.

Mary Stedman

Famous Potato Cookies

1 cup sugar
½ cup butter, softened
1 egg
1 (6 ounce) package buttermilk biscuit mix
1 cup instant potatoes
Dash of salt

Preheat oven to 325 degrees. Cream sugar and butter in a large mixing bowl. Add egg, beating well. Add biscuit mix, instant potatoes, and salt. Mix slowly until dry ingredients are coated. Use teaspoonful amounts of dough to shape into balls and place on ungreased cookie sheet. Bake 10 minutes or until cookie edges begin to turn light brown.

Makes 3 to 4 dozen

Jerry Steed

Submitted by Linda Steed

These are the cookies Jerry enjoyed bringing to the Faith Class bake sale. Hundreds of dollars were raised for Faith Class mission projects with these cookies.

Favorite Oatmeal Cookies

1½ cups all-purpose flour
1 teaspoon baking soda
½ teaspoon salt
1 cup butter or margarine, softened
¾ cup brown sugar
½ cup sugar
1 large egg
1 teaspoon vanilla extract
3 cups uncooked old-fashioned oats
1 cup raisins
1 (6 ounce) package semi-sweet chocolate chips

Preheat oven to 350 degrees. Combine flour, baking soda, and salt. Set aside. In a large bowl, beat butter, brown sugar, and sugar until creamy with mixer on medium speed. Beat in egg and vanilla. Using low speed, gradually beat in flour mixture just until blended. Stir in oats, raisins, and chocolate chips. Drop by heaping tablespoons, 2 inches apart, onto a large ungreased cookie sheet. Bake 13 to 15 minutes or until tops are golden.

Makes 2 to 3 dozen

Good as a gift! Cookies keep up to a week in a tightly covered container.

Carolyn Fondren

Pawtucketts

1 cup butter, softened
1 cup sugar
2 eggs
1 cup all-purpose flour
1 teaspoon nutmeg
1 teaspoon vanilla extract
1 cup chopped nuts
Confectioners' sugar, sifted

Preheat oven to 350 degrees. In a mixing bowl, cream butter and sugar until fluffy. Add eggs one at a time, beating well after each addition. Sift together flour and nutmeg. Fold into butter mixture. Add vanilla and nuts. Pour into a greased and floured 8 or 9-inch square baking pan. Bake 35 to 40 minutes. While still warm, sprinkle with confectioners' sugar. Let cool slightly and cut into small squares.

Makes 16 squares

Lucian Dickerson

Submitted by Martha Fountain

Sinful Brownies

1¼ cups unsalted butter
4 ounces milk chocolate
10 ounces dark chocolate
2 cups sugar
4 teaspoons vanilla extract
1 teaspoon salt
4 large eggs, room temperature
2 large yolks, room temperature
1⅓ cups all-purpose flour

Preheat oven to 350 degrees. Butter a 9x13-inch baking pan. Line bottom of pan with parchment paper and butter paper. In double boiler over simmering water, melt butter and chocolates. Remove from heat and cool slightly. Whisk in sugar, vanilla, and salt. Mixture will be grainy. Whisk in eggs and egg yolks one at a time, whisking after each until blended. Add flour and mix only until blended. Pour into prepared pan and bake 35 to 45 minutes or until toothpick inserted in center comes out with crumbs on it — no batter. Cool on rack making sure sides of brownie are not attached to pan. Flip pan to remove brownies. Cut into squares.

Makes 24 squares

These brownies are called "sinful" because you can't eat just one.

Norma Colbath

Miss Ethel's Fruit Roll

1 (12 ounce) package vanilla wafers, crushed
1 cup chopped candied pineapple
1 cup chopped candied cherries
2 cups chopped pecans or walnuts
1 (14 ounce) can sweetened condensed milk
Confectioners' sugar, sifted

Combine crushed wafers, pineapple, cherries, nuts, and condensed milk. Mix well. Divide into 3 equal portions and roll each portion into an 11-inch log. Roll each log in confectioners' sugar and wrap in plastic. Refrigerate for several hours until firm. Cut into ½-inch slices and serve.

Makes 5 dozen slices

Ethel DeArmond

Submitted by Gene Duren and Charlene Lockhart

Melting Moments

COOKIES

1 cup butter

½ cup sifted confectioners' sugar

2 cups all-purpose flour

TOPPING

½ cup butter, softened

1½ cups sifted confectioners' sugar

2 tablespoons fresh lemon juice

1 tablespoon grated lemon peel

1 drop yellow food coloring

Preheat oven to 325 degrees. Cream butter and sugar together. Slowly add flour. Mix well. Pinch off very small balls of dough and flatten with hand or with glass dipped in flour. Place on a cookie sheet covered with foil. Bake 11 to 12 minutes until lightly browned. Cool. To make topping, combine butter, sugar, lemon juice, lemon peel, and food coloring. Mix until smooth. Spread on top of cooled cookies.

Makes 5 to 6 dozen

Ethel DeArmond

Submitted by Sallie Colwick

Hot Fudge Sauce

5 (1 ounce) squares semi-sweet chocolate

½ cup butter

1 (12 ounce) can evaporated milk

3 cups confectioners' sugar

1½ teaspoons vanilla extract

Melt chocolate and butter in top of double boiler. Remove from heat and add milk and sugar. Bring to boil over medium heat and boil 8 minutes, stirring constantly. Remove from heat and add vanilla.

Makes 3 cups

Sydna Johnson

Luscious Pecan Bars

CRUST

- 1 (18.25 ounce) package butter pecan cake mix
- ½ cup butter, melted
- 1 egg

FILLING

- 1 (8 ounce) package cream cheese, softened
- 1 (16 ounce) box confectioners' sugar
- ½ cup butter, melted
- 2 eggs
- 1 cup finely chopped pecans

Preheat oven to 350 degrees. For crust, combine dry cake mix, one egg, and melted butter until well blended. Press into a buttered 9x13-inch baking pan. Set aside and make filling. Beat cream cheese, confectioners' sugar, butter, and eggs until creamy. Pour over crust. Sprinkle with chopped pecans. Bake 50 to 55 minutes. Cool and cut into 1-inch squares. Bars will be very soft until they cool.

Makes 117 squares

May be prepared ahead. Freezes well.

Helen Middleton

Caramel Crunch Squares

- 1 cup all-purpose flour
- ¼ cup quick-cooking oats
- ¼ cup brown sugar
- ½ cup butter, softened
- ½ cup finely chopped pecans
- 1 (12 ounce) jar caramel ice cream topping
- 4 cups vanilla ice cream, softened

Preheat oven to 400 degrees. Combine flour, oats, and brown sugar. Cut in butter until mixture resembles coarse crumbs. Stir in pecans. Pat mixture into a 9x13-inch pan and bake 15 minutes. Remove from oven and stir while warm to crumble. Cool. Spread ½ of crumbs in a 9x9-inch pan. Drizzle ½ of caramel topping over crumbs. Spread softened ice cream over crumb mixture. Drizzle remaining caramel topping over ice cream. Sprinkle remaining crumb mixture on top. Freeze.

Serves 10 to 12

A wonderful dessert to make ahead and have on hand.

Robbie Burlison

Ohio Peanut Butter Buckeyes

(Peanut Butter Balls)

1 cup margarine, melted
2 cups smooth peanut butter
4½ cups confectioners' sugar
1 (12 ounce) package semi-sweet chocolate chips
¼ (4 ounce) bar of paraffin wax

In a large bowl, thoroughly mix margarine, peanut butter, and sugar. Form into balls and place on wax paper covered tray. Refrigerate 1 hour. Melt chocolate and paraffin in double boiler. When peanut butter balls are chilled, stick a toothpick into each and dip ¾ way into the chocolate. Place back on the wax paper until set. Remove toothpick and smooth over toothpick hole. Store in refrigerator or freezer.

Makes 5 dozen

Mark Stahl

Variation: ½ teaspoon vanilla extract may be added to peanut butter mixture. Dip peanut butter balls in chocolate to completely cover.

Jessie M. Bledsoe

Scottish Oat Cakes – Inverary, Canada

4 cups all-purpose flour
1½ cups sugar
2 teaspoons brown sugar
2 teaspoons salt
2 teaspoons baking soda
6 cups rolled oats
2¼ cups shortening
½ cup butter, softened
½ cup cold water

Preheat oven to 350 degrees. Sift flour, sugar, brown sugar, salt, and soda together. Add oats and mix well. Add shortening and butter. Mix until absorbed. Do not over mix. Add water and mix for 1 minute until absorbed. Roll dough ¼ to ½-inch thick. Cut in desired shape with cookie cutter. Place on baking sheet and cook 10 minutes or until lightly browned.

Makes 5 to 6 dozen

Freezes well. Recipe is easily cut in half.

Jeannette Brewster

Pecan and Date Roll

3 cups sugar
1 cup milk
1 (8 ounce) package pitted dates, chopped
6 whole candied cherries, chopped
1 tablespoon butter
1 cup pecan pieces

Mix sugar and milk in saucepan. Bring to a boil and add dates and cherries. Boil slowly until mixture forms a soft ball in cold water (234 to 240 degrees on a candy thermometer). Add butter and stir. Set pan in cold water and when nearly cooled, beat until thickened. Add nuts and mix well. Place mixture in a damp cloth and roll until a log is formed. Chill and slice.

Makes 30 slices

Ivo Sparkman

Submitted by Sallie Colwick

I was given this recipe around 1970-71 while living in Fayette County. The recipe came from one of Senator Sparkman's campaign workers.

Microwave Pralines

1 pound light brown sugar
1 cup whipping cream
2 cups chopped pecans
2 tablespoons butter
Butter

Mix sugar and whipping cream in a microwave safe bowl. Microwave on high 13 minutes; 9 minutes if microwave is 1000 watts. Remove from microwave and add pecans and butter. Stir vigorously until mixture begins to lose its sheen. Quickly drop onto a buttered cookie sheet or wax paper.

Makes about 2 dozen

Jack Hemby

Rudolph Cookies

- ½ cup margarine, softened
- ½ cup sugar
- 1 egg, beaten
- ½ teaspoon baking soda
- 2 tablespoons milk
- ½ teaspoon vanilla extract
- 2½ cups all-purpose flour
- Pinch of salt
- Confectioners' sugar
- Sprinkles (optional)

Preheat oven to 350 degrees. Cream margarine and sugar. Add beaten egg. Dissolve baking soda in milk and add to mixture. Add vanilla. Slowly stir in flour and salt. Roll into a large ball and cover with plastic wrap. Refrigerate overnight. Divide dough into several pieces. Sprinkle confectioners' sugar on flat surface and roll dough pieces one at a time. Cut into shapes using favorite cookie cutters. Place on greased cookie sheet. Bake 5 to 7 minutes, depending on how thick dough is rolled. Decorate with sprinkles, if desired.

Makes 2 dozen

Anne Forgey

I have made these cookies with my kids and grandkids for over 40 years. Santa loves them!

Pralines

- 2 cups sugar
- 1 tablespoon white corn syrup
- Pinch of salt
- ¾ cup milk
- ¼ teaspoon baking soda
- 1 teaspoon vanilla extract
- 1 cup chopped nuts

Bring sugar, syrup, salt, and milk to a full boil in a large pan. Add soda and stir until mixture reaches 232 degrees on a candy thermometer. Add vanilla and nuts. Beat until thick enough to drop by spoonfuls onto wax paper.

Makes 15 (3 to 4-inch) round candies

Evelyn Dickson

Slow Cooker Chocolate Peanut Clusters

- **1 (16 ounce) container salted dry roasted peanuts**
- **1 (16 ounce) container unsalted dry roasted peanuts**
- **1 (4 ounce) bar German sweet chocolate, chopped**
- **1 (12 ounce) package milk chocolate chips**
- **2 (16 ounce) packages white chocolate almond bark, chopped**

Layer, in order, peanuts, German chocolate, chocolate chips, and almond bark in slow cooker. Turn cooker on low heat for 2 hours. Do not open cooker during this time. After 2 hours, stir the mixture until well combined. Drop by teaspoonfuls on waxed paper. Let cool. Store in tins.

Makes 140 to 150 pieces

Cashews or pecans may be substituted for unsalted peanuts. Semi-sweet chocolate chips may be substituted for milk chocolate chips.

Norma Colbath

Easy Chocolate Truffles

- **1 (1 pound 2 ounce) package cream filled chocolate sandwich cookies**
- **1 (8 ounce) package cream cheese, softened**
- **2 (8 ounce) packages semi-sweet baking chocolate, melted**

Crush 10 cookies in a food processor to fine crumbs. Reserve for later use. Crush remaining cookies to fine crumbs and place in a medium bowl. Add cream cheese and mix until well blended. Roll cream cheese cookie mixture into approximately 36 1-inch balls. Melt baking chocolate. Place truffle balls, 1 at a time, in melted chocolate. Roll to coat. Lift truffle using 2 forks and allow excess chocolate to run off. Place on wax paper. Sprinkle with reserved cookie crumbs. Refrigerate for 1 hour before serving. Store leftover truffles in airtight container in refrigerator.

Makes 36

Recipe may be varied by using chocolate sandwich cookies with mint filling.

Natasha McCrary

Jesus saith unto her,
"Woman, why weepest thou? Whom seekest thou?"
She, supposing him to be the gardener,
saith unto him, "Sir, if thou have borne him hence,
tell me where thou hast laid him,
and I will take him away."
Jesus saith unto her, "Mary."
She turned herself, and saith unto him,
"Rabboni," which is to say, "Master."

John 20:15-17

The renovation and new Wesley Center addition to house the Wesley Worship Center were designed to complement the Romanesque Revival architecture of the existing church building. Soon after construction was completed in 2000, the Wesley Center Prayer Garden was added to offer a place of reflection, beauty, prayer, and quiet in the midst of a busy downtown.

The garden, designed, created, and maintained by members, is in the Classical Garden design of a knot garden, dating to medieval times. It follows two axis lines dividing it into four corners to represent the four corners of the earth, or all creation.

Plants mark the passing of the seasons. There are also symbolic plantings such as rosemary for remembrance; Biblical references such as Burning Bush recalling Moses; dogwoods remembering Jesus's sacrifice on the Cross; and redbud, known as the Judas tree.

A wooden cross and four benches were added to the Garden. On Easter, the children of the church decorate the cross with flowers.

Teas & Receptions

"I AM THE VINE, YE ARE THE BRANCHES;
HE THAT ABIDETH IN ME, AND I IN HIM,
THE SAME BRINGETH FORTH MUCH FRUIT:
FOR WITHOUT ME YE CAN DO NOTHING."

JOHN 15:5

This stained glass window in the 2000 Wesley Worship Center continues the tradition of Christian symbolism found in the windows of the historic Sanctuary across the street. Generations of church members have been inspired by light shining through the windows and reflecting the beauty of God's word portrayed in art. The amber and dark blue replicate the colors from the earlier windows. Sunrise, dogwood flowers, and grapes continue the Christian theme.

Thelma Hooper's Cheese Hermits

- ½ pound sharp Cheddar cheese, grated, room temperature
- 1 cup margarine, room temperature
- 2 cups all-purpose flour
- ½ teaspoon salt
- ¼ teaspoon red pepper (optional)
- 1 tablespoon Worcestershire sauce
- ½ cup chopped pecans

Cream cheese and margarine in mixer. Add flour, salt, red pepper, Worcestershire, and pecans. Mix thoroughly. Chill 45 to 60 minutes. Take dough out of refrigerator and divide into 4 parts. Roll each part into a long roll and wrap in wax paper. Return rolls of dough to refrigerator. Preheat oven to 350 degrees. Bring out 1 roll at a time, slice, and form into 1-inch balls. Place balls 1 inch apart on ungreased cookie sheet. Bake 20 minutes.

Makes 75

Sometimes I use a table fork to press criss-cross on each ball before baking.

Carolyn Hooper Hovik

Cheese Straws

- 1 pound New York State cheese, grated
- ½ cup margarine
- 2 cups all-purpose flour
- 1 teaspoon salt
- 1 teaspoon baking powder
- ¼-½ teaspoon red cayenne pepper

Leave cheese and margarine out overnight to soften. Preheat oven to 375 degrees. Mix cheese with margarine. Add flour, salt, baking powder, and pepper. Mix well. Put in cookie press and use star attachment to form cheese straws into desired length. Bake on an ungreased cookie sheet 10 to 12 minutes.

Makes 4 to 6 dozen

Dorothy Millen

Submitted by Imogene Davis

Salted Pecans

1 pound fresh pecan halves
½ cup butter
Salt

Preheat oven to 275 degrees. Melt butter in a 9x5-inch loaf pan. Add pecans and stir. Bake for 1 hour, stirring every 15 minutes. Drain on paper towels. Salt well, almost to the point of over salting. Cool and store in an airtight container.

Makes 4 cups

Jo Ann Braam

Bacon, Onion, and Pepper Canapés

1½ pounds bacon, cooked to make 1 cup crumbled bacon
½ cup minced onion
¼ cup minced green bell pepper
75 small bread rounds
Homemade mayonnaise
Paprika

Combine bacon, onion, and green pepper with enough mayonnaise to hold together. Spoon on small bread rounds and sprinkle with paprika.

Makes 75

The secret to this spread is using homemade mayonnaise. Mayonnaise recipe provided with Open-Faced Tomato Sandwiches recipe on page 13.

Margaret Anne Whitsett

Party Tea Sandwiches

- **⅔ cup finely chopped carrot**
- **¼ cup finely chopped green bell pepper**
- **¼ cup finely chopped onion**
- **⅓ cup finely chopped cucumber**
- **¼ cup finely chopped celery**
- **1 (8 ounce) package cream cheese, softened**
- **¼ teaspoon salt**
- **2 tablespoons lemon juice**
- **1 tablespoon mayonnaise**
- **1½ (20 ounce) very fresh loaves white sandwich bread**

Combine carrot, green pepper, onion, cucumber, and celery in a small bowl and set aside. With a mixer on low speed, beat cream cheese, salt, lemon juice, and mayonnaise until fluffy. Add vegetable mixture to cream cheese mixture, gently folding in by hand. Chill for several hours or overnight in a tightly sealed container. Using a small cookie cutter, cut 3 circles out of each slice of bread. Discard crust. Spread each round shortly before serving.

Makes 7 to 8 dozen

Bread rounds may be cut the night before if sealed tightly.

Sue Shotts

Submitted by Judy McLaurine

Sue made these sandwiches for our "Needlepoint Bridal Parties" for many years.

SELECTING TEAS

When choosing tea(s) for a tea party, there are many options. Green tea, oolong tea, and black tea are the basic tea types. Green tea is unfermented, oolong is partially fermented, and black tea is fully fermented. In addition, there are flavored, floral, herbal, and scented teas that may or may not be blended with the aforementioned teas. Vast selections within these groups are available from tea purveyors around the world. Often for a formal tea with three courses, one will choose to offer a different tea with each course.

Smoked Salmon Sandwiches

- **1 cup soft cream cheese**
- **20 slices pumpernickel bread, crust removed**
- **½ cup capers**
- **12 ounces thin-sliced smoked salmon**
- **Juice of 1 lemon**
- **Pepper**

Spread cream cheese on 1 side of each slice of bread. Dot with capers. Arrange smoked salmon on 10 bread slices. Brush salmon with lemon juice. Pepper generously. Top with the other 10 slices of bread. Cut each sandwich into 4 triangles or 3 fingers and cover. May be refrigerated up to 4 hours before serving.

Makes 40 tea sandwiches or 30 finger sandwiches

Nancy Barnett Darnall

Nutty Pimiento Cheese

- **1 (8 ounce) package sharp Cheddar cheese, grated**
- **1 (8 ounce) package Pepper Jack Monterey cheese, grated**
- **1 (4 ounce) can chopped ripe black olives**
- **1 (4 ounce) jar chopped pimientos, undrained**
- **½ cup chopped pecans**
- **Garlic powder**
- **1 cup light mayonnaise**
- **½ cup fat-free sour cream**
- **1 tablespoon fresh lemon juice**

Place cheese, olives, pimiento, pecans, and garlic powder to taste in a large bowl. Whisk together mayonnaise, sour cream, and lemon juice and add to cheese mixture. Mix well and refrigerate.

Makes about 1 quart

Malinda Hayes

Louise Powell's Angel Biscuits

- 1 (.25 ounce) package active dry yeast
- ½ cup lukewarm water
- ¾ cup shortening
- 5 cups self-rising flour
- 1 teaspoon baking soda
- 2 cups buttermilk
- 3 tablespoons sugar

Dissolve yeast in lukewarm water. In a large bowl, cut shortening into flour until well mixed. In a small bowl, add soda to buttermilk and mix well. Add buttermilk mixture, sugar, and yeast mixture into flour mixture. Stir until all flour is moistened. Store in an airtight container in refrigerator at least 2 hours before using. Preheat oven to 400 degrees. Grease cookie sheet. On a floured board, roll desired amount of dough to ½-inch thick and cut with a 2-inch biscuit cutter. Place on cookie sheet and bake 12 minutes or until brown.

Makes 5 dozen

Dough will keep 2 weeks in refrigerator

Charles Powell

Kwajalein Banana Bread

- 1 cup sugar
- 1 tablespoon shortening
- 1 egg
- 3 bananas, peeled and mashed
- 1 cup all-purpose flour
- 1 teaspoon baking soda
- 1 cup chopped pecans or walnuts

Preheat oven to 350 degrees. Grease and flour 3 small loaf pans or 1 regular size loaf pan. In a medium mixing bowl, combine sugar, shortening, and egg. Add bananas and mix well. Add flour and baking soda. Mix well. Fold in nuts. Pour batter into pans. Bake 45 to 60 minutes, depending on size of pan. Cool slightly in pan.

May serve with softened cream cheese or butter.

Marsha Arnold

Pumpkin-Orange Cream Tea Sandwiches

BREAD

3⅓ cups all-purpose flour
2 teaspoons baking soda
1½ teaspoons salt
1 teaspoon cinnamon
1 teaspoon ginger
½ teaspoon baking powder
½ teaspoon ground cloves
2⅔ cups sugar
⅔ cup vegetable oil
2 cups cooked mashed pumpkin
4 eggs
⅔ cup chopped nuts
⅔ cup water

ORANGE CREAM CHEESE FILLING

2 (8 ounce) packages cream cheese, softened
¾ cup confectioners' sugar
2 tablespoons frozen orange juice concentrate
Grated peel of 1 orange

Preheat oven to 350 degrees. Sift flour, baking soda, salt, cinnamon, ginger, baking powder, and cloves into a bowl and mix well. Combine sugar, oil, pumpkin, eggs, and nuts in a bowl and mix well. Add flour mixture, stirring until blended. Stir in water. Spoon into 4 greased 8x4-inch loaf pans. Bake 45 to 60 minutes or until a toothpick inserted in center comes out clean. Let stand until cool. Prepare filling. Beat cream cheese until light and fluffy. Add confectioners' sugar, orange peel, and orange juice concentrate, beating until blended. Cut bread into thin slices. Spread with filling and top with another slice of bread. Cut into small tea sandwiches.

Makes 4 loaves of bread and 2 cups of filling.

Virginia Laux

PRESENTING AT A SEATED TEA

A seated tea is a formal event with long-established rituals and presentation. The foods are served on a three-tiered curate stand. If serving a hot dish, it is placed on the top tier and is covered. Otherwise, the top tier holds scones; savories and tea sandwiches occupy the middle tier; and sweets are served from the bottom tier. Lemon may be served in wedges, but preferable in many circles is a thin slice with a clove in the center floating in the tea.

Apricot Tea Loaf

- 2 cups all-purpose flour
- 1 cup sugar
- 1½ teaspoons baking powder
- 1 teaspoon baking soda
- ½ cup margarine
- 1 (8 ounce) container sour cream
- 3 eggs, beaten
- 2 teaspoons vanilla extract
- 1 cup chopped pecans
- 1 (6 ounce) package dried apricots, chopped

TOPPING

- ¼ cup all-purpose flour
- 2 tablespoons sugar
- 2 tablespoons margarine

Preheat oven to 350 degrees. Grease a 9x5-inch loaf pan. Combine flour, sugar, baking powder, and soda in a large mixing bowl. With a pastry blender, cut in margarine until it resembles coarse crumbs. Mix in sour cream, beaten eggs, and vanilla just until flour is moistened. Stir in pecans and apricots. Spoon batter evenly into prepared pan. For topping, combine flour, sugar, and margarine until crumbly. Sprinkle topping evenly over batter. Bake 50 to 60 minutes. Watch time closely, may take less time if baked in a nonstick pan. Cool 15 minutes in pan before removing to wire rack. Cool completely. Freezes well.

Serves 18

Barbie Gardiner

AFTERNOON TEA

Often these terms are used interchangeably, albeit incorrectly. Afternoon tea began in the 1800's as a light meal between lunch, which was consumed at noon, and dinner, which was served between 8 and 9 o'clock. The original menu included tea, bread, and butter served mid-afternoon. The Duchess of Bedford is credited with the origin of this event as she began to invite her friends to share her ritual.

Hazelnut Scones

- **2 cups all-purpose flour**
- **2 teaspoons baking powder**
- **¼ teaspoon salt**
- **½ cup sugar**
- **⅓ cup butter**
- **½ cup chopped hazelnuts**
- **½ cup whipping cream**
- **2 large eggs, slightly beaten**
- **1½ tablespoons hazelnut liqueur**
- **1 tablespoon sugar**
- **18 whole hazelnuts**

Preheat oven to 350 degrees. Combine flour, baking powder, salt, and sugar. With a pastry blender, cut butter into mixture until crumbly. Stir in hazelnuts. Make a well in center of mixture and set aside. Combine cream, eggs, and liqueur. Add to dry ingredients stirring until moistened. Roll out dough on a lightly floured surface to ¾-inch thickness. Cut with a 2½-inch round or diamond shaped cutter. Sprinkle the 1 tablespoon of sugar evenly over all scones. Place a hazelnut in the center of each scone. Bake 15 minutes.

Makes 15 to 18

Freezes well. If hazelnuts are not available already shelled and with the skin removed, the skin can be removed by placing shelled nuts on a jelly roll pan in a 350 degree oven 10 to 15 minutes. Be careful not to burn. While nuts are hot, briskly rub them in a coarse-textured towel to loosen the skins. Separate nuts from skins and chop. Hazelnuts can also be blanched for a few minutes in boiling water to loosen the skin.

Mary Evelyn French

HIGH TEA

High tea sounds more elite, but actually applies to the evening meal served around 6 pm with tea as a beverage. More a man's repast with meats, fish or eggs, bread and butter, and cake, there are debates in the origin of the term. Some say it is because the tea was served at the "high" or main table instead of a smaller, lounge table in a sitting room. Miss Manners responds, "While some unscrupulous restaurants try to make afternoon tea sound more 'high society' by calling it high tea, the word 'high' is actually related to 'It's high time we had something to eat.'" Hosting a "high tea" is more a dinner party than an afternoon diversion primarily for the ladies.

Cranberry Scones

- **2 cups all-purpose flour**
- **1 tablespoon baking powder**
- **½ teaspoon baking soda**
- **¼ teaspoon salt**
- **2 tablespoons sugar**
- **1 tablespoon grated orange zest**
- **½ cup butter**
- **⅔ cup plus 1 tablespoon buttermilk**
- **1 cup dried cranberries**
- **1 tablespoon milk**
- **1 tablespoon sugar**

Preheat oven to 425 degrees. Combine flour, baking powder, baking soda, salt, sugar, and orange zest. Slice butter and add to dry ingredients. Cut in butter with pastry blender. Add buttermilk and cranberries. Mix only until moistened. Turn dough out on a floured surface and knead 5 to 6 times. Dough may be sticky at first. Pat into an 8-inch circle. Cut into 8 wedges and place 1 inch apart on a lightly greased baking sheet. Brush each scone with milk and sprinkle with sugar. Bake 12 to 15 minutes. Freezes well.

Makes 8

Karen Cruze

Lemon Curd Filling or Tarts

- **2 lemons**
- **½ cup butter**
- **1 cup sugar**
- **2 egg yolks, slightly beaten**
- **2 whole eggs**
- **35 baked tiny tart shells**
- **Raspberries**

Grate lemon rind and squeeze juice from lemons. Set aside. In a double boiler, melt butter and stir in sugar. Add egg yolks stirring constantly. After thoroughly mixed, add whole eggs, 1 at a time, stirring constantly. Stir in grated rind and lemon juice. Cook mixture until it reaches the consistency of mayonnaise or until it coats a wooden spoon. Cool and store in a covered glass or plastic container in refrigerator. Mixture thickens as it cools. Spoon into tart shells. Top each tart with a raspberry.

Makes 35 tarts

This filling will keep in the refrigerator for 10 days. Filling may also be used for an 8-inch pie. Freezes well.

Barbie Gardiner

Lemon Poppy Seed Crescents

1 (15-ounce) package refrigerated pie crust
1 (8-ounce) package cream cheese, softened
⅓ cup confectioners' sugar
2 tablespoons poppy seeds
½ teaspoon grated lemon peel

FROSTING
½ teaspoon lemon peel
1¾ cups confectioners' sugar
3 tablespoons lemon juice
Chopped pistachio nuts (optional)

Preheat oven to 350 degrees. Unfold crusts and place on lightly floured surface. Beat cream cheese, confectioners' sugar, poppy seeds, and lemon peel until well blended. Spread on crusts. Cut each crust into 16 wedges and roll up. Bake 20 minutes or until lightly browned. Cool on wire racks. For frosting, combine lemon peel, confectioners' sugar, and lemon juice. Frost and sprinkle with pistachio nuts, if desired.

Makes 32

Cut wedges with pizza cutter and frost with pastry brush.

Gerry Barnes

Snowballs

2 cups all-purpose flour
1 cup chopped nuts
1 teaspoon vanilla extract
¾ cup margarine, softened
5 tablespoons confectioners' sugar

Preheat oven to 350 degrees. In a large bowl, mix flour, nuts, vanilla, and margarine with your hands. Roll into small balls. Bake on a lightly greased cookie sheet 30 minutes or until bottom of balls are slightly brown. Remove from oven and roll each ball in confectioners' sugar. Store in an airtight container.

Makes 30

Pauline Precise

Tea Time Pecan Tassies

PASTRY

1 (3 ounce) package cream cheese, softened
1 cup all-purpose flour
6 tablespoons butter, softened

FILLING

¾ cup light brown sugar
1 egg
½ teaspoon vanilla extract
2 tablespoons butter, softened
⅔ cup chopped pecans
⅛ teaspoon salt

Preheat oven to 325 degrees. Mix cream cheese, flour, and butter together and divide into 24 equal portions. Press each portion into small muffin tins to form shells. To make filling, combine brown sugar, egg, vanilla, butter, pecans, and salt. Fill uncooked pastry shells about ⅔ full. Bake 25 minutes. Cool 10 minutes and remove from tins.

Makes 24

Marie Landers

Submitted by Jo Ann Braam

Cream Cheese Pastry Snack

1 (3 ounce) package cream cheese, room temperature
½ cup butter, room temperature
1 cup all-purpose flour, sifted several times
Apricot preserves

Preheat oven to 450 degrees. Blend cream cheese and butter together. Add flour and blend with fork or pastry blender until mixture forms a ball. Chill pastry about 2 hours. Roll dough thin on a floured surface. Cut dough into 24 circles using a 2-inch biscuit cutter. Spoon ½ to ¾ teaspoon preserves on center of each circle. Fold each circle in half over preserves to form a semi-circle and pinch cut edges together with a fork. Arrange on a lightly greased cookie sheet. Bake 8 to 12 minutes or until lightly browned.

Makes 2 dozen

Your favorite flavor of preserves may be substituted. Great served hot or cooled.

Trudy Striplin

Samplers' Night
Constitution Hall Teacakes

- **5 cups all-purpose flour**
- **1 teaspoon salt**
- **1 teaspoon baking soda**
- **1 teaspoon cream of tartar**
- **1 cup butter, softened**
- **1 cup confectioners' sugar**
- **1 cup sugar**
- **1 cup vegetable oil**
- **2 eggs, slightly beaten**
- **1 teaspoon vanilla extract**

Preheat oven to 375 degrees. Sift flour, salt, soda, and cream of tartar together and set aside. Cream butter, confectioners' sugar, and sugar. Add oil, eggs, and vanilla. Combine with dry ingredients and mix well. On ungreased cookie sheet, drop by tablespoon for large cookie or teaspoon for small cookie. Flatten with fork dipped in sugar. Bake 11 to 12 minutes or until edges are slightly brown.

Makes 4 dozen large or 8 dozen small cookies

Mary Cornell

Submitted by Charlene Lockhart

Pecan Crescent Twists

- **2 (8 ounce) cans crescent rolls**
- **4 tablespoons butter, melted**
- **½ cup chopped pecans**
- **¼ cup sugar**
- **1 teaspoon ground cinnamon**
- **2 tablespoons butter, melted**
- **½ cup confectioners' sugar**
- **2 tablespoons milk**

Preheat oven to 375 degrees. Unroll crescent rolls and separate each can into 4 rectangles, pressing perforations to seal. Brush with 4 tablespoons butter. Stir together pecans, sugar, and cinnamon. Sprinkle 1 tablespoon mixture on each rectangle, pressing in gently. Roll up, starting at long side and twist. Cut 6 shallow ½-inch long diagonal slits in each roll. Place on a lightly greased baking sheet. Brush twists with 2 tablespoons butter. Bake 12 minutes or until golden. Stir together confectioners' sugar and milk until smooth. Drizzle over warm twists.

Serves 8

Sylvia Bruens

Glazed Apple Bars

PASTRY

- 2½ cups all-purpose flour
- 1 teaspoon salt
- 1 cup margarine
- 2 egg yolks, beaten
- Milk

FILLING

- 6-8 Granny Smith apples, sliced
- 1 cup sugar
- 2 tablespoons all-purpose flour
- ½ teaspoon cinnamon

GLAZE

- 1 cup confectioners' sugar
- ½ teaspoon vanilla extract
- 2 tablespoons butter, softened
- 2 tablespoons milk

Preheat oven to 400 degrees. Prepare pastry by mixing flour and salt together in a medium bowl. Add margarine and mix with pastry blender until crumbly. Mix egg yolks with enough milk to make ⅔ cup. Add to pastry mixture and blend well. Divide pastry in half. Roll half of pastry into a rectangle to fit a 15x10x1-inch jelly roll pan. Place pastry in pan. For filling, layer sliced apples over pastry. Combine sugar, flour, and cinnamon and sprinkle over apples. Roll out remaining pastry and place over filling. Cut slits in top pastry to allow steam to escape. Bake 40 minutes. Prepare glaze by whisking together confectioners' sugar, vanilla, butter, and milk. Spread glaze with a pastry brush over warm bars. Cool and cut into small squares and then triangles.

Makes 2 to 3 dozen

Gerry Barnes

Little Cheesecakes

Butter
Graham cracker crumbs
3 egg yolks
¾ cup sugar
2 (8 ounce) packages cream cheese, softened
3 egg whites

FILLING

1 (8 ounce) carton sour cream
¾ cup sugar
½ teaspoon vanilla extract

Preheat oven to 350 degrees. Butter 1½-inch muffin tins and coat generously with graham cracker crumbs. Set aside. Cream egg yolks, sugar, and cream cheese until fluffy. Beat egg whites until stiff and fold into creamed mixture. Spoon cream cheese mixture into muffin tins, filling ¾ full. Bake 20 minutes. Cool 10 to 15 minutes. Center will fall forming an indentation. Carefully remove from muffin tins. To prepare filling, combine sour cream, sugar, and vanilla in a 9-inch pie pan. Stir well. Increase oven temperature to 400 degrees and bake 5 minutes. Stir well and bake an additional 3 minutes. Cool. Spoon 1 teaspoon filling into indentations of baked cheesecakes. Store in refrigerator.

Makes 4 dozen

Carolyn Polk

RECEPTIONS

A reception is a social function, often intended to provide a welcome or greeting. Engagements, weddings, new babies, new ministers, and other life changing events are often marked with receptions.

Ranging from simple finger foods and coffee to elaborate table fare served with sparkling punch, receptions offer a structured setting for a party.

Whether formal with a receiving line and seating plan or casual with few tables and "mingling," receptions are an integral part of our social life.

Sometimes receptions are offered as "coffees" or "teas," with hosts and/or hostesses presenting the honorees.

Luscious Lemon Layers

CRUST

- **1 cup margarine**
- **2 cups all-purpose flour**
- **1 cup chopped pecans**

FILLING

- **1 (8 ounce) packages cream cheese, softened**
- **1 (14 ounce) can sweetened condensed milk**
- **¾ cup lemon juice**
- **2 (3.4 ounce) packages instant lemon pudding mix**
- **3½ cups milk**
- **Frozen nondairy whipped topping, thawed**

Preheat oven to 350 degrees. In a large bowl, mix margarine, flour, and pecans. Press into a 9x13-inch baking pan. Bake 20 to 30 minutes or until light brown. Cool. For filling, mix cream cheese, condensed milk, and lemon juice until light and creamy. Spread over cooled crust. Mix pudding mix with milk and spread over cream cheese mixture. Cover with a thin layer of whipped topping. Chill thoroughly. Cut into squares.

Makes 24 squares

Nancy Kelly

French Mint Tea

- **13 tea bags**
- **¼ cup fresh mint leaves, lightly packed**
- **1 quart water**
- **Juice of 2 lemons**
- **1 (6 ounce) can frozen orange juice concentrate, thawed**
- **1 cup sugar**
- **Mint and orange slices for garnish**

Combine tea, mint, and water in a large pan. Cover and bring to a boil. Immediately remove from heat. Let steep 30 minutes. Add lemon juice, orange juice concentrate, sugar, and enough water to make 2 quarts liquid. Strain and chill. Serve over ice. May garnish with mint and orange slices.

Makes 2 quarts

Gerry Barnes

Claxton Punch

1 (46 ounce) can sweetened orange juice
1 (46 ounce) can sweetened pineapple juice
1 (1 ounce) bottle almond extract
4 cups water, or to taste
4 cups ginger ale

Mix juices, almond extract, and water to taste. Add ice and ginger ale just before serving.

Makes 5 quarts

Nancy Wilkinson Van Valkenburgh

This is the famous "Claxton Punch" served in coastal Georgia. It is a favorite at FUMC in Claxton and was served at my wedding in 1963.

Adonna's Punch

1 (46 ounce) can unsweetened pineapple juice
½ (12 ounce) can frozen lemonade, and water required
1 (12 ounce) can frozen orange juice, and water required
1 teaspoon vanilla extract
2 teaspoons almond extract
2 (2 liter) bottles sugar-free ginger ale

Mix pineapple juice, lemonade, water, orange juice, water, vanilla extract, and almond extract together and chill. When ready to serve, pour over ice ring in punch bowl. Add ginger ale and stir.

Makes 2 gallons

Terry T. Lewis

AND I HEARD A VOICE FROM HEAVEN SAYING TO ME,
"WRITE, BLESSED ARE THE DEAD
WHICH DIE IN THE LORD FROM HENCEFORTH:
YEA," SAITH THE SPIRIT,
"THAT THEY MAY REST FROM THEIR LABOURS;
AND THEIR WORKS DO FOLLOW THEM."

REVELATION 14:13

The Women's Society of Christian Service of First Methodist Church (the forerunner of United Methodist Women of First United Methodist Church) met on May 17, 1965. At that time, the stained glass windows of the chapel were dedicated and presented to the church.

The six windows were given by individuals and Sunday school classes in memory of loved ones. The first was in memory of Rev. Rudolph R. Scott and Rev. William W. Scott and was a gift of the Billie Scott Class. The Esther class gave the second window in memory of Mrs. Mayble Humphrey Metcalfe who organized the class in 1917. The children of Mrs. Margaret Powell Van Valkenburgh gave the third window in her memory. The fourth window is in memory of Mr. and Mrs. Horace W. Esslinger. The fifth and sixth windows are in the chancel. The fifth was given in memory of Miss Martha Louisiana Houston with a plaque honoring the family of Mr. and Mrs. Earle R. Ford. The sixth window was dedicated to the Women's Society of Christian Service and the two Wesleyan Service Guilds. The windows embody many Christian symbols.

Menus

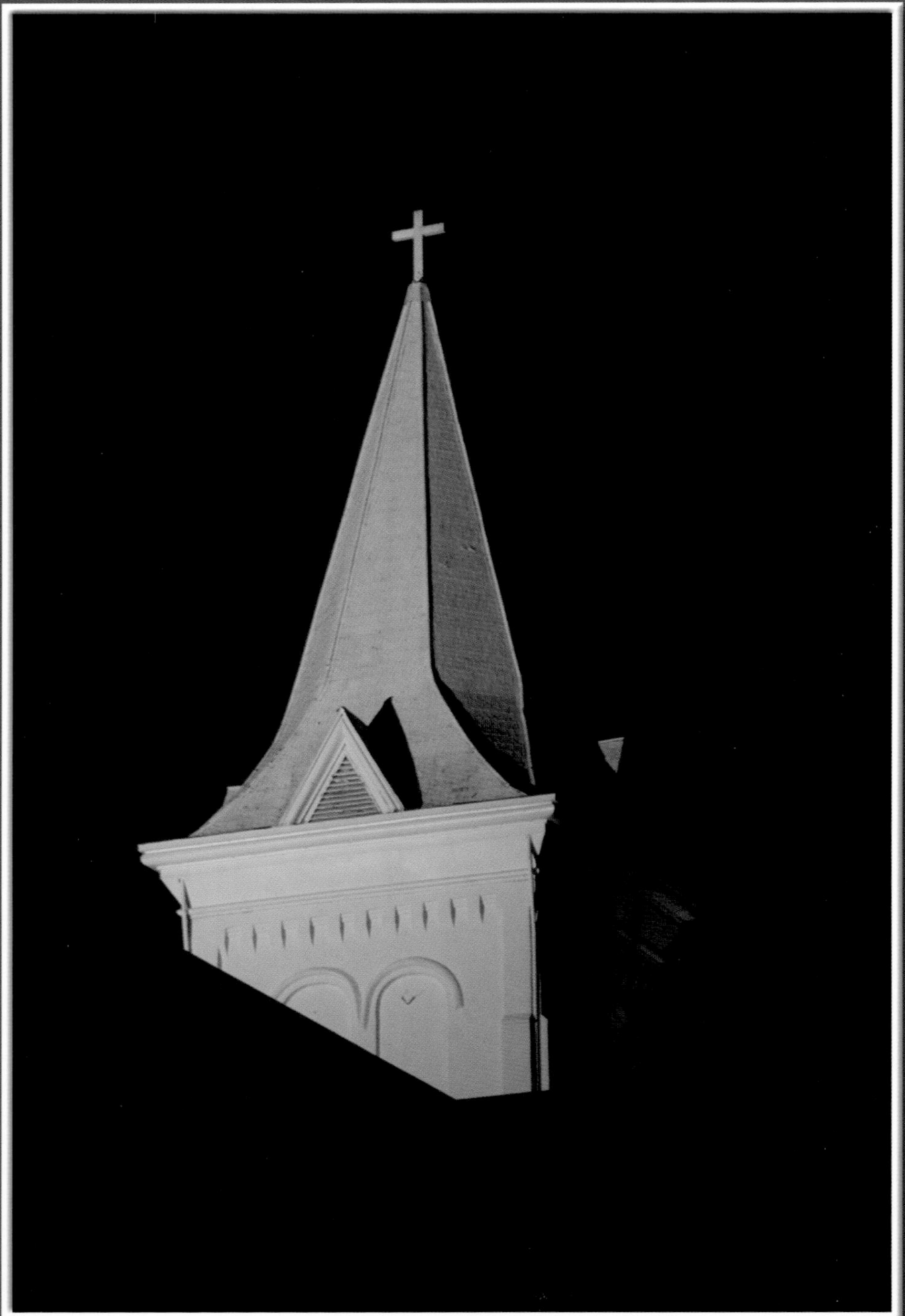

THE NAME OF THE LORD IS A STRONG TOWER: THE RIGHTEOUS RUNNETH INTO IT, AND IS SAFE.

PROVERBS 18:10

The church tower is massive and sturdy, calling to mind God who is a strong tower. The steeple and cross were added to the building in the late 1890's. The steeple pointing toward the blue of Heaven is a silent witness to the one true God whom people come to worship in the church. The cross at the top is a symbol that God loves the world and is reconciling the world and himself through worship, meditation, and prayers of the people in the church below. Shown here, the steeple at night is a beacon to God's word.

Bells rang out from the Methodist church tower from 1834 until 1859, when the Methodist, Episcopal, Presbyterian, and Cumberland Presbyterian churches gave their bells to be cast into the "Bell Battery of Huntsville," a cannon to defend the city. After the church burned in 1864, it was rebuilt. On May 12, 1868, a new bell was installed in the belfry. In the summer of 1942, a scrap metal drive was inaugurated in order to help the war effort in World War II. Continuing tradition, another church bell was donated to this drive.

A few years later, Dr. and Mrs. A. L. Hipp and their son, Raymond, donated a Schulmerich carillon in memory of Dr. Hipp's son, Arville. Organist Kenneth Turvey played this carillon until 1986 when the responsibility was passed to Preston Hayes. About 1988, age caused the faithful little carillon to sound its last note.

Preston Hayes, wanting to continue the tradition of bells at First Methodist, purchased new equipment and recorded the bell in his home church, the Oakmont Methodist Church in Oakmont, Pennsylvania. In 1997, he gave the church a new carillon as a tribute to his family. It is a state-of-the-art digitally sampled electronic instrument manufactured by Schulmerich Bells, Inc. of Sellersville, Pennsylvania, the same company that made the carillon given by Dr. Hipp and his family. Once again the bells ring over downtown Huntsville.

New Year's Day

Applewood Julep
Dirty Rice with Hoppin' John
Beans and Greens Under Cornbread
Don's Never Fail Cornbread
Cranberry Pound Cake

Dinner for Two

Baked Salmon
Fiesta Zucchini
Spinach Salad "My Way"
Too-Easy Peach Cobbler

Youth Supper

Sunday Night Chili
Best Grilled Cheese Ever
Vegetable Tray*
Mary's Dishpan Cookies

Easter Brunch

Crème Brûlée French Toast
Bacon*
Fresh Fruit*
Two-Fruit Frosty

***Recipes not provided**

Seated Tea

Cheese Straws

Cranberry Scones

Hazelnut Scones

Lemon Poppy Seed Crescents

Party Tea Sandwiches

Nutty Pimiento Cheese on Angel Biscuits

Smoked Salmon Sandwiches

Pumpkin Orange Cream Tea Sandwiches

Tea Time Pecan Tassies

Samplers' Night Tea Cakes

French Mint Tea

Assorted Teas*

Celebration Dinner

Châteaubriand with Roasted Vegetables

Pesto Pine Nut Asparagus

Shoepeg Corn Salad

Sally Lunn

Fudge Pie

Baptism Lunch

Poulet de Normandy

Basil Green Beans

Black Cherry Congealed Salad

Virginia's Amaretto Cheesecake

***Recipes not provided**

Reception

Chinese Meatballs
Open-Faced Tomato Sandwiches
Four-Cheese Pâté
Assorted Crackers*
Cheese Olivettes
Zucchini Appetizers
Chili Cheese Bites
Toasted Microwave Pecans
Slow Cooker Chocolate Peanut Clusters
Sweet Dreams Chocolate Chip Cookies
Little Cheesecakes
Adonna's Punch
Hot Cranberry Punch
Coffee*

Father's Day Lunch

Spicy Meatloaf
Fiesta Romaine Salad
Louisiana Smashed Potatoes
Mahan's Rolls
Kim's Chocolate Cake

***Recipes not provided**

July 4th Picnic

Slow Cooker Barbeque Pork
Cowboy Beans
Potato Salad
Coleslaw with Cranberries
Peppermint Ice Cream
Mer's Sour Cream Pound Cake

Ladies' Lunch

Crab Louis
Tomato Aspic
Marinated Vegetable Salad
Parsley Crescent Ring
Berry Trifle
Plantation Tea

Tailgate Party

Grilled Slow Cooker Ribs
Sausage Loaf
Marinated Potatoes
Sweet and Sour Cucumber Salad
War Eagle Pickled Eggs
Tuna Log
Zesty Pimiento and Cheese
Favorite Oatmeal Cookies

First Dinner Party

Mushroom Crab Melts

Joy's Chicken

Potato Pie

Glorified Green Peas

Aunt Hazel's Layered Dessert

Ladies' Brunch

Tomato Juice Appetizer

Quick Three-Vegetable Frittata

Cinnamon Roll-ups

Orange Fruit Cup

Thanksgiving Dinner

Chicken and Cornbread

Cranberry Orange Marmalade

Sweet Potato Dream

Laura's Spider Beans

Easy Baked Mac and Cheese

Apple Pie

Casual Supper

Shrimp and Grits

Gourmet Salad and Dressing

Hot Biscuits*

Cinnamon Ice Cream

Christmas Dinner

Roast Beef with Blue Cheese Marinade

Company Rice

Bundle of Beans

Pink Arctic Salad

Rudd's Mother's Rolls

Mary Spencer's Sugar Plum Cake

Come, dear Lord Jesus, be our guest and bless what thou has given us. Amen
~Unknown

***Recipes not provided**

A

B

D